THE NEW CURRY BIBLE

THE NEW CURRY BIBLE

THE ULTIMATE MODERN
CURRY HOUSE RECIPE BOOK

PAT CHAPMAN

metro

Published by Metro Publishing,
an imprint of John Blake Publishing,
3 Bramber Court, 2 Bramber Road,
London W14 9PB, England

www.blake.co.uk

First published in paperback in 2006

ISBN-13: 978 1 84358 159 8
ISBN-10: 1 84358 159 0

British Library Cataloguing-in-Publication Data:

A catalogue record for this book is available from the British Library.

Design by www.envydesign.co.uk

Printed in Hong Kong by Phoenix Offset Ltd

1 3 5 7 9 10 8 6 4 2

Papers used by John Blake Publishing are natural, recyclable products made from
wood grown in sustainable forests. The manufacturing processes conform to the
environmental regulations of the country of origin.

Every attempt has been made to contact the relevant copyright-holders,
but some were unobtainable. We would be grateful if the appropriate people
could contact us.

I had such a privilege during the writing of this book, to dine at London's elegant top Indian restaurant, La Porte Des Indes, at Marble Arch, and I asked photographer Colin Poole to accompany me. First we had a delicious lunch, then it was on with the whites and into the kitchens. Executive Chef Mehernosh Mody watched me through a recipe for Sri Lankan Shellfish (see page 137), and you can see how I got on with this, and other dishes, in the black and white sequences that appear on pages 198 and 199.

THE CURRY

BIBLE MENU

THE A TO Z OF SPICES

Your definitive alphabetical guide to the thirty-five whole spices, and other important ingredients (★) used in curry cooking.

CURRY BIBLE

INTRODUCTION

I own a huge collection of cookery books, and I've written a good few myself, but I have tried to make this one different. Most cookery books are a curious mixture of fantasy and fact. The recipes must be factual and unambiguous, and they must work. In fact, providing they *do* work, a cookbook needs little else. My first book, *The Curry Club Indian Restaurant Cookbook*, has little else. It does not even have a single photograph. In subsequent books, I've added photographs, historical facts and culinary backgrounds. Researching this information is, for me, one of the most satisfying and interesting stages in the process of writing. From the appreciative letters I receive, it is also of interest to my readers. To research the topic thoroughly, my wife Dominique and I regularly undertake long overseas trips to the country, or countries, under scrutiny. This is enjoyable, of course, but it is hard work too, often the journeying taking more time than the actual stay, which is always eventful and packed with assignments and appointments. Such trips also have their funny side. Dom makes it her business to observe and 'collect' such incidents as they occur. Some of these anecdotes find their way into my books. Again, I receive complimentary mail on these anecdotes. I've also found out something well known to the publishing trade – that not everyone who buys cookbooks, actually cooks from them. A surprising amount of people just buy them for a good read!

There is no doubt that most people prefer cookery books with interesting photography, with the food looking good enough to eat, but there is more to it than that. To prevent the photographs from being dull, they must be presented in a stylised way. Food photographers are highly skilled, their lighting specialised and complex. I am lucky enough to have teamed up with Colin Poole. He is one of the few photographers who is prepared to put the food first, and shoot everything 'on location' at my purpose-built studio kitchen in Haslemere, where we have completed several magazine and book projects together, this one being the largest.

Presenting food for photography is an expertise in its own right. And this is where a little fantasy creeps in. Just as all cats are grey in the dark, many curry dishes, delicious though they may taste, are, in effect, no more than stews, or stir-fries in thick gravy, and turn out somewhat similar in appearance. In the real world, diners build up an expectation and salivation enhanced by delicious aromas, so that by the time the meal is served, its appearance is just one factor contributing to its appeal. Pictorially, on the printed page, however, the food is in a permanently static state, untouchable, untasteable, unsmellable, and unreal, simply there to be stared at, never to be eaten. We must replace these missing senses, and make the dishes tempting, by enhancing or 'styling' them with garnishes and other visual tricks of the trade. Most cookery-book writers leave this entire process to specialist food stylists and cooks. The results are sometimes breathtaking, but equally, sometimes, the food takes second place. In some cases, the specialists may take a short-cut, and not even cook the dish properly, and even if they do, it may bear no resemblance at all to the item when it is made at home, by the book's reader. Of course, it is the author who, quite rightly in my view, gets the flack when this happens. Unlike most authors, I particularly like a hands-on involvement, so I have always undertaken to cook and style all the food that appears in the photographs in my books myself. I do not do this alone. I have very considerable professional assistance from Dominique, as anyone who has been to any of our demonstrations, tastings, cookery courses, gourmet nights and hotel or restaurant guest-chef sessions, will testify. What this guarantees is that the food is cooked properly and looks correct, and I am confident that what you see on the page is what you'll cook at home.

The decorative side of food photography is usually shared amongst a number of specialists, such as designers, scenic artists, construction people and prop suppliers. Take a look at the photographs in any modern cookery book. One finds the food enhanced by ornaments, attractive utensils, cutlery, handicrafts and backgrounds. These are called 'props'. Yet again, this is where Dominique excels. Over the years, she has built up an unrivalled collection of props, collected on our book-researching travels to such diverse destinations as India, Pakistan, Bangladesh, Thailand, Singapore, Australia, Mexico and America. In every town we visit, Dom drags me round as many shops and markets as she can, no matter how tired we are, nor how hot it is, nor how much our feet hurt, and she unerringly spots this pan, or that knick-knack, or that utensil and this piece of material, and has me haggling over

it, and dozens like it, then lugging it all home, in bulging suit-cases, as excess baggage. Were we ever stopped at Customs, just how we'd explain why we are carrying all this valueless junk, I do not know! If I ever whinge to her, about her seemingly endless energies in this process, I soon desist when the next photoshoot occurs.

We have used this unique, ever-growing collection in our photographs for many years, ensuring there is a correct 'ethnic' atmosphere in each shot. The first thing we do when planning a shot is to decide which dish or dishes are going to appear. Props are then ear-marked, and a 'story-board' is sketched, involving ancillary ingredients if they help the 'story', and to decide the physical dimensions of the photograph. Possibly some construc-tion or art work must be done to the small scenic set. On 'shoot' day, the food is prepared and cooked, and it is 'offered' to Colin, the photographer. He decides how to position everything, and at what angle the camera will best 'see' the subject. He then lights it, shoots Polaroids, and when we are all happy, he shoots several large colour positive transparencies. Since all this can take up to two hours per photograph, it is sometimes necessary to cook a second batch of food, just prior to final shooting.

And so to this book. It is the biggest, most lavishly illustrated book I have ever had the privilege to be involved in. Once Hodder and Stoughton's Senior Editor, Rowena Webb, decided to go ahead with a big book, it was necessary to come up with a plan. To do so, I decided to find out what the curryholic cook-book reader actually wants. I have been conducting surveys on Curry Club members, from time to time, since 1982. Amongst

other questions, we ask regular curry diners to name their favourite dishes, in descending order of popularity. Over all these years, the results have hardly varied. Starting from number one, this is the top sixteen: Tikka Masala Curry, Korma, Bhoona, Balti, Roghan Josh, Dhansak, Medium Curry, Madras, Jalfrezi, Vindaloo, Pasanda, Masala, Keema, Kofta, Patia and, hottest of the hot, Phall.

With all of that in mind, I decided to lay out this book unconventionally. It starts normally enough, with a pictorial sec-tion depicting utensils and ingredients, followed by a short kitchen workshop section, with step-by-step photographs. The recipe section begins with starters and ends with desserts. The usual cookbook convention is to divide the recipes into the groupings of meat, poultry, fish and seafood, and vegetables. However, at the restaurant, most curries are offered in all these groups. How much easier for the reader to find all the recipes for one particular curry placed together. To the regular curry diner, this is a familiar format, being the standard curry-house menu lay-out. As you can see on pages 6-7, selection is as easy as it is at the Indian restaurant. Each of the favourite top sixteen curries appears in alphabetical order, with up to four recipes, including, in sever-al cases, a curry-house style recipe and a traditional one. For example, four different recipes for Bhoona (Chicken, Meat, Prawn and Vegetable) are together on pages 64-65, while four Dhansaks appear on pages 68-69. As any curryholic knows, there are many more curries offered on the standard menu, than the top sixteen. I decided to deal with these in three groups of sixteen, with each curry allocated one recipe. I've called the first group 'Sixteen Favourite Curries'; the second group 'Sixteen House Specials' (and this is where I've placed some of my favourite dishes, grouped into four themes, Moghul, Maharaja, Raj and south Indian); the third group comprises sixteen of the most popular curry-house vegetable and dhal dishes. The recipes conclude with rice, breads, chutneys and desserts. The quick route to find the curry, ingredient or item you want, is to use the index on pages 207-208.

Another novel feature, which runs throughout the book, is the A to Z of Spices. No less than thirty-five whole spices, plus rice, wheat, salt and jaggery, are defined in detail, with each subject appearing, full size, in its own colour photograph. Incidentally, although Indian food uses more spices than any other style of cooking, it uses very few herbs. Despite this slight drawback, Dominique's herb garden, home to over 60 different herb species or varieties, supplied many of the garnishes used in the book's photographs.

To transform all these elements of text and picture into a visually attractive book, every book needs its designer. In this case, we were extremely fortunate to be in the experienced and talented hands of Peter Ward. Finally, the book's title had to be selected. Throughout its year-long planning stage, Rowena had given it the working title of the 'Curry Bible'. Just as the writing began, she recommended that it be the final title. I was concerned that it might be a trifle pretentious. 'Bible' is a mighty big word. So I looked it up in my Collins Dictionary, to find that it means 'an authoritative book'. The word derives from the Greek *biblos*, and has a number of further derivatives. 'Bibliomania', for example, is an extreme fondness of books. A 'bibliopole' is a dealer in books, while a 'bibliophile', is a person who loves collecting and reading books. Rowena does indeed have the situation perfectly defined: I love writing books, and in this one I have included as much 'authoritative' information as I can. Dealers sell to 'book-loving' readers. In a nutshell: I'm a bibliomaniac whose bible is sold via bibliopoles to you bibliophiles!!!

And that word 'Curry'? It is not so mighty, of course. Some Indian people abhor the word, believing it disparages their food. There is some truth to this. No matter how popular curry becomes, nor how many up-market restaurants open, curry, it seems, cannot escape its down-market connotations. But I believe 'curry' to be a wonderful word. It is so precise and concise. It performs a function, unique in the world of culinary definitions. It is better than a one-liner; it is a one-worder, and I make no apologies for saying this all the time: curry refers to a single dish, a whole meal, and the entire food of India, the subcontinent, and beyond. It also comprehensively refers to a niche market sector, in the retail and restaurant trades. What other single culinary word does that? We have problems when we try to avoid using the word 'curry'. We can say Indian food. But 'Indian' is itself a misused word, from colonial days. In the sixteenth century, almost every newly discovered land was described as being populated by 'Indians'. In America they were 'red Indians', in Latin America,

south), which having little taste, some small quantity of a much more savoury preparation is added as a relish'. What exactly was this savoury preparation? Was it, perhaps, the Gujarati soup-like dish with gram flour dumplings, called *khadi*, whose yellow gravy is made with turmeric, spices and yoghurt? An Iranian stew is called *koresh*. The Moghuls had Persian ancestry, and *korma* was their signature dish. Hawkins undoubtedly ate Korma, if not Koresh, at court. Hawkins travelled up and down India during his two-year stay, with the court and on his own. A dish he must have met in the south was *kari*, a southern Indian Tamil spicy stew, or another version called *turkuri*. Some of the dishes he ate would have included the leaves of the neem tree, *kari patta* (now also called curry leaves). And let us not forget the two-handled wok-like cooking pot, the *karahi* or *karai*. The inquisitive Hawkins would have seen and enquired about this ubiquitous utensil. He undoubtedly tried all these dishes, and he clearly enjoyed his spicy food. We will never know just which derivation convinced him to write: '*Curry consists of meat, fish, fruit or vegetables, cooked with a quantity of bruised spice and turmeric, called masala. A little of this gives a flavour to a large mess of rice.*' Since no one has come up with a better definition or word in four centuries, let's stick to 'curry'.

Many people are keen to know what differences there are, if any, between standard restaurant curries and their authentic counterparts, cooked in the subcontinental home. This book explains these differences, with numerous recipe examples, such as the two Kormas on pages 84-85, the two Roghan Josh Goshts on pages 112-113, and the Vindaloos on pages 120-121. Such differences are a bone of contention amongst the purists. They fret that the 'unfortunate' British public is being duped by some elaborate confidence trick. I certainly do not agree with anything as ludicrous as a conspiracy theory. At many restaurants, no matter what their 'nationality', commercial necessities and rapid service require catering techniques different from those at home. The great British roast is vastly different at the hotel carvery from Mum's home-made version, and Tex-Mex, adored by some, bears little relation to real Mexican cooking. The fact is, some restaurants do things better than others. The curry house is no different. Some do superb standard 'formula' restaurant-style curries. A few, preferring to be called 'Indian restaurants', sell wonderful Indian food, as nearly authentic as possible. It is the same in the home. Some people are marvellous home cooks, some are appalling!

I hope you find my *Curry Bible* enjoyable. Let's open the curry storecupboard to reveal its spicy secrets.

'native Indians'. The Caribbean islands became the West Indies, the Indonesian islands, the East Indies. India itself derived its name from the river Indus, and from its Hindu people. It called itself Hindustan, until its invaders changed it to India. As India grew under British rule to incorporate Burma, Sri Lanka and Nepal, it became known as the subcontinent. But all that changed in 1947. Today, as well as India, there is Pakistan, Nepal, Bhutan, Bangladesh, Burma and Sri Lanka, all of whose people eat curry.

Until a new food word, or words, develops to replace 'Indian', 'Asian' and 'ethnic', I'll continue to use 'curry', even though the word sticks in some people's craw. Far from being derogatory, I think it is just fine. But just how did the word 'curry' come into use? It is a word which has no direct translation into any of India's 15 or so languages. True, today, everyone in India uses the word, but it was coined by an English mariner, a captain William Hawkins, who in 1608 was sent there, by the newly formed East India Company, as Britain's first diplomat. He landed in Gujarat, and stayed long enough to open negotiations with Moghul emperor Jehangir, for British trading rights in India. Hawkins described Indian food '*as cereal (wheat in the north and rice in the*

THE BASICS

UTENSILS

To cook the recipes in this book, you will need a stove top (any type), a grill with tray and rack, and an oven and baking trays, plus the following standard items: knives, boards, rolling pin, various-sized non-metallic mixing bowls, lidded casserole dishes and lidded saucepans, sieve(s), deep-fryer, slotted spoon and tongs. Much Indian cooking and serving is done in the two-handled karahi or balti pan, available in iron, stainless steel, or silvered beaten copper and brass (illustrated here and on page 31). Several other examples of karahi appear in some of the photographs in this book. Alternatively, you can use a wok. The 20 cm (8 inch) diameter wok (illustrated here, top right) is ideal for roasting spices and for small portion items. The 30 cm (12 inch) size is the all-purpose workhorse for stir-fries. For those who have one, a slow cooker is excellent for cooking many curries, especially meat. Useful for bread-making is the heavy metal flattish tava (shown here, bottom left). For grinding spices I recommend an electric coffee grinder (see page 29) or a spice mill attachment. To create the smooth texture needed in certain curry gravies, a blender or a purpose-designed hand blender is really useful. An example appears in the top centre of the picture here. See it in use on page 31.

Also depicted in this photograph are some interesting but non-essential items. Bottom right is the traditional spice *dabba*, a stainless steel container inside which are seven smaller dishes. Illustrated right is a small tandoori skewer. A nutmeg grater is really useful. A decorative mortar and pestle can be useful if you just need to grind a few spices. Top left is a decorative *pan* box, without which no Indian home is complete. It stores the *pan* leaves and other ingredients needed for this after-curry chew. Note the betel nut cutter and flower petals alongside.

GROUND SPICES

Many Indian gourmets compare the cook's use of spices to that of the artist who uses a palette of colours to create a unique and satisfying result. So it is with curry. Selective use of these pungent or aromatic substances makes curry cooking unique. Many spices are available, and just as with colours, some are rarely used, whilst others are used in almost everything. Some dishes need just one or two spices to acquire their distinctive flavour, whilst others need a greater number.

Spices are seeds, berries, pods, capsules, bark, leaves, flower buds, petals, stigmas or stamens. One spice (asafoetida), is the gum of a particular tree. After cropping, the spice is dried in the sun or artificially to preserve it. This encapsulates the essential or volatile oils for months or even years. These oils are released by frying, roasting or boiling the spice, and the result is flavoured food.

So far we have only considered whole spices. Ground spices are essential to curry cooking. Some, such as garam masala (see page 29), are best ground freshly at home. Others are too difficult to grind at home – chilli because it gets in the eyes; dried ginger and turmeric because they are too brittle. Coriander and cummin can be home-roasted and ground, for a different flavour from the factory-ground versions that we also need. Pictured here are the top 20 factory-ground spices, plus four impostor food colours (see page 56), and in the centre, two mixes – garam masala and the 'curry masala', described on pages 30 and 31 respectively.

Clockwise from the brown spice next to the thumb hole:

allspice	clove	mustard	*Food colourings:* yellow, orange, red and green
asafoetida	coriander	nutmeg	
bay	cummin	paprika	
beetroot	fenugreek	pepper, black	*In the centre:* curry masala (right) and garam masala
cardamom	garlic	pepper, white	
chilli	ginger	turmeric	
cinnamon	mango		

The A TO Z OF SPICES, interspersed alphabetically throughout this book, studies each of the whole spices we need for curry cooking. To locate a particular whole spice, and to find out more about the ground spices illustrated here, please refer to the index.

BULBS, ROOTS, RHIZOMES AND TUBERS

The ingredients shown alongside, known as bulbs, roots, rhizomes, or tubers, all grow underground, and they provide some of the most important flavours in Indian cooking.

Clockwise from bottom left:

Galangal is a rhizome, and a relative of ginger, used in Thai cookery. Its flesh is white, and its flavour quite distinctive.

Lesser or stem ginger, with its cluster of yellowy brown fingers, has pale yellow flesh and is milder and sweeter than ginger. It too is used in Thai curries.

Ginger originated in India, where it grows to a considerable size. Its beige-pink skin should have a bright sheen or lustre. The flesh should be moist and a creamy-lemon colour, with no trace of blue (a sign of age).

As the two varieties of *turmeric* depicted here (top right) indicate, when it is halved its gorgeous yellow colour is a clue that turmeric's primary use, in powder form, is to give curry its distinctive golden colour.

The three types of *onion* illustrated are the best for curry cooking – the pink onion, also very decorative for fresh chutneys and garnishing; the equally attractive white onion (bottom right); and, ideal for cooking because it caramelises so well, the larger, quite mild 'Spanish' onion.

Shallots are miniature onions which grow as bunches of bulbs. Though fiddly to peel, they are ideal for dishes where onions predominate, such as the Onion Bhaji or Pakora (page 40), or Dopiaza Curry (page 128), and for garnishing. Three types are illustrated here. Spring onions or scallions (not pictured) are not used in traditional Indian cooking, but are excellent where a fresh taste is required such as in Jalfrezi or Balti, and for garnishing.

The potato, a tuber, was 'discovered' in South America in the sixteenth century, and it eventually found its way as a 'newcomer' to India and her cooking. The *sweet potato* is readily available in the West, and it makes an excellent and colourful potato substitute.

FRESH HERBS AND LEAVES

The French use the word *aromate* (aromatics) to describe any fragrant vegetable matter that is used for flavouring. Indian cooking uses a few leafy herbs for this purpose, the best known of which are coriander and mint. But there are others, which are becoming available in the West.

Top row, left to right:

Flat-Bladed Parsley

No Indian name

This resembles coriander, but since it lacks its flavour, it is used as a garnish rather than in cooking.

Curry Leaf

Neem or *Kari Phulia*

Used to great effect in south Indian cooking, this small, edible, soft leaf, available fresh at Asian stores, has a lemony rather than curry fragrance; indeed the small tree it comes from is related to the lemon family. The dried leaf is widely available as a substitute and is described on page 92.

Mint

Podina

There are many species of fresh mint available from the greengrocer. Though mint is not widely used in Indian cooking, it is very effective in such dishes as Balti and Podina Gosht. It is also the backbone of Tandoori Chutney, or Mint Raita. Illustrated here are spearmint and apple mint (shown below the curry leaf).

European Sweet Basil

Tulsi

There are 40 varieties of basil, but the one you are most likely to find at the supermarket is European sweet basil (shown top right). Thai basil (*horappa*, below right of the spearmint), with a more aniseed-like taste, is available at the Asian or Thai store. Both have a fabulous fragrance, giving basil, quite rightly, its Greek name 'king of herbs'. Though indispensable to Thai curries, basil is hardly used in Indian cooking at all, but it does add magic to certain dishes, such as Balti.

Lemon Grass

Takrai

Only the bulbous stalky end of this grass is used in Thai, though not Indian, curries, to which it imparts a sweet, vaguely lemony flavour. See also page 116.

Bottom row, left to right:

Rocket

No Indian name

A light and fragrant, slightly pungent, small, herby vegetable, rocket is now very widely available. It enhances salads, can be lightly cooked, and makes a fine garnish.

Chive

No Indian name

Familiar, fine, long chive leaves are a member of the onion family. Although not traditionally used in Indian cooking, they make an excellent and easy garnish.

Coriander Leaf

Hari Dhania

Coriander, undoubtedly the most prevalently used spice in Indian cooking, is described on page 84. The leaf has a very distinctive and rather musky taste which, once acquired, is indispensable to many curries. Fresh, the leaves are used whole, chopped or ground. Soft stalks can also be used, but thicker stalks should be discarded. In Thai cooking the roots are used too. Flat-bladed parsley resembles coriander leaf in appearance. To identify one from the other at the greengrocer's, crush a leaf in your fingers – only coriander has that musky smell.

Spinach

Sag or Palak

Baby spinach leaves, washed and cleaned, are so tender that they can be used raw as a herb and garnish, in certain curry dishes, and, of course, lightly cooked as the main flavouring in other important dishes from the Punjab, such as Sag Gosht, and from the east in Palak Paneer. In the subcontinent there are many spinach varieties, including red spinach which you can substitute when seasonally available.

Middle row, dead centre:

Fenugreek

Methi

Fresh fenugreek leaves are available from Asian stores, for use in small quantities in certain pungent and savoury dishes from the Punjab. The stalks are discarded, being too pithy and bitter. Dried leaves (see page 108) are more readily available and more commonly used. Fenugreek seeds are described on page 104.

Onion or Garlic Chive, budding and flowering

No Indian name

Increasingly available, and interesting, especially as a garnish, the flavour of onion chive is similar to that of chive; garlic chive is more pungent.

CHILLIES

The cooking of India predates Greek and Roman civilisations. Even before those times, pepper was traded as a valuable commodity, being the spice which gave food its sparkle or 'heat'. Little wonder it is still India's biggest export crop, earning itself the title 'king of spice'. See page 144.

When many people think of curry, it is its 'heat' which springs first into their minds, with chilli being the heat giver. Yet chilli is a relative newcomer to Indian cooking. It was 'discovered' in the Americas by mistake, by explorers, of whom Columbus was the first, who were seeking the source of pepper. Indeed it was they who gave the chilli and allspice their confusingly similar names, *pimiento* and *pimento*, both derived from the Spanish for 'pepper'. Chilli pepper soon caught on and it was taken around the world to become adored, and grown by countries like India. See also page 72.

There are thousands of varieties of chilli, ranging in heat from zero to incendiary. Depicted here are some of the ones readily available in the West. Of them, working clockwise from bottom left, the chilli most commonly used in Indian cooking, is the quite hot cayenne chilli. Top left are strands of fresh green peppercorns, which will quickly go black (shown below the green strands) and detach themselves from their vine to become peppercorns.

Clockwise from the peppercorns are medium-heat, long green chillies; a zero-heat orange bell pepper; medium-heat African Snubs, similar to American Jalapeños, and the most commonly available chilli at the supermarket. Next, top right, the world's hottest, the Scotch Bonnet; below them are fairly hot Thai short red cayennes; and bottom right, mild large green Anaheims. Left of them are slightly hot Dutch green above a group of three dark green Serranos; then medium-heat Kenyan reds; above them and centre, the really hot miniature Thai cayennes; then one example each of a red, green and yellow Penis Pepper. Left of them are medium Indian red chillies, and above them quite mild lemon-yellow Hungarian wax chillies.

22

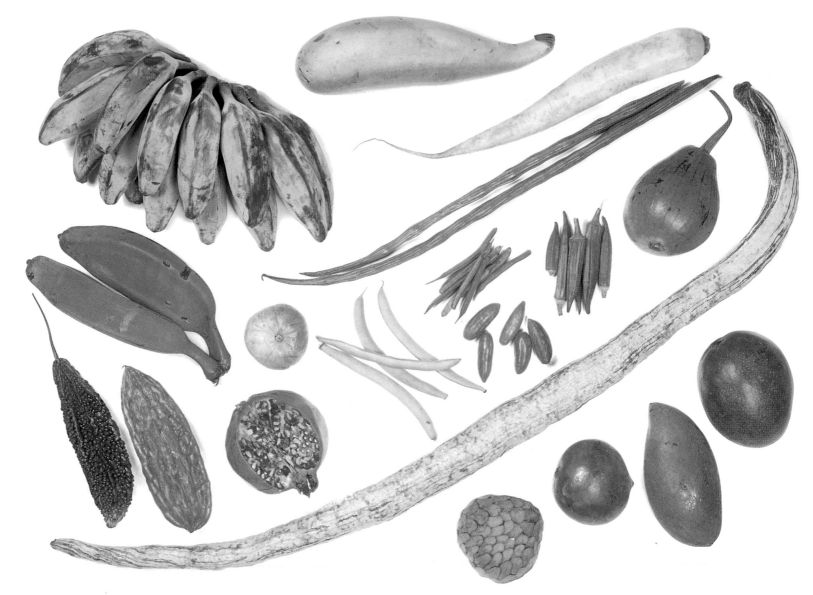

EXOTIC FRUIT AND VEGETABLES

The exotic fruit and vegetables shown in this photograph were purchased one winter's day in Southall, Britain's longest established Asian community. From time to time you will encounter one or more of them at the Indian restaurant. If you can obtain them, you may like to try experimenting with them yourself, so I have used some of them in a few of the recipes in this book.

Clockwise from left centre:

Two green cooking bananas or *plantains* and, above, a bunch of smaller *plantains*. Next is a bottle gourd, or long *doodi*, a member of the marrow or squash family;

the white radish or *mooli* can be eaten raw as a garnish or lightly cooked. The two long thin items, a type of marrow with a hard, ribbed casing, are called drumsticks or *sajjar*, and are really popular in south India, chopped and curried. To eat them, cut them open and spoon or suck out the soft delicious flesh. See page 153 for a recipe.

Next, is the aptly named snake gourd. Another squash, it grows hanging down from its tree, until, like this one, it reaches about a yard or metre in length. Cook as for drumsticks.

Next are three mangoes. The red one is

ideal for sweet mango chutney, the centre one is ideal for eating (see page 197) and the small green one is for tart pickle. At the bottom of the picture is a custard apple, a fruit beloved of all Indians.

Bottom left are two types of bitter gourd, or *karela*, very much an acquired taste, being very bitter indeed. Next is a pomegranate, cut open to expose its luscious red seeds (see also page 148). Directly above it is a small round gourd called *papdi*, and to its right are white beans and green valor beans. The little green oval vegetables are *tindoora* and right of them are okra or *bindi*, then a round *doodi*.

Most of the vegetables in this picture are aubergines. On the left, from top to bottom, are Thai varieties, and it is easy to see why they are also called eggplants. The tiny berry-like ones are called pea aubergines.

Indian aubergines are invariably a beautiful shiny purple boot-black colour and come in a variety of shapes and sizes. The item in the middle is a banana flower, and is relished especially in Bengali curries.

NUTS AND MISCELLANEOUS INGREDIENTS

Grouped together here are what can best be described as a miscellaneous assembly of important ingredients in the curry larder. These are nuts (including coconut), tamarind and oils.

Starting on the grinding stone at the bottom left, is an array of coconut products. At the stone's top is a halved coconut. Next, working clockwise, are dried coconut chippings, then thick coconut cream taken from a can of coconut milk, then coconut oil. Desiccated coconut is in the centre of the stone, with coconut milk powder bottom left. Top left of the stone is coconut water, and right of that is part of a block of creamed coconut. Immediately above the stone is a familiar brown hairy coconut, but on its left is a coconut in its less familiar green outer casing.

The small group of three items to the left of the green coconut are, top, chirongi nuts, then sunflower kernels, below right, and charoli nuts, to their left.

Right of the hairy coconut are blanched polished peanuts, followed by redskin peanuts and pistachio nuts. In the next row are pale-skin peanuts, blanched almonds and blanched cashews. Left to right in the third row are almond flakes, ground almonds and whole shelled almonds.

Immediately under the almonds are melted ghee and solid ghee. On the shiny tray is tamarind in pod form and seeds. Left of that are mustard oil, sesame oil and sunflower oil.

LENTILS

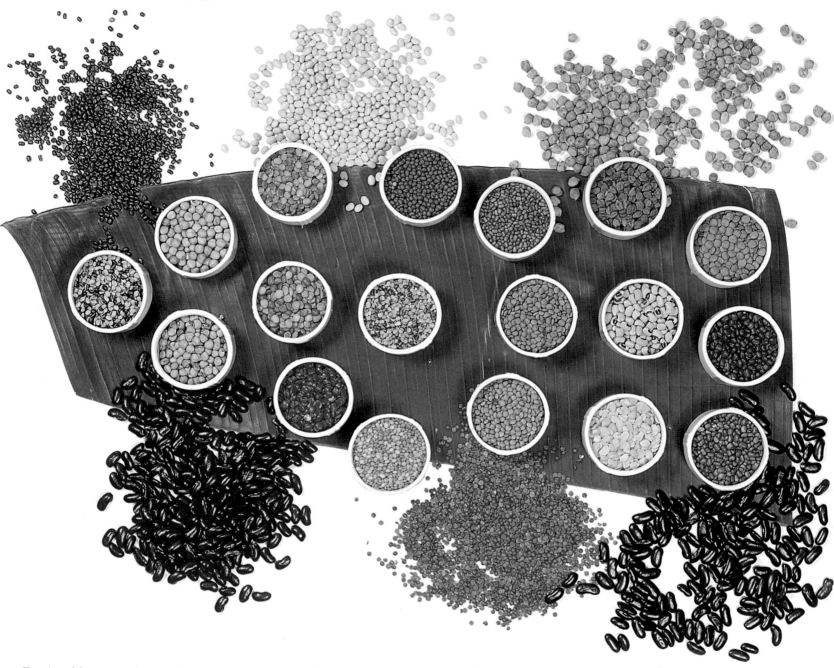

Depicted here on a banana leaf are the most popular types of lentil and bean. All are readily available but, unless you are devoted to lentils, you only need to stock three or four types. You will find more information about lentils (or *dhal*) on page 166, and about banana leaf on page 151.

Clockwise from top left, loose around the leaf:

Whole black *urid dhal*, white haricot beans, chick peas, black kidney beans, split and polished red *massoor* lentils, and red kidney beans.

Clockwise from the far left, in bowls:

Split *urid*, whole yellow peas, split *chana*, whole green *moong*, whole *mooth*, black chick peas (*kala chana*), whole green lentils, whole red *chori*, whole brown *chori*, split *val*, whole *massoor*, split and polished *moong*, split *toovar*, and whole pigeon peas (*gungo*).

Centre row from the left:

Yellow split peas, split green *moong*, whole brown lentils, and black-eyed (*lobhia*) beans.

AROMATIC SALT

Throughout this book, recipes call for aromatic salt. You can, of course, use ordinary salt, but aromatic salt adds a little more 'magic' to your cooking. The light version, shown on the right, is complete in itself, but it can be developed into a spicier version, shown top left. In each case, grind, and then store in an airtight jar.

Lightly Spiced Aromatic Salt

MAKES 100 G (3½ OZ)

100 g (3½ oz) coarse sea salt
1 teaspoon freshly ground allspice
1 teaspoon ground cinnamon

Spicier Aromatic Salt

MAKES 100 G (3½ OZ)

1 quantity lightly spiced aromatic salt
1 teaspoon dried mint
½ teaspoon ground fenugreek
1 teaspoon ground almonds
½ teaspoon turmeric

PANCH PHORAN

At the front of the photograph is panch phoran, a Bengali mixture of five (*panch*) whole aromatic seeds, used alone in certain dishes. Celery and/or caraway seeds can be substituted for cummin. Simply mix together and store in an airtight container.

MAKES ABOUT 75 G (2½ OZ)

1 tablespoon cummin seeds
1 tablespoon aniseed
1 tablespoon wild onion seeds
1 tablespoon black mustard seeds
1 tablespoon fenugreek seeds
25 g garlic powder

FRAGRANT STOCK

The subtler authentic Indian recipes often need water added at some stage in their cooking. More effective is a light fragrant stock, known in India as *akhni* or *yakhni*. It is really easy to make and surplus can be frozen in yoghurt pots.

MAKES ABOUT 700 ML (1¼ PINTS)

10-12 green cardamoms
10-12 cloves
5-6 bay leaves
6-8 pieces cassia bark
2 tablespoons dried onion flakes
1 tablespoon ghee
750 ml (1½ pints) water

Simply simmer all the ingredients together for about 20 minutes, then strain the stock and discard the solids. The stock can be frozen in small batches, in disposable moulds, such as yoghurt pots.

NOTE: Dried onion flakes (dehydrated onion) are much quicker to use than fresh onion.

GARAM MASALA

Garam means 'hot' and *masala* means 'mixture of spices'. Whole spices are cooked by dry-frying (with no oil or liquid) or 'roasting'. They are then cooled and ground. There are as many recipes for the actual spice mixture as there are cooks in the Indian subcontinent. Garam masala is used in various ways. It can be sprinkled on finished cooking, added to yoghurt dips, or added to certain curries towards the end of cooking (to retain the aromatics), particularly those curries from north India. Or it can be used to cook with, from the beginning of the process, as in Balti curries. This example is a traditional Kashmiri garam masala. Compare it with any factory-made garam masala of your choice and you will always make it fresh from now on, I guarantee! And of course, you are at liberty to vary the ingredients to your taste.

MAKES ABOUT 250 G (9 OZ)
WHEN GROUND

60 g coriander seeds
50 g cummin seeds
40 g fennel seeds
25 g black peppercorns
15 g cloves
15 g brown cardamoms
3 pieces mace
25 g cassia bark pieces
4 bay leaves
5 g ground ginger

1. Omitting the ground ginger, mix the remaining nine whole spices together in your pan. Keeping it dry, stir the mixture continuously as it heats up.

2. Very soon the mixture will give off steam, rather than smoke. The process is called 'roasting'. The volatile oils, or aromas, are now being released into the air. Stir for a few seconds more, then transfer the spices to a cold pan or bowl, to stop them cooking. They must not burn. If they do, your cooking will have a bitter, carbonised taste. If they burn, discard them and start again.

3. Allow the garam masala to go completely cold for two reasons. Firstly, it will become brittle, so will grind more easily. Secondly, if the mixture is hot when you grind it in an electric grinder, the blades could overheat the spices, and burn off the very volatile oil you are striving to capture.

4. Whether you use a mortar and pestle or an electric grinder (here it is a coffee grinder), do so in small batches. This avoids overloading the machine.

5. Grind until all the clattering noises change to a softer similar sound, then grind on until the mix is as fine as you want it, or as fine as the grinder will achieve.

6. Thoroughly mix all the ingredients together, including the ground ginger. Store it in an airtight jar in a dark, dry place. Like all ground spices, though it will last for many months, it will gradually lose fragrance until eventually it tastes of little or nothing. It is best to make garam masala freshly in batches even smaller than this example.

CURRY MASALA AND TANDOORI MASALA

Indians call any mixture of spices 'masala'. Its simplistic name, 'curry powder', helped give Indian food a poor reputation. To this day, certain Indian foodies refuse ever to use it. Indeed, many of the recipes in this book do not need such a mixture. However, there are other recipes which can benefit from a ready-prepared, good-quality, home-made masala curry. It is easy to make, so please avoid factory-made alternatives, and use this well-tried and trusted masala of 15 ground spices. If you cannot weigh these amount precisely, 5 g equals about 1 teaspoon ground spice.

MAKES ABOUT 250 G (9 OZ) CURRY MASALA

Top row, left to right:

60 g coriander
30 g cummin
20 g fenugreek
25 g gram flour (besan)
25 g garlic powder

Middle row, right to left:

20 g paprika
20 g turmeric
20 g garam masala (see page 30)
5 g bay leaf
5 g asafoetida

Bottom row, left to right:

5 g ginger
5 g chilli powder
5 g yellow English mustard powder
5 g black pepper
5 g cinnamon

For a tandoori masala, use the following ingredients (all ground):

MAKES ABOUT 250 G (9 OZ) TANDOORI MASALA

40 g coriander
30 g cummin
40 g garlic powder
40 g paprika
20 g ginger
20 g mango powder
20 g dried mint
20 g beetroot powder
10 g anatto seed powder
10 g chilli powder
5 g red food colouring powder (optional)

Top left: Put the curry masala ingredients into a bowl.

Top right: Mix well.

Bottom right: Add just enough water to make a paste thick enough to drop sluggishly off the spoon.

Bottom left: The same technique is used to make the tandoori masala paste.

To use either of the above masala pastes, heat the amount of ghee specified in the recipe, add the masala paste and stir continuously (*above right*) until after a few minutes its colour has gone much darker, and the ghee separates and 'floats' (*above left*, note the spoon). Remove from the heat and leave the mixture to stand for a while.

CURRY MASALA GRAVY

MAKES ABOUT 1.3 KG (3 LB)
CURRY MASALA GRAVY

110 g (4 oz) ghee
150 g (5½ oz) garlic cloves, finely chopped
110 g (4 oz) ginger, finely chopped
(optional)
1 kg (2¼ lb) Spanish onions, chopped
600 ml (1 pint) water
250 g (9 oz) curry masala paste
(see page 31)

Like any restaurant, the Indian restaurant has found a foolproof method which enables it to produce, very rapidly, any amount of different dishes, in its case 'formula' curries. Every day, it pre-cooks meat, chicken and certain vegetables, then chills them. And it makes a large stock-pot of thick curry masala gravy. The next part of the process is to fulfil individual customers' orders, on a person-by-person, dish-by-dish basis, using these main ingredients, pinches of appropriate spices, and a ladleful or two of the gravy.

At home, we are unlikely to cook for upwards of 100 diners each evening, so for recipes in this book I have modified restaurant techniques to produce four-portion dishes, by, for example, oven casseroling some meat dishes and stir-frying others. However, in order to recreate the smooth texture of restaurant curries, some recipes do need a curry masala gravy. This recipe makes enough for about 12 individual curries, each of which requires about 110 g (4 oz) gravy. Since, as I say, most of my recipes are for four portions, this gravy will therefore make enough for about three recipes. I keep saying 'about' because the exact gravy content can be varied according to taste, and the ginger is an optional ingredient. To save on time, washing-up and smells, you might prefer to make several batches of this gravy at once.

1. Heat the ghee in a wok and stir-fry the garlic and optional ginger for the minute or two it takes for them to go translucent (*above right*). Lower the heat and add the onions, bit by bit as they reduce in size in the wok, stir-frying as needed until they have all become browned and caramelised (*above left*).

2. Add the water, then mulch the mixture down in a blender, or using a hand blender, until you achieve a smooth purée.

3. The curry masala paste can either be added to the gravy (*above right*) or, to be more flexible, you can keep the paste and the gravy separate until needed in a particular recipe. To preserve the finished gravy, fill three large yoghurt pots, pop on their lids and freeze. Each pot gives about 450 g (1 lb), or enough gravy for one of my recipes for four people.

Shown in the rear wok (*above left*) is onion tarka. This is onion which is fried on a very low heat until it is really brown and crispy.

PANEER

Paneer is the only form of cheese made in India. It is really simple to make at home by heating and curdling milk, and then separating the solids. It is used in curries and sweetmeats (see index), either crumbled or in its denser cubed form. It goes hard and rubbery if kept so it should always be freshly made.

MAKES ABOUT 225 G (8 OZ) PANEER

2 litres (3½ pints) full cream milk
freshly squeezed juice of 1 or 2 lemons
or 3-6 tablespoons white distilled vinegar

1. Bring the milk just up to boiling point. Careful it doesn't boil over!

2. Take it off the heat, and add lemon juice or vinegar until the milk starts to separate. Stir to assist the separation.

3. Using a clean tea-towel and a large sieve, strain off the liquid (the whey). Relative to the solids (the curds), there is always a lot of whey, and whilst you can use some for stock or soup, you will probably discard most of it.

4. Fold the tea-towel over the curds, and form them into a flat disc which must now be compressed. The easiest way to do this is to fill a saucepan full of water, and put it, with a weight on its lid, on top of the disc.

5. For crumbled paneer, remove the weight after 15-20 minutes and crumble the paneer as shown. For cubes, leave the weight in place for at least an hour, maybe two, then the disc can be cut into cubes or chip shapes.

GHEE

Ghee is clarified butter, which is very easy to make and gives a distinctive and delicious taste. When cooled and set, it will keep for several months without refrigeration.

900 g (2 lb) slightly salted butter

1. Place the butter blocks whole into a non-stick pan. Melt at a very low heat.
2. When completely melted, raise the heat very slightly. Ensure it does not smoke or burn, but don't stir. Leave to cook for about 1 hour. The impurities will sink to the bottom and float on the top. Carefully skim off the floating sediment with a slotted spoon, but don't touch the bottom.
3. Turn off the heat and allow the ghee to cool. Then sieve it through kitchen paper or muslin into an airtight storage jar. When it cools it solidifies, although it is quite soft. It should be a bright pale lemon colour and it smells like toffee.

STARTERS

One of the pleasures of Indian food is contemplating the marvellous array of unique starters in its repertoire. Anyone who has roamed the streets of the subcontinent's towns and cities will have enduring and mouth-watering memories of tantalising smells emanating from the multiplicity of street stalls, all vying for your rupees in exchange for this or that tasty morsel. Ranging from simple roast peanuts, still hot and smouldering, to complex cold concoctions, or from delicious deep-fried offerings to grilled burger-type items, and the wonders of the clay oven, it is not surprising that India claims to have invented 'fast food'.

Starters are the wonders of the Indian restaurant. Where else can you get that fabulous spicy, luscious fritter, the celebrated onion bhaji, or its close relative the lightly battered pakora? What can possibly be better than the famous tri-cornered samosa, with its stunning curry fillings? And where else will you find seven distinctly different types of kebab? The more adventurous will try speciality cold snacks such as Chaat (it literally means 'a snack'), spicy chick peas with diced chicken or vegetables, or Dahi Vada, a spicy dumpling bathed in yoghurt, or Bhel Puri, a divine combination of tang, spice and crunch. But the true jewels in the crown, the king and queen of the curry kitchen, are indisputably tandoori and tikka, divinely fragrant and savoury, infinitely satisfying, and now a world-class product, from Tokyo to Tallahassee, Brisbane to Brighton, Cape Town to Canterbury, and Alaska to Australia.

The very thought of such delights works up the appetite, especially since all these wonderful dishes can be made at home.

And there are two more masterpieces to make your mouth water – Papadom and Bombay Mix. Who can resist nibbling away at those intriguing spicy mixes with an aperitif to hand? And who at the restaurant can say no to a crisp, crackling Papadom, dripping with an array of sweet, hot and tart chutneys, whilst pondering what to order for their curry meal?

Alkanet

Ratin Jot

ALKANNA TINCTORIE

Alkanet is a wild, deep-rooting plant with yellow flowers, related to borage. Its root stem is a remarkable purple-beetroot red in colour, and once dried, it forms a wafer-thin bark. In medieval Europe, and until recently, it was used to make a deep red dye to colour make-up, pharmaceuticals, clothing and artifacts. It is still used for this purpose in contemporary India. Alkanet got its name from the Arabic *al-henne*, the deep red-brown dye from the mignonette tree, still used to dye hair, hands and feet in India and Arabia. *Al-kenna* is simply a diminutive word for the less versatile alkanet dye.

But alkanet has a further use in Kashmir, as a food colouring. Though it has no flavour, it is important in achieving a deep reddy-brown colour in certain dishes. Alkanet is not alone in giving a red colour to Kashmiri food. Another plant, a type of amaranth, with feathery red flowers, called *maaval* in Kashmiri, which translates to 'cockscomb' (so called because it exactly resembles that part of the domestic chicken's anatomy in shape and colour), also gives off a gorgeous red colour when soaked in water. The deep red Kashmiri chilli also performs this function (see page 73).

The unique feature of alkanet is that it is impervious to water. However, fry it briefly in hot oil, and the result is spectacularly different. At once the oil changes colour to deep red. Examples of its use are in Gurda or Kaleji Kebab (page 57) and Roghan Josh Gosht (page 112).

NIBBLES

The best known Indian 'nibble' is Bombay Mix. It obtained this name at a Southall factory in 1970. It is in fact a mixture of several traditional items made from a spicy gram flour dough called *ompadi*. This is extruded in various shapes, through a brass press called a *murukus*, and then deep-fried. Different shapes have different names, and though they can be made at home, they can all be bought in packets. They are *ganthia*, *teekah* and thick, medium or thin *sev*. Other packet items include crisp chick peas, green peas, puffed rice (*mamra*), *chana dhal*, *moong dhal* and peanuts.

It is fun to make up your own nibble mixes, using packet items. Here are four examples. In each case, mix together all the ingredients, including the masala. Store in an airtight container (for up to 8 weeks) and eat with drinks before your meal.

Bombay Mix

MAKES 900 G (2 LB)

225 g (8 oz) *ganthia*
225 g (8 oz) thick (*teeka*) *sev*
175 g (6 oz) *chana dhal*
110 g (4 oz) chick peas
110 g (4 oz) green peas
50 g (2 oz) peanuts

Masala

2 tablespoons garam masala (see page 30)
2 tablespoons roasted cummin seeds
1 tablespoon lovage seed
1 teaspoon chilli powder
1 teaspoon aromatic salt (see page 29)

Chevda or Chewra

MAKES 900 G (2 LB)

450 g (1 lb) *mamra* (puffed rice)
350 g (12 oz) *chana dhal*
75 g (2½ oz) peanuts
25 g (1 oz) sultanas
25 dried curry leaves
2 tablespoons granulated white sugar
1 tablespoon aromatic salt (see page 29)

Mooth

MAKES 900 G (2 LB)

675 g (1½ lb) *chana* or *moong dhal*
225 g (8 oz) almonds
100 ml (4 fl oz) vegetable oil
1 tablespoon sunflower seeds
1 tablespoon mustard seeds
1 teaspoon aromatic salt (see page 29)

Special Mix

2 parts Bombay Mix
1 part Chevda
½ part Mooth
¼ part chick peas
¼ part green peas
⅛ part cashew nuts
⅛ part chirongi nuts

Add to taste:

roasted cummin seeds
roasted lovage seeds
aromatic salt (see page 29)
granulated sugar
chilli powder

PAPADOM

Whichever way you spell 'papadom', and there are many ways, from 'papard' to 'pup-puddum', it is an unparalleled piece of south Indian culinary magic which has been around for a long time.

Each is made by hand, from a lentil flour dough ball, which is slapped, in a trice, into a thin flat disc, and laid out on huge trays to dry in the sun. This is usually done by women who have spent a lifetime learning their skill. When the papadoms are hardened, they are put in dozens or twenties into packets and it is in this form that most people buy them. At this stage, the papadom is about as edible as a disposable plastic plate. The magic comes about when they are cooked, whereupon they become light, crisp, crunchy wafers. At the restaurant, they are served as an appetiser, in much the same way as the Anglo-French bread roll, Italian *grissini*, or Chinese prawn cracker, to fill a gap while customers place their orders.

Papadoms come in many sizes, from mini to large, and their flavours vary from plain and unspiced, to those spiced with black pepper, cummin seed, chilli, whole lentils, etc. There are three ways of cooking them.

DEEP-FRYING: Preheat some oil to 170°C/340°F. Deep-fry one papadom at a time in the hot oil for about 5 seconds. Remove from the oil with tongs, shaking off the excess. Allow to cool, but keep in a warm, damp-free place for no more than a few hours until each is crispy and oil-free.

GRILLING: Preheat the grill to about medium-high. Grill one or two papadoms at a time, for about 10 seconds, with the grill tray in the midway position. Ensure that the edges are cooked. Being oil-free, grilled papadoms can be served at once or stored until ready.

MICROWAVING: Papadoms can also be microwaved, though their flavour is not as good as when they are grilled. Most microwaves are power-rated at 650 watts. Place a papadom on a plate and cook for about 30 seconds on full power. Inspect and apply more heat if necessary. Serve at once or store.

SERVING STARTERS

Starters of all types are ideally served on a bed of salad. Choose from a combination of the following, and arrange artistically on your serving dish.

SHREDDED LEAVES: Iceberg lettuce, Chinese leaf, endive top, radicchio, spinach, white cabbage, etc.

STRIPS: Red, green, yellow, orange, black or white bell pepper, carrot, white radish (mooli), celeriac, chillies, fresh coconut

LEAVES: Whole, chopped or shredded coriander (stalks removed), parsley, dill, chives, fennel, mustard and cress, watercress and basil

GARNISHES

Most salad vegetables can be used to garnish curry dishes, just prior to serving. The following items can also be used.

NUTS: Pistachios, almonds and cashews, for example, can be added whole or chopped, raw, toasted or fried. Do not use salted nuts.

ONIONS: Onion rings are attractive raw or fried crispy brown, but try spring onion or leek rings. Dried fried onion flakes are attractive and crunchy.

LEAFY HERBS: Coriander leaves, for example, can be used raw, but for a fascinating change try deep-frying them in hot oil at 190°C/375°F. It only takes a few seconds. They whoosh and turn dark green almost at once. Promptly remove from the oil and drain on kitchen paper. They will crisp up quite soon. Serve immediately.

OTHER GARNISHES: Ginger strips, raw or deep-fried; green chillies, sliced and deep-fried; red chilli, roasted in strips; tomato, grilled and sliced; bottled beetroot in strips; cucumber, dipped in egg white and fried; eggs, hard-boiled, crumbled or sliced; red cabbage, deep-fried; mushrooms, grilled or sautéed in thin slices; lime or lemon slices, battered and fried.

Onion Bhaji

The onion bhaji, pronounced 'bargee', is a spicy fritter made from a batter whose essential ingredient is gram flour or *besan*. Made from ground *chana dhal*, this fine blond flour gives the bhaji its distinctive taste. A touch of spice, some salt, fresh coriander, thinly sliced onion and water are mixed into the batter, blobs of which are deep-fried. Any raw ingredient can be used as well as, or instead of, the onion; chopped carrot, cauliflower, broccoli, mushroom, bell pepper, chilli, marrow, parsnip, mooli and celeriac are amongst the vegetables which work well. Thin strips of raw chicken breast or prawns work equally well.

Pakora

The pakora is the close relative of the bhaji. The batter and spicing is the same, as is the deep-frying. But their appearance is different. Like Japanese tempura, the main ingredients, usually raw vegetables as listed for Onion Bhaji, should be suitable for holding in the fingers, so they are kept whole, not chopped. For example, rather than using thinly sliced onion, an onion ring might be used. The batter lightly coats the vegetables to form a crisp outer shell after frying. Like bhajis, pakoras should be served piping hot. In the photograph, the bhajis are at the top in the tongs; below are pakoras in the form of onion rings, chillies, broccoli, cauliflower and mushrooms.

Samosa

The samosa probably originated in the ancient Middle East, where thin stuffed pastries called *borek* have been formed into various shapes and deep-fried for many enuries. Only triangles reached India. Samosa fillings are traditionally keema curry or mashed vegetables. There are a number of ways of achieving the triangle. The method described on page 41 is one of the simplest.

Chutneys go very well with these starters. Depicted are podina, imli, raita, tomato and coconut (see pages 186-189).

Allspice *or* Pimento

Seenl or *Kababchini*

PIMENTA DIOCA

Allspice is a spherical, dark purple berry, from a tree related to myrtle, native to the West Indies. Once dried, it becomes a dark brown, slightly abrasive, spherical seed, about 5 mm (¼ inch) in diameter, a little larger and smoother than a black peppercorn. Indeed, allspice got its alternative name, pimento, thanks to the errant Christopher Columbus, whose quest for pepper led to his 'discovery' of the Americas in 1492. Though the native seed was clearly not pepper, Columbus named it *pimienta*, Spanish for pepper, thus creating confusion ever since. So popular did it become in seventeenth-century English cookery, and in an attempt to avoid this confusion, it became known as the 'English spice'. The name 'allspice' was adopted later, because, being related to the clove family, its aroma, deriving from the eugenol in its oils, seems to combine those of clove, cinnamon and nutmeg. Despite these properties, and despite being planted in the East Indies by the British, allspice never became as important a revenue earner as other more traditional spices. To this day, the best allspice comes from Jamaica, and, although it is grown in India, mainly for export, it is little used in Indian cookery, although it can be used to give a wonderful aroma to such dishes as Dhansak and Biriani.

Onion Bhaji

MAKES 8–10 BHAJIS

MAIN INGREDIENTS

225 g (8 oz) onion, chopped into fine 2.5 cm (1 inch) strips
vegetable oil for deep-frying

TRADITIONAL BATTER

85 g (3 oz) gram flour
2 garlic cloves, chopped
1 tablespoon curry masala (see page 31)
1 tablespoon lemon juice
1 teaspoon garam masala (see page 30)
½ teaspoon lovage seeds
½ teaspoon cummin seeds, roasted
1 teaspoon dried fenugreek leaves
1 tablespoon chopped fresh mint
2 tablespoons fresh coriander leaves, chopped
1 teaspoon aromatic salt (see page 29)

TYPICAL RESTAURANT BATTER

85 g (3 oz) gram flour
1 egg
3-4 tablespoons natural yoghurt
1 tablespoon fresh or bottled lemon juice
1 teaspoon salt
2 teaspoons garam masala (see page 30)
2 teaspoons dried fenugreek leaves
½-2 teaspoons chilli powder

1.   Choose one of the batters. Mix the ingredients together, adding sufficient water to achieve a thickish paste which will drop sluggishly off the spoon. Mix in the onion, then leave to stand for at least 10 minutes, during which time the mixture will fully absorb the moisture.

2.   Meanwhile, heat the deep-frying oil to 190°C/375°F. This temperature is below smoking point and will cause a drop of batter to splutter a bit, then float more or less at once.

3.   Inspect the mixture. There must be no 'powder' left, and it must be well mixed. Scoop out an eighth of the mixture and place it carefully in the oil. Place all eight portions in, but allow about 15 seconds between each one so the oil maintains its temperature.

4.   Fry for about 10 minutes each, turning once. Remove from the oil in the order they went in, drain well and serve with salad garnishes, lemon wedges and chutneys. Or they can be allowed to cool, and then frozen. Reheat in deep hot oil for about 2 minutes, but don't let them get too brown. Serve hot.

VARIATION
Restaurant Method

1.   Mix the batter as above but use less water to achieve a drier, mouldable texture. Add the onion and leave to stand, as above.

2.   Heat the deep-frying oil, as above.

3.   Roll the mixture into smooth balls about 5 cm (2 inches) in diameter. You will need to wash your hands frequently while doing this.

4.   Deep-fry the bhajis for 2-3 minutes to set the batter firmly, then remove them to go cold for later cooking. Alternatively, continue cooking.

5.   The part-cooked bhajis can be left spherical, or when cool enough they can be flattened into discs with the heel of your hand.

6.   When required, reheat the deep-frying oil and fry the part-cooked bhajis for 5-7 minutes. Serve hot.

Pakora

one of the onion bhaji batter mixes
225 g (8 oz) any of the raw vegetables listed on page 39
vegetable oil for deep-frying

1.   Mix the batter ingredients, adding sufficient water to achieve a thickish paste which will drop sluggishly off the spoon. Let it stand for at least 10 minutes, during which time the mixture will absorb the moisture.

2.   Add your chosen vegetables, mix in well and leave again for about 10 minutes to absorb the batter mixture.

3. Meanwhile, heat the deep-frying oil to 190°C/375°F. This temperature is below smoking point and will cause a sliver of batter to splutter a bit, then float more or less at once.

4. One by one, place the coated items carefully in the oil, allowing about 15 seconds between each one so the oil maintains its temperature.

5. Fry for 10 minutes, turning once. Remove from the oil, drain well and serve with salad garnishes, lemon wedges and chutneys.

Samosa

It is worth making a largish batch of samosas. Make the filling first. Freeze any spare for future use. Here are three filling options. Each makes 20-24 samosas.

VEGETABLE SAMOSA FILLING

900 g (2 lb) mashed potatoes
4 teaspoons salt
450 g (1 lb) frozen peas
1 teaspoon ground black pepper
2 teaspoons chilli powder
2 teaspoons ground coriander
1 teaspoon ground cummin
2 tablespoons dried fenugreek leaves

MEAT SAMOSA FILLING

450 g (1 lb) keema curry (see page 76)
225 g (8 oz) frozen peas, thawed
1-2 chopped chillies (optional)
1 teaspoon aromatic salt (see page 29)
1 teaspoon garam masala (see page 30)
2 teaspoons dried fenugreek leaves

SAG PANEER SAMOSA FILLING

450 g (1 lb) spinach, fresh, frozen or canned
2-4 garlic cloves, finely chopped
110 g (4 oz) spring onions, finely chopped
1 tablespoon curry masala (see page 31)
110 g (4 oz) crumbled paneer (see page 33)
or cottage cheese
4 tablespoons chopped fresh coriander

4 tablespoons chopped fresh mint
1 tablespoon garam masala (see page 30)
½ teaspoon aromatic salt (see page 29)
up to 4 green chillies, finely chopped
(optional)

1. To ensure the filling will be dry enough, strain off any excess liquid from the ingredients. Keep for another use.

2. Mix together the ingredients. Allow the mixture to go cold before using it.

SAMOSA PASTRY

2 tablespoons vegetable oil
450 g (1 lb) strong plain white flour
vegetable oil for deep-frying

1. Mix the oil, flour and enough water to make a dough which, when mixed, does not stick to the bowl. Leave it to stand for about an hour.

2. Divide the dough into four pieces, then shape each piece into a square. Roll it out and cut it into four rectangles measuring 7.5 x 20 cm (3 x 8 inches). Remember, the thinner you roll the pastry, the crispier the samosas will be.

3. Take one rectangle and place a teaspoon of filling at one end. Fold one corner diagonally over the filling to form a triangle, then fold the triangle over and over again.

4. Open the pouch and top up with some more filling. Do not overfill or the samosa will burst during frying.

5. Brush some flour and water on the remaining flap, and seal. Trim off excess pastry.

6. Preheat the deep-frying oil to 190°C/375°F. Put one samosa into the oil, and after a few seconds add the next, until about six are in. This maintains the oil temperature. Fry for 8-10 minutes, then remove, shake off excess oil, and drain on kitchen paper.

7. Serve hot or cold with tamarind chutney (*imli*); see page 44.

NOTE: You can substitute ready-made sheets of spring roll or filo pastry or samosa pads for home-made pastry at stage 2.

Chaat

Chaat is a general term meaning 'snack'. There is also a dish called Chaat. It is based on curried chick peas served either with diced chicken breast (Murghi Chaat, illustrated here, top of the basket tray), or diced potatoes (Aloo Chaat, shown here, right, using canned *kala chana* (black chick peas)). Either can be served hot, but they are also among India's few dishes which benefit from being served chilled with a salad and a lime wedge, plus some tasty chutneys. You can buy packets of ready-mixed *chaat masala* at Asian food stores. The distinctive feature of these mixes is that they contain tart mango powder and black salt, both an acquired taste.

Dahi Vada

Also using *chaat masala* and also served chilled, is Dahi Vada. *Dahi* is natural yoghurt and *vada* is a small dumpling-like ball, in this case made from lentil (*urid dhal*) flour, which is mixed with chilli and spices, then made into a dough which is either steamed or deep-fried. It is then cooled before being immersed in the pre-spiced yoghurt. A short marination, then a sprinkling of garnish is all that is needed before serving.

Bhel Puri

Little known outside Bombay, where it is a favourite kiosk food, Bhel Puri is a tantalising cold mixture of crisp, chewy textures laced with sweet, hot and sour sauces. Crunchy squiggly savoury biscuits share a bowl with diced potato, *sev*, puffed rice (*mamra*) and fresh coriander. Serve together with separate tamarind and chilli sauces and you have it. Its close relative, Sev Batata Puri, is similar, but the biscuits are replaced by flakes of crisp *puri*. Yoghurt is incorporated and the whole dish is topped with *sev* (see page 34). London boasts a few successful Bhel Puri houses, where for some decades they have served their very fresh and very cheap Bhel, and some of the smarter Indian restaurants charge infinitely more for the same equally delicious dishes.

Aniseed

Saunf or *soonf*

PIMPINELLA ANISUM

This tiny oval, striped, grey-brown seed, about 2 mm long, with a little tail, grows on an annual plant with a yellow-white flower. Aniseed is a very ancient spice, native to the Middle East, where its use was recorded by the ancient Egyptians, Greeks and Romans. It was used in English cooking in the Middle Ages, though it has less use in India than its near relative, the larger but slightly less aromatic fennel seed (see page 100) with which it is frequently confused. It is a member of the same family (Umbelliferae) as fennel. It even shares the same Hindi name, *saunf*. The similarity in taste, though not in appearance, comes about because aniseed also shares with fennel, and with star anise (see page 168), its very distinctive essential oil, anethole, of which aniseed contains a huge 90 per cent. It is this that gives aniseed its sweet and aromatic flavour, best known as the principal flavouring in such alcoholic drinks as ouzo and pastis. Aniseed is an occasional but important spice in dishes requiring an aromatic conclusion. It is also a major ingredient in *supari* mix, the digestive mixture of spices eaten after a curry meal, sometimes being coated with a highly colourful sugar coating. It is definitely worth having in stock.

Chicken Chaat

SERVES 4 AS A STARTER

2 tablespoons vegetable oil
1 teaspoon white cummin seeds
2 teaspoons white sesame seeds
2 teaspoons curry masala (see page 31)
1 teaspoon *chaat masala* (see page 43) or
½ teaspoon mango powder and
½ teaspoon black salt
1 teaspoon finely chopped garlic
2 tablespoons finely chopped onion
400 g canned chick peas
200 g (7 oz) skinned chicken breast fillet, cut into thin strips
1 tablespoon tomato purée
3 tablespoons tomato juice
2 tablespoons chopped fresh coriander
aromatic salt to taste (see page 29)

1. Heat the oil, and stir-fry the seeds and masalas for a few seconds. Add the garlic and stir-fry for a further 30 seconds, then add the onion and stir-fry for 2 minutes more.
2. Add all the remaining ingredients, and stir-fry for about 10 minutes, adding a little water if needed.
3. Remove from the heat and serve hot, or allow to cool.

Aloo Kala Chana

Potato with black chick peas

SERVES 4 AS A STARTER

2 tablespoons vegetable oil
1 teaspoon white cummin seeds
1 teaspoon curry masala (see page 30)
1 teaspoon *chaat masala* (see page 43) or
½ teaspoon mango powder and
½ teaspoon black salt
1 teaspoon garlic purée
2 tablespoons finely chopped onion
400 g canned curried black chick peas
200 g (7 oz) cooked potato, cubed
chopped green chilli to taste
aromatic salt to taste (see page 33)

1. Heat the oil, and stir-fry the seeds and masalas for a few seconds. Add the garlic purée and stir-fry for a further 30 seconds, then add the onion and stir-fry for 2 minutes more.
2. Add all the remaining ingredients and stir-fry for about 5 minutes.
3. Remove from the heat and serve hot, or allow to cool.

NOTE: If you wish to use dried chick peas, cook them as follows:

1. Check that the chick peas are free of grit, then rinse them and soak them in twice their volume of water for 6-24 hours.
2. Drain the chick peas, rinse with cold water, then boil them in ample water for 40-45 minutes until tender.

Dahi Vada

MAKES 4 VADAS

100 g (3½ oz) polished *urid dhal*
1 teaspoon chopped green chillies
⅓ teaspoon cummin seeds, crushed
⅓ teaspoon ground black pepper
⅓ teaspoon salt
1 tablespoon finely chopped onion
6 fresh curry leaves, chopped
vegetable oil for deep-frying

YOGHURT MASALA

225 g (8 oz) creamy natural yoghurt
1 teaspoon *chaat masala* (see page 43) or
½ teaspoon mango powder and
½ teaspoon black salt
½ teaspoon chilli powder

1. Grind the *dhal* (dry) into a flour (in a coffee grinder, small quantities at a time), and put in a bowl with the chillies, cummin, black pepper, salt, onion and curry leaves.
2. Make the mixture into a dough with a little water, and allow to stand for 20 minutes.
3. Roll the dough into four equal-size balls. Heat the deep-frying oil to 180°C/350°F, and

fry the vadas for 10 minutes, or until golden. Remove from the oil and allow to go cold.

4. Mix the yoghurt masala ingredients together, add the cold vadas and leave in the fridge for an hour or two. To serve, sprinkle a little extra chilli and *chaat* masala on the dish.

Bhel Puri

SERVES 4

60 g (2 oz) puffed rice (*mamra*)
25 g (1 oz) *sev*
2–3 matthis, broken into small pieces
(see page 181)
2 large cold boiled potatoes, chopped
3 tablespoons chopped onion
2 green chillies, chopped
2 tablespoons chopped fresh coriander
1–2 teaspoons *chaat masala* (see page 43)
aromatic salt to taste (see page 29)

SAUCE

150 ml (¼ pint) *imli* (see below)

1. Mix all the ingredients, except the imli, together and put in serving bowls.

2. Serve the *imli* separately, allowing the diner to add it to taste. Serve cold.

3. Optionally, in addition serve red and green chilli sauces (see page 189) and/or plain yoghurt.

Tamarind Purée

MAKES: AMPLE PURÉE

300 g block packet tamarind

1. Roughly break the tamarind block into a saucepan. Cover with ample water and bring the simmer. Work the tamarind with the back of a spoon, until the husks and seeds have separated from the flesh.

2. Strain through a sieve, returning the husks and seeds back to the saucepan with more water to repeat the process.

3. If the brown liquid is very thin and watery place in a saucepan and simmer until the liquid has reduced. Use within 1 week. Freeze in ice cube moulds, transferring to double wrapped bags.

Imli

Add to the above purée:

2 or more tablespoons sugar to taste
1 teaspoon ground white pepper or chilli powder

Prawn Butterfly

The key ingredient of this effective starter is a gigantic king prawn known to the trade, despite metrication, as the 'U5', i.e. there are under five such prawns to the pound weight (450 g). Put another way, they clock in at a massive average of 110 g (4 oz) each. Fished from the Bay of Bengal by Bangladeshis and Thais, they are also available as 'jumbo' or 'tiger' prawns, at quite a price, from specialist fishmongers. But, for taste and texture, they are worth it for that special occasion. Apart from its tail, each prawn is peeled and carefully flattened. It is then dipped in bhaji batter and deep-fried. It was originally called 'batter-fry', but someone changed the name to the rather prettier 'butterfly'.

Prawn Puri

This simple notion combines two well-established items from the menu. The *puri*, that delightful deep-fried puff-ball Indian bread (see page 179) forms the base for a small portion of prawn curry. The Patia from page 104 is the perfect partner.

Chana Puri

This vegetarian version of Prawn Puri, above, uses chick peas (*kabli chana*) as the curry subject (see page 167). There are other variants of this dish: for example, you could use the Chaat recipes from page 44 as the curry.

Aloo Tikki

These are breadcrumbed, lightly spiced mashed potato rissoles, optionally encasing a walnut-sized amount of *chana* curry. Although time-consuming to make, they are worth the effort, and can be eaten alone with chutneys, or in the traditional Southall Punjabi fashion, with a good serving of *chana* curry (see page 168) along with plain yoghurt and carrot chutney from page 189.

Asafoetida

Hing

FERULA ASAFOETIDA

This spice is extracted from the carrot-shaped rhizome of a giant perennial plant of the fennel family, called *ferula*, native to Kashmir. When the *ferula*'s rhizome is between 12 and 15 cm (5 and 6 inches) in diameter, it is mature enough to yield a milky-white sap when cut. Up to 1 kg (2¼ lb) sap slowly oozes out, over the period of a few days, and solidifies into a brown resin-like substance, pictured opposite. This is factory-ground into a grey-brown or bright greeny-lemon powder (depending on species).

The Persian word *aza*, 'resin', and Latin *foetidus*, 'stinking', indicate that asafoetida has an obnoxious, disagreeable odour, giving rise to its other names, 'devil's dung' and 'stinking gum'. This is due to the presence of sulphur in its composition. It was so highly prized, and highly priced, by the Romans, that culinary writer Apicius advised great thrift in its use, and care in its storage. Today, because of its smell, it is a good precaution to store it in its factory packaging, inside a second airtight container.

Its use is confined to Iranian and Indian cooking, where it is particularly specified in fish and lentil dishes. Fortunately, its unpleasant odour disappears once cooked, to give a further distinctive and pleasant fragrance and sweetish taste. Used in small quantities, it is supposed to aid digestion by combating flatulence.

Prawn Butterfly

SERVES 4

3 tablespoons gram flour
2 tablespoons plain flour
1 teaspoon salt
1 teaspoon garam masala (see page 30)
½ teaspoon chilli powder
4 large raw king prawns, each weighing about 110 g (4 oz)
vegetable oil for deep-frying

1. Mix the flours, salt, garam masala and chilli with enough water to form a creamy batter which drops slowly off the spoon.
2. Remove the heads and shells from the prawns, leaving the tails, and remove the 'veins' by cutting all along the back of each. To create the butterfly shape, flatten the prawns gently with a cleaver.
3. Heat the deep-frying oil to 190°C/375°F (chip-frying temperature).
4. Immerse the prawns in the batter.
5. Deep-fry the coated prawns for about 10 minutes until the batter is a golden orange colour.
6. Serve at once on a bed of salad, before the batter goes soggy and chewy.

Prawn Puri

Prawn curry on fried bread

SERVES 4 AS A STARTER

2 tablespoons ghee
1 garlic clove, finely chopped
6 tablespoons very finely chopped onion
175 g tub peeled prawns in brine
1 tablespoon coconut milk powder
1 tablespoon tomato purée
2 tablespoons bottled prawn ballichow pickle (see page 104)
1½ tablespoons jaggery or brown sugar
2 tablespoons chopped fresh coriander
aromatic salt to taste (see page 29)
4 puris (see page 180)

MASALA

1 teaspoon mustard seeds
½ teaspoon turmeric
½ teaspoon ground cummin
½ teaspoon garam masala (see page 30)

1. Heat the ghee and stir-fry the garlic and masala for 1 minute. Add the onion and continue to stir-fry for about 2 minutes more.
2. Drain the prawns and rinse them.
3. Add the remaining ingredients to the pan, including the prawns but not the puris, and stir-fry for a further 3-4 minutes.
4. Deep-fry the puris, following the method on page 180.
5. Serve very hot with the prawn curry on top of the puris.

Chana Puri Curry
Chick pea curry on fried bread

SERVES 4 AS A STARTER

2 tablespoons vegetable oil
1 teaspoon white cummin seeds
2 teaspoons white sesame seeds
1 teaspoon finely chopped garlic
225 g (8 oz) canned chick peas
2 tablespoons chopped fresh coriander
1 teaspoon dried mint
1 teaspoon dried fenugreek leaves
1 tablespoon curry masala paste (see
page 31)
2 fresh tomatoes, chopped
1 tablespoon tomato purée
100 ml (3½ fl oz) canned tomato soup
salt to taste
4 *puris* (see page 180)

1.   Heat the oil and stir-fry the seeds for a
few seconds, then add the garlic and cook for
a further minute. Add all the remaining ingredients, except the *puris*, and stir-fry for about
5 minutes.

2.   Deep-fry the *puris*, following the method
on page 180.

3.   Serve the *chana* curry over the *puris* whilst
both are piping hot.

Aloo Tikki
Potato and lentil rissoles

MAKES 8–10 RISSOLES

450 g (1 lb) mashed potatoes
175 g (6 oz) frozen peas
1–2 green chillies, finely chopped
½ teaspoon salt
110 g (4 oz) cooked cold *dhal* (see
page 169)
breadcrumbs
vegetable oil for frying

MASALA

½ teaspoon ground coriander
½ teaspoon cummin seeds
½ teaspoon chilli powder

1.   Mix together the potatoes, peas, chilli, salt
and masala.

2.   Make the mixture into cup shapes of 5–6
cm (2–2½ inches) in diameter. Depending on
the size of your 'cups', the recipe should give
eight to ten rissoles.

3.   Put a little of the *dhal* mixture in each
'cup' and enclose it in the potato by gently
squeezing. Flatten each filled cup into a
conventional rissole shape, and cover in breadcrumbs.

4.   Heat the oil in a frying pan. Fry the
rissoles on one side until brown, then turn
over and brown the other side.

5.   Aloo Tikki can be served hot or cold, on
their own with chutneys.

VARIATION
Aloo Tikki Chana

Hot or cold Aloo Tikki can be covered with
hot or cold Chana Chaat, and topped with
yoghurt masala (see page 45). Serve with
carrot chutney (see page 189).

KEBABS

It was the early Turks who perfected the technique of marinating meat cubes before grilling them. *Kebab* literally means 'cooked meat' in Turkish. The Turks also developed the method of pounding flavoured meat and shaping it over skewers, originally their swords. The celebrated *doner* (meaning 'to turn') is a mixture of pounded mutton, fat, garlic and herbs which is rotated on an upright skewer in front of a flame. Somehow India missed out on this particular delight, but nowhere else is there such a variety of kebabs available than in the subcontinent. These are the most popular kebabs:

Boti and Chaamp

Bite-sized cubes of tender lean leg of lamb or pork are marinated in yoghurt, oil, garlic and chilli, then grilled (top skewer). Lamb chop (Chaamp) is marinated as for Boti, then grilled.

Hassina or Shashlik

Shashlik originated in Armenia, now independent once again from the USSR. The word in Armenian means 'grill'. Marinated meat or chicken cubes are interspersed with onion and pepper on a skewer and grilled. The simple concept was taken by invading armies into India where the dish, with a different marinade, is called Hassina Kebab. Both versions are to be found in Indian restaurants.

Sheek, Shami and Katori

Ground meat is moulded round skewers (*sheek* in Turkish), though my foolproof method (see page 53) works without skewers. Other spellings include Shish, Sis, Sheesh and Sheik. The Shami kebab is disc-shaped. Katori kebabs are tiny and very soft (shown in the small bowl). Nargis kebabs are like scotch eggs (here using quail and chicken eggs).

Bay Leaf

Tej Patta Laurel

LAURIS NOBILIS

Bay, or laurel leaf, is pointed and oval in shape, and grows to an average 7 cm (3 inches) in length. It can be used fresh or dried. Fresh, it is glossy, smooth, quite fleshy, and dark green in colour. Dried, it is paler, and quite brittle. The leaf grows on an evergreen tree or bush, found worldwide, and especially in Europe. In fact bay is one of the few spices to be grown and used in England, though not in India. There, it is *tej patta cassia*, the slightly larger leaf of the cassia tree, which is used, not the bay leaf (see page 188). Considerable confusion exists about these two leaves, since both are called 'tej patta', or 'bay', in India and Indian cookbooks. In fact they have different flavouring attributes. Whole bay, though quite different, is a familiar spice to most people in the West, and since *tej patta cassia* is virtually unobtainable outside India, bay makes a perfectly acceptable substitute in subtle, aromatic curries, such as Korma, and in Birianis. Fresh, it is more powerful than dried, with a slightly more bitter undertone. Ground bay is an ingredient in masalas.

Boti Kebab

SERVES 2 AS A STARTER

ten 3 cm (1¼ inch) cubes lean meat or skinned chicken breast
2 tablespoons fresh lemon juice

MARINADE

110 g (4 oz) natural yoghurt
2 tablespoons vegetable oil
1 tablespoon tomato purée
2-3 teaspoons finely chopped garlic
1½ teaspoons ground coriander
1 teaspoon chilli powder
1 teaspoon aromatic salt (see page 29)

1. Prick the meat or chicken cubes with a sharp, pointed knife, then rub in the lemon.
2. Mix the marinade ingredients together, then add the meat. Cover and leave to stand overnight.
3. To cook, preheat the grill to medium hot.
4. Thread five cubes of meat on to a skewer, leaving a small gap between each piece. Repeat with a second skewer.
5. Cook under the grill in the midway position, or over charcoal, until ready, turning once or twice.

VARIATION

Chaamp

Lamb Chop Kebabs

SERVES 4

8 lamb chops, each weighing about 110 g (4 oz)

Follow the Boti recipe, using its marinade. Cook the chops under the grill or over charcoal for 10-20 minutes, depending on the size and thickness of the chops, turning at least once.

Hassina Kebab

SERVES 2 AS A STARTER

ten 3 cm (1¼ inch) cubes lean meat or skinned chicken breast
200 g (7 oz) red tandoori marinade
½ red bell pepper
½ green bell pepper
½ Spanish onion
2 garlic cloves, peeled
2 fresh green chillies

1. Add the cubes of meat or chicken to the tandoori marinade in a large non-metallic bowl, ensuring they are well coated. Cover the bowl and refrigerate for 24-60 hours.
2. After the meat has marinated, cut each bell pepper into four 2.5 cm (1 inch) diamonds or squares, discarding the seeds. Separate the layers of the onion and cut ten pieces into the same-sized shapes.
3. Preheat the oven to 220°C/425°F/Gas 7. Meanwhile, thread half the items on to a skewer as follows: onion, meat, green pepper, meat, onion, red pepper, meat, onion, green pepper, meat, onion, red pepper, meat, onion. Repeat with the remaining items and a second skewer. Put one clove of garlic and one green chilli on to each skewer.
4. Place the skewers on a wire rack on an oven tray. Baste with any excess marinade.
5. Cook in the oven for 8-10 minutes for rare meat, 10-15 minutes for medium and 15 minutes more for well done. Alternatively, cook under a medium grill, with the rack at the lowest level, or over charcoal for the same amounts of time.

VARIATION

Shashlik Kebab

SERVES 2 AS A STARTER

Use the Hassina ingredients, minus the tandoori marinade. Using the Boti marinade, thoroughly mix together all the marinade ingredients in a large, non-metallic bowl, then follow the method for Hassina Kebabs.

Sheek Kebab
Restaurant style

Best-quality lean lamb, skinned chicken breast, etc., can be used instead of beef.

SERVES 4

675 g (1½ lb) topside of beef, or fillet steak
4-6 garlic cloves, chopped
2.5 cm (1 inch) piece fresh ginger, chopped
2-4 fresh green chillies
2 tablespoons chopped fresh coriander leaves
10 fresh mint leaves, chopped
2 tablespoons curry masala (see page 30)
1 teaspoon aromatic salt (see page 33)
⅓ teaspoon red food colouring (optional)

1. Inspect the meat and remove all fat, skin, gristle, etc. Chop the meat coarsely.
2. Mix the meat with all the other ingredients, then put it into a food processor in several small batches (to avoid overloading the machine), or through a mincer. Run each batch through the machine several times. This achieves a fine texture, and the finer the mince, the softer the kebab.
3. Put the batches of mixture in a bowl and mix again thoroughly, using your fingers.
4. Divide the mixture into four and shape each portion on a metal skewer in a long sausage of at least 15 cm (6 inches) in length.
5. Preheat the oven to 190°C/ 375°F/Gas 5. Place the skewers on an oven tray, and cook in the oven for 12-15 minutes. Alternatively, cook under the grill at a medium-high heat, rotating the kebabs a few times.

VARIATIONS
Shami Kebab

The ingredients given above will make eight Shami kebabs.

Follow the recipe above, to the end of stage 3, then divide the mixture into eight portions. Roll them into balls, then flatten them into rissole-shaped discs. Bake in the oven for 10-12 minutes, or grill as above.

Soft Sheek, Shami Kebab
A quick version

Mash 8-10 tablespoons Tarka Dhal (see page 169) and add it to the Sheek Kebab ingredients at stage 3. Follow the rest of the recipe.

Nargis Kebab
Indian scotch egg

SERVES 4

8 quail eggs or 2 chicken eggs
1 batch finely minced Sheek Kebab mixture

1. Hard-boil the quail eggs for exactly 4 minutes (chicken eggs for exactly 15 minutes), then shell.
2. Preheat the oven to 190°C/375°F/Gas 5.
3. Divide the kebab mixture into eight for quail eggs, and two for chicken eggs
4. Carefully wrap it around the shelled eggs, to achieve a round or egg-like shape. Place the kebabs on a foil-lined oven tray.
5. Bake the kebabs in the oven for 8-10 minutes for the quail-egg version, or 12-15 minutes for the chicken-egg version.

Katori Kebab
Silky smooth kebabs

To get a melt-in-the-mouth smoothness and softness, you need a pâté-like texture. Here is my 'cheats'' method, letting the delicatessen do the hard work.

To the soft kebab recipe above: reduce the meat quantity by about 150 g (5½ oz), and replace it with an equal weight of fine-textured pâté (any type). Proceed with either recipe to the shaping stage.

Katori kebabs should be really small, so roll the mixture into 'marbles' or 'acorns'. Cooking time is thereby reduced to less than half the time, whether baked or fried.

Rashmi Kebab
Kebabs in egg nets

These should be Shami Kebabs wrapped in threaded egg nets, but at some restaurants, Rashmis simply come wrapped in omelettes.

TANDOORI AND TIKKA

It is hard to believe that tandoori, and its off-spring tikka, meaning 'a little piece', did not become widely known in Britain until the 1970s. In fact tandoori was equally unknown in India until 1947. Until that time it had been an unintentionally well-kept secret in its place of origin, the North-West Frontier, that rugged inhospitable area now well inside Pakistan. There, the custom of rapidly baking a uniquely spiced marination of meat or chicken in a high-temperature, vertical, clay oven called a *tandoor*, had been going on for centuries, having previously evolved from the Egyptian *tonir* via the Persian *tanoor*. *Nane* bread and *Tikkeh*, spicy meat on a skewer, certainly originated in Iran, but it was definitely the Moghuls who developed tandoori flavours as we know them today.

The secret lies in the combination of spices, herbs and yoghurt which penetrates and tenderises the meat during marination. The longer the marination, the better the penetration and thus the taste. The *tandoor* itself adds its own smoky flavour to the food as it is cooked.

Having eventually reached Britain, it was not surprising that tandoori cooking spread rapidly during the 1970s to nearly every curry house in the land, and beyond. Being low in fat and served with salads and yoghurt dips, tandoori food is unquestionably good for health, apart, that is, from one ingredient, tartrazine food colouring. The bright red and orange of Britain's tandoori food play no part in its place of origin, where natural colourings were, and still are, sufficient. But if you are amongst the many who say they prefer bright colours, all is explained overleaf. The comparison in the photograph is really striking. The big platter, of course, contains restaurant-style Tandoori Chicken Leg, Lamb Tikka and Chicken Tikka. The adjacent plate contains two naturally coloured Chicken Tikkas, one the original orange colour, the other an authentic Herbal Green Chicken Tikka. The third plate contains Gurda and Kaleji Kebab (kidney and liver kebabs).

Caraway

Shia, Shahi or *Siya Jeera* or *Zira*

CARUM CARVI

Caraway may well be the world's most ancient spice, with evidence of its use going back over 5,000 years. Seeds have been discovered amongst pottery remains in a number of archaeological sites in the Levant, the area where both argriculture and literacy, as well as caraway, originated. The Romans added it to their bread, as do contemporary Germans and Austrians.

Caraway grows as a biennial plant, yielding small seeds about 3 mm (⅛ inch) in length, coloured dark grey-brown, with five lighter-coloured ridges. It is a member of the same family (Umbelliferae) and is similar in appearance to black cummin (see page 196), though it is paler in colour and a fraction larger, and has no similarity in flavour. Caraway has an aromatic, agreeably warm aroma, with a hint of astringency due to the presence of caravone in its essential oil. In England, it is best known as a cake-making spice. It grows well in cooler climates, such as northern Europe, Russia and the northern subcontinent, especially the Himalayas. In India, it is used more medicinally than in traditional Indian cookery. As in Europe, it is enjoyed in bread and cakes, cheese and distilling. As far as curry cookery goes, it is a minor spice, but it gives an interesting flavouring option to bread (see Matthi, page 181) or rice dishes. A tiny pinch adds depth to aromatic curries.

Tandoori Paste

The tandoori masala on page 31 creates 250 g (9 oz) dry mix. This quantity can be made into a paste weighing 675 g (1½ lb) which stores in the bottle indefinitely. But you can reduce this pro-rata for smaller batches.

Red Marinade

MAKES 400 G (14 OZ)

150 g (5½ oz) natural yoghurt
2 tablespoons vegetable oil
2 tablespoons fresh lime juice
2-3 garlic cloves, finely chopped
2-3 fresh red chillies, finely chopped
2 tablespoons chopped fresh coriander leaves
1 teaspoon white cumin seeds, roasted
1 teaspoon garam masala (see page 30)
2 tablespoons red tandoori paste (see above)
1 tablespoon tomato purée
½ teaspoon aromatic salt (see page 29)

1. Put all the ingredients into the blender and start pulsing.
2. Gradually drizzle in enough water to make a purée that is easy to pour, and as smooth as you can get it. Refrigerate until needed.

NOTE: To achieve the restaurant red or orange look, simply add ½ teaspoon red and/or orange food colouring (tartrazine food dyes). Made from coal tar, they are said to have 'side-effects', particularly affecting children, such as allergies, asthma attacks and hyperactivity. These dyes appear, of course, in numerous other factory-produced foods, such as ready meals, confectionery, sauces, bakery, etc. The food tastes no different, with or without them, but if you wish to have vibrant-coloured tandoori and rice dishes, purchase them in powdered form, and remember, they are extremely concentrated, so use just a tiny amount. See also page 173.

Green Marinade

An unusual, herby, natural marinade.

MAKES 400 G (14 OZ)

150 g (5½ oz) natural yoghurt
2 tablespoons mustard blend oil
3-4 garlic cloves, finely chopped
225 g (8 oz) spring onion leaves
225 g (8 oz) fresh coriander leaves
20-30 fresh mint leaves, finely chopped
20-30 baby spinach leaves and soft stalks, finely chopped
2-4 green chillies, finely chopped
½ teaspoon aromatic salt (see page 29)
1 tablespoon garam masala (see page 30)

Make a purée as for Red Marinade, above.

Chicken Tikka

SERVES 2 AS A STARTER

ten to twelve 4 cm (1½ inch) cubes skinned chicken breast
200 g (7 oz) red or green marinade (see above)

1. Mix the chicken into the marinade in a non-metallic bowl. Cover and refrigerate for 24-60 hours.
2. To cook, preheat the grill to medium and divide the chicken between two skewers.
3. Place the skewers on the grill rack above a foil-lined grill pan and place this in the mid-way position. Alternatively, the kebabs can be barbecued.
4. Cook for 5 minutes, turn, then cook for a further 5 minutes.
5. Cut through one piece of chicken to ensure that it is fully cooked; it should be white right through with no hint of pink. If not, cook for a while longer. When fully cooked, raise the pan nearer to the heat and singe the pieces to obtain a little blackening.

Meat Tikka

SERVES 2 AS A STARTER

ten to twelve 4 cm (1½ inch) cubes
lean meat
200 g (7 oz) red or green marinade

1. Mix the meat into the marinade in a non-metallic bowl. Cover and refrigerate for 24-60 hours.
2. To cook, preheat the oven to 220°C/425°F/Gas 7. Line an oven tray with foil and place a rack over the tray.
3. Divide the meat between two metal skewers and place them on the rack. Cook in the oven for 15-20 minutes, or until the meat is cooked to your liking. A degree of pinkness or 'rareness' in the middle of the meat may be preferred, and this is acceptable (except for pork which should be fully cooked) – adjust the cooking time accordingly

VARIATIONS

Tandoori Chicken Legs

These can be oven cooked using the same times as the Meat Tikka above.

Tandoori Mixed Grill

A favourite restaurant presentation is Tandoori and Tikka Mixed Grill. You can create your own mixed grill by choosing a selection of recipes from this book. Adjust quantities to suit the number of people you are serving. It's ideal for parties and barbecues.

Tandoori Fish

SERVES 2

2 whole trout or mackerel, each weighing
about 350 g (12 oz), cleaned and gutted
200 g (7 oz) red or green marinade

1. Lightly slash the fish with a sharp, pointed knife, then cover the fish with the mari-nade in a non-metallic bowl.
2. Cover and leave to marinate in the refrigerator for at least 6 hours.
3. Preheat the oven to 190°C/375°F/Gas 5. Place the fish on foil on wire racks over foil-lined oven trays, and cook in the oven for about 20 minutes, turning at least once. Keep a close eye on the fish at all times as it may need slightly less or more than 20 minutes' cooking.
4. Alternatively, cook over the barbecue until ready (10-15 minutes, depending on heat and thickness of fish).

Gurda or Kaleji Kebabs

Kidney or liver kebabs

SERVES 4

4 tablespoon butter ghee
about 1 teaspoon (several flakes) alkanet
root (see page 42)
225 g (8 oz) lamb kidneys or liver, cut
into bite-sized pieces
aromatic salt to taste (see page 29)

1. Heat the ghee, add the alkanet root and stir-fry it for about 30 seconds. Note how the ghee turns deep red.
2. Using a metal sieve, strain the hot ghee into a wok or karahi. Discard the alkanet root.
3. Reheat the red ghee, add the seeds, and, as soon as they start to pop, add the kidney.
4. Stir-fry for 8-10 minutes or until cooked, adjusting the heat as necessary. Salt to taste and serve hot.

THE TOP SIXTEEN CURRIES

Between this page and page 121 are the Top Sixteen Curries, i.e. those most in demand at the curry restaurant. I have arranged them in alphabetical order, and in each case I have given a main recipe, which is illustrated in the accompanying photograph, and a selection of alternative recipes.

BALTI

In my introduction on page 9, I discuss the most popular curry dishes. It probably comes as no surprise to find that Tikka Masala is always the most popular curry, with Korma a close second. But to find that Balti is now the nation's third most popular curry does come as a surprise because, up until the early 1990s, hardly anyone had heard of it outside its place of origin in northern-most Pakistan, and it only started to become popular in Birmingham's suburbs in the 1970s. Its main attraction is its price; it is inexpensive. Served authentically with no cutlery, in a two-handled pan, the Balti pan or *karahi*, it is eaten Pakistan-style with naan bread. Being of Kashmiri origin, it is aromatic and herby, using garam masala spices and plenty of coriander and/or mint to accompany freshly cooked main ingredients. Diners are free to mix any number of main ingredients, so combinations such as Balti Chicken Mushroom and Dhal, or Balti Meat and Prawns, or Balti Aubergine with Spinach, Sweetcorn and Chana Dhal are typical. For those who wish to study the history of Balti in depth, and its remarkably rapid spread around the UK and beyond, I refer you to my book, the *Curry Club Balti Curry Cookbook*, with its 100 Balti recipes.

Illustrated left is Balti Keema with Paneer, Spinach and Chick Peas, a good, attractive example of a Balti combination dish (recipe overleaf).

Cardamom

Elaichi

CARDAMOMUM: ELETTARIA
(GREEN AND WHITE);
AFRAMOMUM (BROWN/BLACK);
AMOMUM (THAI)

Cardamom grows in south India, Sri Lanka, Thailand and Guatemala, on a herbaceous perennial plant related to the ginger family, whose pods contain slightly sticky black seeds, their familiar flavour coming from the cineol in their oils. Cardamom is one of the most elegant, aromatic and expensive spices, and is one of India's most exported spices, earning the country considerable revenue, and the spice itself, the title 'the Queen of Spice'. There are three main cardamom types, all of which can be used whole or ground.

Natural white cardamoms are much in demand for flavour. The Thai species (at the top of the photograph opposite), are darker in colour, rounder and larger than Indian whites (bottom). These are of the same species as the green, having a similar flavour, which is rather more delicate than the brown. But beware bleached cardamoms, which are old specimens 'livened-up'.

Green cardamoms, *chota elaichi*, have a smooth, ribbed, pale green outer casing, about 1 cm (½ inch) long. The greener the cardamom, the fresher it is, though use of food dyes is not unknown to 'freshen-up' older specimens. They are used whole or ground, with or without casing.

Brown, also called black, cardamom, *bara elaichi*, have a rather hairy, husky, dark brown casing about 2 cm (¾ inch) long. Used in garam masala, kormas and pullaos, they are astringent and aromatic.

Balti Masala mix

This simplified mix is the key to obtaining aromatic fresh Balti tastes. It makes enough for 8-10 Balti recipes, and will keep for months in an airtight screw-topped jar. For easier measuring, 5g equals 1 teaspoon.

> MAKES 200 G (7 OZ)
>
> 10 g aniseed
> 10 g fennel seeds
> 10 g allspice
> 70 g garam masala (see page 30)
> 60 g curry masala (see page 31)
> 20 g garlic powder
> 10 g ground ginger
> 10 g chilli powder

1. Roast and grind the aniseed, fennel seeds and allspice (see page 30 for method).
2. Mix with the other ingredients and store.

Balti Keema

Aromatic mince curry

> SERVES 4
>
> 675 g (1½ lb) minced meat
> 2-3 tablespoons butter ghee or vegetable oil
> 3-6 garlic cloves, finely chopped
> 3 tablespoons Balti masala (see above)
> about 200 ml (7 fl oz) fragrant stock (see page 29)
> 225 g (8 oz) onion, very finely chopped
> 3 tablespoons chopped fresh coriander leaves
> 1 tablespoon chopped fresh mint leaves
> 1 red bell pepper, chopped
> aromatic salt to taste (see page 29)

1. Preheat the oven to 190°C/375°F/Gas 5.
2. Heat the ghee or oil in a karahi or wok on high heat. Add the garlic and stir-fry for 30 seconds, then add the masala with just enough stock to make a paste, and continue to stir-fry for a further minute. Add the onion, reduce the heat, and stir-fry for about 10 minutes more, allowing the onion to become translucent and begin to brown (see tarka method on page 31).
3. Add the mince to the pan. Raise the heat again and bring to a brisk sizzle, stir-frying to seal as needed for about 5 minutes.
4. Transfer the mixture to a lidded casserole dish and cook in the oven for 20 minutes. Inspect and stir, adding a little stock as needed. Cook for 20 minutes more, then repeat, adding the fresh coriander and mint, red pepper and aromatic salt to taste.
5. Cook for a final 20-30 minutes, after which time it is ready to serve.

VARIATIONS

Balti Keema with Paneer, Spinach and Chick peas

SERVES 6

To make the dish pictured on the previous page, make the Balti Keema as above, then add the following ingredients after stage 5:

> 200 g (7 oz) paneer cubes (see page 33)
> 20-25 baby spinach leaves and their soft stalks, chopped
> 200 g (7 oz) canned chick peas, drained

They only need time to heat up, which they will do if given a few minutes in the casserole dish, with its lid on. Note in the picture that the Paneer is attractive if some of it is treated like a garnish, and not immersed in the curry.

Balti Meat

Diced lamb or stewing steak can be substituted for the mince. the remaining ingredients and method are the same.

Balti Chicken and Mushroom

500 g (1 lb 2 oz) skinned chicken breast
fillet, cut into 3 cm (1¼ inch) cubes
2–3 tablespoons butter ghee
1 teaspoon white cummin seeds
½ teaspoon lovage seeds
3–6 garlic cloves, finely chopped
3–4 tablespoons Balti masala (see left)
200 ml (7 fl oz) fragrant stock (see page 29)
225 g (8 oz) spring onions, leaves and
bulbs, chopped
1 tablespoon chopped red bell pepper
1–2 fresh green chillies, chopped
350 g (12 oz) button mushrooms, cleaned
and sliced
1 teaspoon garam masala (see page 30)
2–3 tablespoons finely chopped fresh
coriander leaves
1–2 tablespoons finely chopped fresh
basil leaves
aromatic salt to taste (see page 29)

1. Heat the ghee in a karahi or wok on high heat and stir-fry the seeds for a few seconds. Add the garlic and stir-fry for a further 30 seconds.

2. Add the Balti masala with just enough stock to make a paste, and continue to stir-fry for a further minute.

3. Add the chicken, and stir-fry at the sizzle for 8–10 minutes, drizzling in more stock, little by little, so that it thickens, but never overwhelms the dish.

4. Add the onion, red pepper, chillies and mushrooms with any remaining stock, and simmer for about 5 minutes more.

5. Test that the chicken is cooked right through by removing a piece and cutting it in two. If there are any traces of pink, replace the halves in the pan and continue cooking. Keep testing until cooked, then add the remaining ingredients and salt to taste. Simmer for a minute or two further, then serve.

VARIATION
Balti Prawns

Raw prawns or king prawns can be substituted for the chicken. The remaining ingredients and method are the same.

Balti Chi-Dhal-Sweetcorn-Aub

Balti mixed vegetable curry

This is a delicious all-vegetable combination, as its Balti-house name suggests. For the uninitiated, it means chick pea, *dhal*, sweetcorn and aubergine curry.

2 tablespoons Balti masala (see left)
2 tablespoons vegetable oil
150 g (5½ oz) Tarka Dhal (see page 169)
150 g (5½ oz) Brinjal Bhajee (see
page 161)
150 g (5½ oz) canned sweetcorn kernels
150 g (5½ oz) canned chick peas, drained
2 tablespoons chopped brinjal pickle
175 g (6 oz) baby leaf spinach
6 cherry tomatoes, halved
1–2 fresh red chillies, chopped
1 teaspoon garam masala (see page 30)
2–3 tablespoons finely chopped fresh
coriander leaves
aromatic salt to taste (see page 29)

1. Add just enough water to the Balti masala to make a paste.

2. Heat the oil and stir-fry the paste for a couple of minutes.

3. Add all the remaining ingredients, except the aromatic salt, to the pan and combine well. Heat it right through, salt to taste, garnish and serve hot accompanied by a Balti Karak Naan and Balti chutney.

BHOONA

Bhoona is the Hindi and Urdu term for the process of cooking a wet ground masala or ground spice paste in hot oil. It is the most important part of curry cooking, since it is this process that removes the raw taste of the spices and releases the essential oils, creating that wonderful well-rounded taste that we expect of our curry, in which no one spice jars the taste-buds or predominates.

We saw how to carry out this process on page 30. As soon as it is complete, i.e. when the oil 'floats', it is essential to add small quantities of water or stock to the pan. This prevents sticking, lowers the temperature and helps to prevent burning. Incidentally, the process of frying whole spices is called *bargar*.

The Bhoona process is extended to cooking an entire curry by stir-frying it right through to completion. In the case of a meat curry, Bhoona Gosht, this can take over an hour of virtually continuous stir-frying with almost drip-by-drip addition of liquid throughout all that time. What should emerge is a meat curry which is very tender but quite dry, certainly with no excess gravy. The meat, usually mutton or goat leg, is invariably sawn into small pieces on the bone from a cut which is not available in the West. Indians greatly prefer meat on the bone, and there is a lot to be said for sucking every last bit of flavour from such pieces, including the marrow. On-the-bone chicken pieces can be deliciously cooked by the Bhoona process, taking about half the time of meat. Either way, the traditional Bhoona results are wonderful, needless to say, but the effort is excruciating.

It would be totally impractical to stir-fry anything for an hour in a restaurant. As with the chicken version shown here, the Bhoona is presented as a mild, dryish curry, usually cooked with a little coconut and coriander.

Cassia Bark

Jangli Dalchini

CINNAMOMON CASSIA

This is the corky, outer bark of a tree, with a sweet fragrance, related to cinnamon (see page 76). Indeed there is considerable confusion between the two. Many spice manufacturers insist on labelling 'cassia bark' as 'cinnamon'. Cassia originated in Burma and is now widely grown in Indonesia and south China, giving rise to its alternative name, Chinese cinnamon.

Cassia is an ancient spice, known to the ancient Egyptians. It grows as a large, evergreen, tropical-forest tree, the leaves of which are used as a spice (see Tamala Leaf, page 188). Branches are cut down and their bark is scraped off and formed into reddish-brown quills about 1 metre (3 feet) long. These are fragile, and by the time it is packed, cassia is usually in chips, averaging 5 cm (2 inches) in length. Cassia's essential oil contains cinnamic aldehyde, giving it a sweet, clove-like, musky flavour. Cassia bark is usually much less fragrant, coarser, thicker and tougher than cinnamon, and it stands up to more robust cooking. It is also cheaper. It is used as an aromatic flavouring in subtle meat and poultry dishes, and as a major flavouring in pullao rice and garam masala. Although widely used in cooking, the bark cannot be eaten.

Bhoona Chicken

SERVES 4

675 g (1½ lb) chicken breast, skinned and cut into large bite-sized cubes
2 tablespoons ghee or vegetable oil
½ teaspoon turmeric
8 tablespoons curry masala gravy (see page 32)
2 tablespoons chopped fresh coriander leaves
2 tablespoons natural yoghurt
salt to taste

MASALA ONE

4 bay leaves
6 small pieces cassia bark
6 cloves

MASALA TWO

1 tablespoon garam masala (see page 30)
2 teaspoons chilli powder

1. Heat the ghee or oil and stir-fry the Masala One ingredients for a few seconds. Add the turmeric and continue stirring for a few more seconds.
2. Add the chicken pieces and stir-fry for 3-4 minutes to seal it. Add 2 tablespoons curry masala gravy, stir it in for about a minute, until it is absorbed, then add more. Repeat this process until the gravy is all in. The chicken should be fairly dry and nearly cooked after about 15 minutes.
3. Add Masala Two to the pan with the fresh coriander and the yoghurt. Stir-fry for a further 2-3 minutes. Check that the chicken is cooked right through by cutting a piece in half. It must be white right through. Salt to taste and serve.

Bhoona Meat

SERVES 4

675 g (1½ lb) lean meat, cut into 3 cm (1 ¼ inch) cubes, and weighed after discarding unwanted matter
2 tablespoons ghee or vegetable oil
2 tablespoons curry masala (see page 31)
225 g (8 oz) onions, roughly chopped, or 225 g (8 oz) onion tarka (see page 32)
2 tablespoons chopped fresh coriander leaves
salt to taste

1. Preheat the oven to 190°C/375°F/Gas 5.
2. Heat the ghee or oil in a flameproof casserole dish of between 2.25 and 2.75 litre (4 and 5 pint) capacity, and stir-fry the curry masala mix for a minute, adding a little water to achieve a paste. Add the onions or onion tarka, and continue to stir-fry for 3 minutes more. Add the meat, put the lid on the casserole dish, and put it in the oven.
3. After 20 minutes' cooking, inspect, stir and taste. Add a little water, if required, remembering it should be dryish. Replace in the oven.
4. After a further 20 minutes, again inspect and taste the casserole. The meat should be tender. Add more water if needed, add the coriander leaves and salt to taste. Replace the casserole in the oven for a final 20-30 minutes, or until the meat is very tender. Turn off the heat and leave the casserole in the oven for 10 minutes before serving.

Bhoona Prawns
Fried prawn curry

SERVES 4

675 g (1½ lb) medium to large raw prawns, weighed after removing shells and heads
3 tablespoons ghee or vegetable oil
2–3 garlic cloves, finely chopped
2 tablespoons curry masala (see page 31)
110 g (4 oz) onions, finely chopped
1 tablespoon chopped fresh coriander leaves
aromatic salt to taste (see page 29)

1. De-vein the prawns and wash them.
2. Heat the ghee or oil in a karahi or wok and stir-fry the garlic for 30 seconds. Add the masala with just enough water to make a paste, and stir-fry for a couple of minutes more. Add the onion and continue stir-frying for 5 minutes.
3. Add the prawns and stir-fry briskly for 2–3 minutes, then reduce the heat and simmer for about 5 more minutes or until cooked. The larger the prawns, the longer they will take to cook. During cooking, add small amounts of water as needed, remembering the dish should be quite dry.
4. Add the coriander and salt to taste, and simmer for a couple more minutes before serving.

Vegetable Bhoona

SERVES 4

450 g (1 lb) mixed vegetables, weighed after stage 1, below
3 tablespoons vegetable ghee or oil
5 cm (2 inch) piece fresh ginger, thinly sliced into matchsticks
1 tablespoon curry masala (see page 31)
200 g (7 oz) onion, thinly sliced
2 tablespoons chopped fresh coriander leaves
aromatic salt to taste (see page 29)

1. Clean and prepare the vegetables as appropriate.
2. Heat the ghee or oil in a karahi or wok and stir-fry the ginger for 20 seconds. Add the masala and stir-fry for a further minute. Add the onion and stir-fry for about 5 minutes.
3. Meanwhile, steam, boil or microwave the vegetables until just cooked but still crunchy. Drain well.
4. Add the hot vegetables and the coriander to the fried onions and mix in well. Simmer for a couple of minutes more, then salt to taste and serve.

DHANSAK

Eleven centuries ago a tribe was forced to flee Persia for religious reasons. Some time later they settled in Gujarat in India, where they became known as Parsees (from Persia), specialising as traders. Later they migrated south to Bombay in time to use their business acumen in a supporting role to the activities of the British Raj. About 100,000 Parsees still live in Bombay, a tiny proportion of that city's 12 million population, but they are still at the hub of all things commercial, their original faith intact, their food unique in India, still showing its Persian origins. Meat mixed with vegetables and fruit, for example, is typical of Persian and Parsee food, though the latter has now incorporated the Indian spice palette. One such speciality dish is lamb cooked with dried apricots; another is Patia, a hot, sweet and sour curry (see page 103). But the most celebrated and popular of all Parsee dishes is Dhansak. At the restaurant, this dish is interpreted as meat, chicken or prawns merged with pre-cooked *massoor dhal*. Additional flavours are achieved by using dried fenugreek leaf for savoury, though this is not a traditional Parsee flavouring, and varying amounts of sugar, lemon and chilli for sweet, sour and hot tastes.

The traditional Parsee Dhansak always combines meat with up to four types of lentil (polished *moong*, *massoor*, *chana* and *toovar*). Slow cooking amalgamates the flavours. During the cooking, a kind of ratatouille of aubergine, tomato, spinach and fresh chillies is added. Sweet and sour comes from jaggery (see page 112) and a slight overtone of sour from fresh lime. The apt derivation of the name of this dish comes from *dhan*, meaning 'wealthy' in Gujarati, and *sak*, meaning 'vegetables'. Pronounced slightly differently, *dhaan* means 'rice', and this sumptuous dish is traditionally eaten as a Sunday special with brown rice (see page 171).

The dish shown here is a simplified version of the traditional Dhansak, with, overleaf, some restaurant versions too.

Celery Seed

Ajmud or *Shalari*

APIUM GRAVEOLENS

This is an ancient spice, native to Europe, Asia and Africa. In recent centuries it has been taken to America. It is a herbal plant of the parsley family, which grows up to 1.5 metres (5 feet) in height, and yields tiny (1 mm) oval olive-greenish-brown seeds, with five paler-coloured ribs. From the same family (Umbelliferae) comes aniseed, caraway, coriander, cummin, dill, lovage (*ajwain*), fennel and parsley. The celery seed used as a spice is only distantly related to domestic celery, which is a 'recent' (mid-sixteenth century) development from Italy and France. Wild celery, also called smallage, was used as a herb and a spice by both the Greeks and the Romans, who were convinced it had aphrodisiac qualities. Be that as it may, it has a savoury, aromatic, slightly bitter taste, and when fried or 'roasted', its 'celery' taste is intensified. It is little used in Indian cookery, though it can make an interesting substitute for one of the Bengali five spices (see Panch Phoran, page 29). Celery seed has a further use in medication, for the treatment of asthma, liver disorders and rheumatism.

Meat Dhansak

A traditional method

SERVES 4

400 g (14 oz) lean lamb, cut into 3 cm (1¼ inch) cubes, weighed after stage 2, below
25 g (1 oz) *chana dhal*, split and polished
25 g (1 oz) *moong dhal*, split and polished
25 g (1 oz) red *massoor dhal*, split and polished
50 g (2 oz) split oily *toovar dhal*
4 tablespoons butter ghee
225 g (8 oz) onions, finely chopped
2 garlic cloves, finely chopped
200 g (7 oz) canned tomatoes, drained
1 tablespoon jaggery or brown sugar
3-4 pieces red or green bell pepper
1 small to medium aubergine, chopped
1 large potato, peeled and chopped
110 g (4 oz) fresh baby spinach leaves
2 tablespoons chopped fresh coriander
aromatic salt to taste (see page 29)

MASALA ONE

1 teaspoon cummin seeds
1 brown cardamom
5 cm (2 inch) piece cassia bark
½ teaspoon black mustard seeds

MASALA TWO

1 teaspoon turmeric
1 teaspoon ground coriander
1 teaspoon ground cummin
¼ teaspoon fenugreek seeds, ground
½ teaspoon chilli powder

1. Mix together all the lentils and wash them. Cover with cold water and leave to soak overnight.
2. Trim the meat of any unwanted matter, and preheat the oven to 190°C/375°F/Gas 5.
3. Drain the lentils and simmer in twice their volume of fresh water for about 30 minutes, then coarsely mash them in the pan.
4. While the lentils are cooking, heat 2 tablespoons ghee in a lidded flameproof casserole dish of 2.25-2.75 litre (4-5 pint) capacity, and fry the meat at high temperature for 5-8 minutes to seal it.

5. Heat the remaining ghee in a wok and fry Masala One for about 30 seconds. Mix Masala Two with just enough water to make a paste, add it to the wok and stir-fry for about a minute. Add the onions and garlic, and continue to stir-fry for about 10 minutes or until golden.
6. Add the stir-fry to the meat in the casserole. Put the lid on and cook in the oven for 20 minutes, then inspect, stir and taste. Add a little water if required. Replace in the oven and, after a further 20 minutes, inspect, stir and taste again, this time adding the tomatoes, sugar, mashed lentils and the other vegetables.
7. Continue cooking for 20-30 minutes, or until the meat is really tender. Add the coriander and salt to taste. Turn off the heat and leave the casserole dish in the oven to rest for 10 minutes, or until ready to serve.

Chicken Dhansak
Restaurant style

SERVES 4

400 g (14 oz) chicken breast, skinned and
cut into bite-sized cubes
4 tablespoons vegetable oil
½ teaspoon turmeric
450 g (1 lb) curry masala gravy (see
page 32)
1–2 teaspoons chilli powder, or to taste
2 teaspoons dried fenugreek leaves
2–3 canned or fresh pineapple cubes
225 g (8 oz) cooked Tarka Dhal
(see page 169)
2 teaspoons sugar
2 teaspoons fresh lemon juice
salt to taste

1.   Heat the oil in a wok or karahi and stir-fry the turmeric for a few seconds. Add the chicken and stir-fry to seal it and colour it yellow.

2.   Add the gravy, chilli and fenugreek leaves, and simmer for 12–15 minutes, then check to see whether the chicken is cooked. Cut a piece in half. It must be white right through. When it is, add all the remaining ingredients, and mix well. When simmering, it is ready to serve.

VARIATION
Kaju Paneer Dhansak

Instead of chicken, use paneer for a vegetarian option. Use the same ingredients as for the above recipe, but replace the chicken with the following:

225 g (8 oz) pre-fried paneer cubes (see
pages 33 and 164)
50 g (2 oz) raw cashew nuts

1.   Heat the oil in a wok or karahi and stir-fry the turmeric for a few seconds.

2.   Add the gravy, chilli and fenugreek leaves, and bring to a simmer, then add the remaining ingredients, except the paneer and nuts, and mix well. When simmering again, it is ready to serve.

3.   Add the pre-fried paneer and cashew nuts as a garnish, and serve with brown rice (see page 172).

Dhal Dhansak
A quick method

SERVES 4 AS AN ACCOMPANIMENT

250 g (9 oz) cooked Tarka Dhal
(see page 169)
400 g (14 oz) can of ratatouille in oil
1 tablespoon brinjal pickle, finely chopped
1 tablespoon coconut powder
2 teaspoons garam masala (see page 30)
1 teaspoon dried mint
1 tablespoon chopped fresh coriander
leaves
sugar and salt to taste

Simply mix everything together in a saucepan. Bring to a simmer, stirring, and serve.

JALFREZI

In the Chittagong hills in the former Indian state of West Bengal, now part of Bangladesh, a Buddhist tribe called the *mogs* can still be found. In the Anglo-Indian days of the Raj, *mogs* became household cooks, particularly in the nearby Calcutta district. It was they who interpreted their memsahibs' demands for good old plain English cooking, such as roasts and pies and mountains of boiled vegetables, to be served in endless courses at lunches, dinners and banquets in stifling heat and humidity. Naturally, given a chance, the *mogs* added a little spice here and there, and a wonderful food style evolved. My own ancestors were part of this, and for those who want to know more about the life and times of the British in India, and their food in particular, please refer to my book *Pat Chapman's Taste of the Raj*.

Apart from being obliged to cook strange alien food in totally unsuitable conditions in those days, often without any form of oven or decent kitchen equipment, the other concept equally alien to all Indians, to this day, is the notion of using leftovers for another meal. In the days of the Raj there were no refrigerators and *jal farajee*, or *jal frezi*, or *jalfri*, became a dish for using up cold cooked meat or poultry leftovers. *Jal* or *jhal* in Bengali means 'pungently spicy' and *frezi*, 'stir-fry.'. I well remember my grandmother's delicious version, for which I give a recipe overleaf.

But the dish has evolved in recent times to become a rapidly cooked stir-fry, the best rendition of which uses chicken breast or prawns. Meat takes too long to cook by this method. At the restaurant, however, because they have pre-cooked meat to hand, Meat Jalfrezi can be whipped up in moments, as can any other dish requiring a pre-cooked main ingredient. My Chicken Jalfrezi recipe overleaf takes about 15 minutes to cook from scratch and is delicious with plain rice.

Chilli

Hari Mirch (green)
Lal Mirch (red)

CAPSICUM ANNUUM

Chilli is the fleshy pod of shrub-like bushes of the capsicum family. There are five species, and thousands of varieties, some of which are shown on pages 22 and 23. Fresh, chilli can be green, white, yellow, orange, red or purple in colour. Dried, it is nearly always red, and is available whole, crushed, or ground to a fine powder. Though this is simply called 'chilli powder', and is available in different 'heat' grades, confusion exists about cayenne pepper. This originally came from French Guiana, but is now blended from many types of chilli, and is indistinguishable from 'chilli powder', though it is often dearer. Paprika (Hungarian for 'pepper'), is simply a capsicum variety, which is best known in a mild powdered form, though some varieties can be hot. 'Hot', in this context, is an ambiguous word, having nothing to do with temperature. 'Piquancy' is better, meaning the burning sensation in the mouth, which is caused by the alkaloid capsaicin, present to a greater or lesser degree, in equal amounts, in the flesh and the seeds of all members of the capsicum family, irrespective of their colour, except bell peppers. Capsaicin is related to caffeine, nicotine and morphine, which explains why chilli is mildly addictive. Rich in vitamin C, fresh chilli, like onion and garlic, actively helps to reduce blood pressure and cholesterol. The chillies in the photograph opposite are Kashmiri chillies, used as much for their red colouring properties in curries like Roghan Josh Gosht (see page 112) as for their heat.

Chicken Jalfrezi

Taking just 15 minutes from start to finish, this is one of the easiest curries in the book.

SERVES 4

675 g (1½ lb) chicken breast, boned and skinned
4 tablespoons ghee or vegetable oil
½ teaspoon turmeric
1 teaspoon white cummin seeds
1 teaspoon mustard seeds
4 garlic cloves, finely chopped
5 cm (2 inch) piece fresh ginger, finely chopped (optional)
2 tablespoons curry masala (see page 31)
1 large Spanish onion, chopped
2 or more fresh green chillies, sliced
½ green bell pepper, coarsely chopped
½ red bell pepper, coarsely chopped
2 tablespoons chopped fresh coriander leaves
2-3 fresh tomatoes, chopped
2 teaspoons garam masala (see page 30)
salt to taste
lemon juice

1. Cut the chicken into bite-sized pieces.
2. Heat the ghee or oil in a karahi or wok and fry the turmeric and seeds for about 30 seconds. Add the garlic and optional ginger, and stir-fry for about 30 seconds more, then add the masala, with just enough water to make a paste, and stir for a further minute.
3. Add the chicken pieces and stir-fry for about 5 minutes.
4. Add the onion, chillies and peppers, and continue to stir-fry for about 5 minutes more.
5. Add the coriander, tomatoes and garam masala, and stir-fry for about 5 minutes on medium heat. Add a little water if needed.
6. Test that the chicken is cooked. Cut a piece in half. It must be white right through. When it is, salt to taste, and serve. It's nice with a squeeze of lemon juice over the top.

Raj-style Jalfrezi

SERVES 4

450-675 g (1-1½ lb) cooked beef, lamb or chicken, etc.
up to 225 g (8 oz) cooked vegetables (e.g. chopped roast or boiled potatoes, peas, carrots, etc.)
2 tablespoons vegetable oil
1 small onion, finely chopped
1 garlic clove, finely chopped
450 g (1 lb) curry masala gravy (see page 32)
salt to taste

1. Heat the oil in a wok and fry the onion and garlic for at least 10 minutes, or until starting to go golden.
2. Add all the other ingredients to the pan. Mix well and simmer for about 5 minutes to soften the meat. Salt to taste, then serve with rice or breads.

Balti Jalfrezi Cod

SERVES 4

675 g (1½ lb) filleted cod steaks
1½ teaspoons cummin seeds
½ teaspoon lovage seeds
½ teaspoon coriander seeds
2 tablespoons vegetable ghee or oil
2 tablespoons Balti masala (see page 60)
2 garlic cloves, finely chopped
110 g (4 oz) spring onions, bulbs and
leaves, sliced
1 or more fresh red chillies, chopped
1 green bell pepper, cut into small
diamond shapes
2 tablespoons coconut milk powder
3 tablespoons freshly chopped coriander
leaves
freshly squeezed juice of ½ lemon
1 teaspoon garam masala (see page 30)
aromatic salt to taste (see page 29)

1. Cut the cod into bite-sized pieces.
2. Dry-roast the seeds in a wok (see page 30 for method), then set aside.
3. Heat the ghee or oil in the wok and stir-fry the Balti masala for 2 minutes, adding just enough water to create a paste. Add the garlic and stir-fry for a further 30 seconds. Add the onions, chilli and pepper and stir-fry for 3 minutes more.
4. Add the cod chunks, and bring to a simmer. Cook for about 10 minutes, adding the coconut, and water as needed to keep things mobile.
5. Add the seeds, coriander, lemon juice and garam masala, and simmer until everything is cooked to your liking. Salt to taste and serve with plain rice.

KEEMA

For some reason, Keema, which means 'minced meat curry', is not in the top five curries. This is strange because, in my view, it creates one of the best curries of all time. Let me give you my reasons. Firstly, mince is the ideal subject for a novice curry cook because it is quite simply indestructible. It cannot be overcooked, unlike cubes of meat which can be tough if incorrectly cooked, or can disintegrate into stringy pieces if overcooked. Secondly, mince has a formidable texture, although I should say that I prefer a coarsely ground mince to a finely ground version. It will shrink during cooking and, if it is too fine, it gives, for me, an unsatisfactory, almost purée-like, texture, having nothing to chew on. Thirdly, it accepts any spice flavour you care to give it, so technically there is absolutely no reason why you cannot use mince for any of the other curries in this book. Fourthly, it is cheap and economical. However, I do make the proviso here that you must buy good-quality mince. There are grades of mince with relatively high amounts of fat and gristle permitted. Please avoid these; they are a false economy and will result in a greasy, gristly curry. Please use lean, meaty mince. Of course, as with all things, you will get the best results by doing it yourself. Buy whole meat of the quality of your choice, divest it of all unwanted matter, but leave a little fat, then mince it yourself. You can get an inexpensive hand mincer, or use an electric mincer attachment if you have the appropriate unit. Fifthly, you can mince any meat you like for keema: beef, lamb, mutton, veal, venison or, as shown in the photograph alongside, pork, and all poultry (skin-off please), such as chicken, turkey, duck and game.

Finally, vegetarians need not miss out. There is a dried minced soya bean substitute which is so like the texture of real mince that some vegetarians don't enjoy it.

Cinnamon

Dalchini

CINNAMOM ZELYANICUM

Cinnamon has been used to flavour food for thousands of years, its sweetish aromatic flavour adding a haunting quality to dishes. In Roman times, Arabs were the middlemen between the Chinese and Romans. To protect their trade routes, and their monopolies, the Arabs used to invent tall stories. They claimed, for example, that cinnamon bark came from the nest of a great, man-eating, horned eagle, the size of a horse, located on top of a single, high mountain peak. It is because the Romans believed this sort of story that they paid outlandish prices, squandering their gold reserves, and ultimately bankrupting their empire, in exchange for such 'luxuries' as spices.

Cinnamon is native to Sri Lanka, and though it now also grows in the Seychelles, Brazil, the West Indies and Indonesia, Sri Lankan cinnamon is still regarded as the best. Like cassia (see page 64), with which it is sometimes confused, cinnamon is the inner bark of a tropical tree. It is cropped in the same way as cassia, yielding more delicate, parchment-thin, tightly rolled, pale brown quills of around 1 cm (½ inch) in diameter by 10-12 cm (4-6 inches) in length. These quills are more aromatic than cassia but, unlike that spice, cinnamon can break up in robust cooking. Little pieces of cinnamon are inedible with an unpleasant mouth-feel, so quills are best confined to infusing drinks and flavouring pullao rice. Ground cinnamon is used in some dishes.

Keema

Traditional mince curry

SERVES 4

675 g (1½ lb) lean meat, weighed after removing all unwanted matter, finely minced
2 tablespoons butter ghee
1 large onion, finely chopped
2 garlic cloves, finely chopped
5 cm (2 inch) piece fresh ginger, finely chopped
400 g (14 oz) canned tomatoes, drained
1 tablespoon tomato ketchup
225 ml (8 fl oz) canned tomato soup
1 tablespoon red bell pepper, chopped
1-2 fresh green chillies, chopped
2 teaspoons garam masala (see page 30)
1 tablespoon chopped fresh coriander eaves
1 tablespoon chopped fresh mint leaves
aromatic salt to taste (see page 29)
6 quail eggs, hard-boiled, shelled and halved
fresh mint sprig to garnish

MASALA

1 teaspoon turmeric
1 teaspoon ground coriander
½ teaspoon chilli powder
4 cloves
1 brown cardamom

1. Heat 1 tablespoon ghee in a lidded flameproof casserole dish of 2.25-2.75 litre (4-5 pint) capacity, add the mince and fry for 5-10 minutes to seal.
2. Heat the remaining ghee in a karahi or wok and stir-fry the onion, garlic and ginger over a medium heat until golden. Add the masala and simmer for a couple more minutes. Add a little water if it dries up too much.
3. Preheat the oven to 190°C/375°F/Gas 5. Add the stir-fry to the casserole dish with the tomatoes and ketchup. Cover and cook in the oven for 20-30 minutes.
4. Bring the dish out of the oven and stir in the tomato soup, red pepper, chilli and garam masala. Continue to cook in the oven for a further half an hour.
5. Switch off the oven. Mix the coriander and mint leaves into the keema with salt to taste. Put the dish back into the oven for a few more minutes.
6. Garnish with the eggs and a sprig of mint, and serve with *puris* or *parathas*.

VARIATIONS

Punjabi Keema Mattar

For a more savoury tasting mince curry with peas, follow the above recipe with the following modifications:

1. Reduce the meat quantity to 600 g (1¼ lb).
2. Omit the canned tomatoes, tomato ketchup, tomato soup and red pepper.
3. Add to the masala: 4 bay leaves, 1 teaspoon *chaat masala* (see page 42), ½ teaspoon lovage seeds.
4. Add sufficient water or fragrant stock (see page 29) in stage 4 to prevent the curry from drying out.
5. Add 1 tablespoon dried fenugreek leaves at stage 4.
6. Add 350 g (12 oz) frozen peas, thawed, at stage 5.

Keema Paneer

Instead of, or as well as, the peas in the above recipe, paneer cubes (see page 33) can be added to create another traditional keema variation.

Restaurant Keema

Follow the Medium Meat Curry recipe on page 96, substituting mince for the meat.

Balti Keema

A recipe for this is on page 60.

Tikka Masala Keema

Yes, there is such a combination! Simply use 675 g (1½ lb) mince with 450 g (1 lb) tikka tandoori masala curry gravy from page 116, using the oven temperature and cooking times given in the Keema recipe.

Keema Samosa Filling

Any of these keema recipes can be used for samosa filling. Strain off excess gravy for use elsewhere, and remove any whole spices. See page 41.

Murghi Keema

Chicken keema

Skinless chicken meat (or turkey) makes an ideal subject for keema. The recipes work without modification.

Vegetarian Keema

Use 450 g (1 lb) soya mince granules in place of the meat. Also add 225 g (8 oz) diced mixed vegetables. Soak the granules for 20 minutes, then drain them. Cook for just 20 minutes in the oven.

Nepalese Keema

Also called Shak Shu Ka, this is finely ground meat cooked in a creamy sauce.

SERVES 4

450 g (1 lb) lean lamb or beef, chopped
4 tablespoons butter ghee
1 tablespoon very finely chopped fresh ginger
110 g (4 oz) onions, very finely chopped
4 fresh green chillies, chopped
2 tablespoons chopped fresh coriander
175 ml (6 fl oz) single cream
2 eggs
4 tablespoons almonds, toasted and coarsely chopped
aromatic salt to taste (see page 29)

MASALA

2 teaspoons garam masala (see page 30)
½ teaspoon mango powder
1 teaspoon garlic powder

1. Grind the meat down as finely as possible either by mincing three times or by pulsing it in a food processor.
2. Heat the ghee in a karahi or wok, and stir-fry the masala for 30 seconds. Add the ginger and stir-fry for a further 30 seconds, then add the onions and continue to stir-fry for 4 minutes. Add the chilli and coriander, and continue frying until everything is soft.
3. Add the mince with about 175 ml (6 fl oz) water. Stir-fry for 10-15 minutes or until the water has evaporated, lowering the heat to maintain a gentle sizzling simmer.
4. Whip the cream with the eggs and add to the pan. Stir-fry for 10-15 minutes more, then add the almonds with salt to taste. The dish should by now be cooked and nicely creamy in texture. Serve with naan bread.

KOFTA

Kofta simply means '(meat) balls'. Invented by the Arabs, variations of the concept are found all over the Middle East, Greece and the Moslem world. Any number of kofta curries can be savoured in the subcontinent. The balls themselves can be made from ground meat or poultry, fish or shellfish, and from mashed potatoes or other pliable cooked vegetables. They can also be made from flour-based mixtures used alone or with any of the above ingredients added.

Taking these ingredients one by one, I have found the meat recipe overleaf and pictured alongside to be very easy if you start with whole meat and grind it yourself, rather than using bought mince. It *is* possible to use bought mince, but it needs a binding ingredient such as egg or flour to keep it intact while it is cooking in the curry sauce. Grinding the meat in a food processor is a swift and effortless task (apart from the washing-up). You can and must add spices to the mixture as for Sheek and Shami Kebabs (see page 51), and I prefer to par-bake the koftas in the oven. This absolutely guarantees that they will not disintegrate when cooking in the gravy.

As with the previous keema method, you can grind any meat you like for kofta: beef, lamb, mutton, pork, veal, venison and all poultry (skin-off please), such as chicken, turkey, duck and game. Fish and shellfish, such as king prawns, can be ground and shaped and par-baked, but are far more delicate during the gravy stage, so stir carefully.

Vegetable koftas are the most delicate of all to cook, but they do not need prolonged cooking in the gravy, since they only need to heat through with minimal stirring. Flour-based balls can be steamed to readiness or fried, then added to the gravy, but my foolproof method (overleaf) is to coat them in batter, then deep-fry them, onion bhaji-style, so that they do not break up in their gravy. Pictured alongside are batter-coated Maachli Kofta (left), with Meat Kofta.

Clove

Lavang

EUGENIA AROMATICA

Clove is Britain's most familiar spice, having been used continuously since the Romans brought it here. We still use it in apple pies, and to ease toothache because of its pain-killing essential oil, eugenol. Clove grows on a smallish tropical evergreen tree, related to the myrtle family, which thrives near the sea. Originally native only to two neighbouring tiny Indonesian Moluccan 'spice islands', Ternate and Tidore (now called Soasiu), in the East Indies, wars were fought over the acquisition of clove. Today, clove is found in India, Sri Lanka, Zanzibar, Madagascar, Brazil and Grenada.

The clove itself is the unopened bud of the tree's flower. It is bright green at first, and must be picked just as it turns pink. The flower, if allowed to bloom, is dark pink and about 1 cm (½ inch) in diameter.

Dried clove is dark red-brown, bulbous at one end (this is the bud, where the flavour is, so watch out for 'headless' cloves), with tapering stalks about 1 cm (½ inch) in length. The Romans thought they resembled nails – 'clavus' being the Latin for 'clout' or 'nail'. Clove is the world's second most important spice, earning India alone some £20 million a year. It takes some 8,000 to 10,000 cloves to make up 1 kg (2 ¼ lb).

Meat Kofta

SERVES 4

675 g (1½ lb) lean stewing steak
2 large garlic cloves, finely chopped
1 egg yolk
2 tablespoons chopped fresh coriander
gram flour for rolling
3-4 tablespoons vegetable oil

SAUCE

2 tablespoons butter ghee or vegetable oil
225 g (8 oz) onion, finely chopped, or
350 g (12 oz) curry masala gravy (see page 32)
150 ml (¼ pint) fragrant stock (see page 29) or water
aromatic salt to taste (see page 29)

MASALA ONE

1 teaspoon ground coriander
½ teaspoon mango powder
¼ teaspoon chilli powder
2 teaspoons cummin seeds
2 teaspoons gram flour

MASALA TWO

1 teaspoon garlic powder
1 teaspoon turmeric
¼ teaspoon asafoetida
1 teaspoon garam masala (see page 30)
1 teaspoon dried fenugreek leaves
¼ teaspoon caraway seeds

1. To make the meatballs, put the meat, garlic, egg yolk, coriander and Masala One through a mincer, or pulse in a food processor.
2. Mix well, then divide the mixture into four equal parts. Roll each part into six small balls (koftas) to get 24 equal-sized balls. Keep washing your hands to help make the balls smooth. Roll them in gram flour.
3. To cook, heat the oil in a karahi or wok and fry the balls for 2 minutes each. Put them aside.
4. To make the sauce, heat the ghee or oil in the karahi or wok and fry Masala Two for 1 minute, then add the onion and stir-fry for about 10 minutes, or until golden. If using the masala gravy, it just needs to be brought to the simmer.
5. Simmer for about 10 minutes, adding the fragrant stock or water until the sauce starts to thicken. The sauce should be neither too thick nor too runny. Add salt to taste. Keep simmering, then add the meatballs. Simmer for a further 20 minutes, but avoid vigorous stirring as you might break up the balls
6. Serve with a green vegetable curry and rice.

Tikka Kofta Curry

Meatball curry with a tandoori flavour

675 g (1½ lb) uncooked Sheek Kebab mixture (see page 53)
1 tablespoon ghee or vegetable oil
2-3 garlic cloves, finely chopped
450 g (1 lb) tikka tandoori masala curry gravy (see page 116)
1 tablespoon tomato purée
175 g (6 oz) canned tomatoes, drained
1 tablespoon white granulated sugar
½ teaspoon dried fenugreek leaves
salt to taste
fresh coriander leaves to garnish

1. Preheat the oven to 190°C/375°F/Gas 5.
2. Divide the sheek kebab mixture into four equal parts. Roll each part into six small balls (koftas). Put the 24 koftas on a foil-lined oven tray and bake them in the oven for 15 minutes.
3. Meanwhile, heat the ghee or oil in a karahi or wok, and stir-fry the garlic for 30 seconds. Add the tandoori gravy and bring to a simmer.
4. Add the tomato purée, tomatoes, sugar, fenugreek and salt to taste. Bring back to a simmer and add the koftas. Stir-fry for about 5 minutes more or until cooked to your liking. Garnish with coriander.

Maachli Kofta
Fish balls

MAKES 8 LARGE OR 16 SMALL KOFTAS

semolina or cornflour
oil for deep-frying

FISH MIXTURE

450 g (1 lb) skinless cod or salmon fillet
225 g (8 oz) mashed cooked potato
2-3 large spring onions, leaves and bulbs,
chopped
1 tablespoon chopped fresh coriander
leaves
1 teaspoon chopped fresh red chilli
2 teaspoons panch phoran (see page 29)

BATTER

110 g (4 oz) gram flour
1 tablespoon curry masala (see page 31)
½ teaspoon aromatic salt (see page 29)

1. Mix the fish ingredients together in a food processor to achieve a mouldable mixture.
2. Mix the batter ingredients with just enough water to achieve a pourable batter.
3. Divide the fish mixture into eight for larger koftas or 12-16 for smaller ones. Sprinkle semolina or cornflour on the work top, and roll the koftas on the top to achieve balls. Keep washing your hands to help this process.
4. Preheat the oil in a deep-fryer to 190°C/375°F (chip-frying temperature).
5. Immerse the koftas in the batter, then lower them, one by one, into the hot oil, allowing some seconds between adding each one to maintain the oil temperature.
6. Deep-fry for 8-10 minutes, after which the koftas will be golden and cooked. Remove and drain on absorbent kitchen paper.
7. Serve hot or cold as a snack, or add to the curry sauce made for Malai Kofta (right). Serve with lemon rice and *chupattis*.

Malai Kofta
Vegetable balls in cream sauce

SERVES 4

KOFTAS

450 g (1 lb) mashed cooked potato
1 tablespoon raisins
2 tablespoons cashew nuts, coarsely ground
1 tablespoon curry masala (see page 31)
1-2 fresh red chillies, finely chopped
1 teaspoon sugar
½ teaspoon aromatic salt (see page 29)

SAUCE

4 tablespoons mustard blend oil
1 tablespoon curry masala (see page 31)
2 garlic cloves, finely chopped
200 g (7 oz) onions, finely chopped
150 ml (¼ pint) fragrant stock (see page 29)
1 teaspoon tomato purée
200 ml (7 fl oz) single cream
6 tablespoons vegetable oil
110 g (4 oz) paneer, cut into 5 mm
(¼ inch) cubes (see page 33)
12 whole cashew nuts

1. Mix together all the kofta ingredients. The mixture should be glutinous enough to form into 'dumpling' balls. Set aside.
2. For the sauce, heat the oil in a pan and stir-fry the masala for 1 minute, then add the garlic and stir-fry for 1 minute, then add the onion and stir-fry for 5 minutes. Add the stock and tomato purée, and simmer for a further 10 minutes or so, until the mixture starts to thicken, then stir in the cream.
3. Meanwhile, heat the vegetable oil in a wok or karahi, and stir-fry the paneer and nuts together until both are golden. Strain well, reserving the oil, and put the paneer and nuts into the sauce. Keep warm.
4. Heat the same oil in the pan, and very carefully fry the koftas for 4-5 minutes or until they are hot right through and golden.
5. To serve, place the balls in a serving dish and pour the warm sauce over them.

KORMA

Many people are keen to know what differences, if any, there are between standard restaurant curries and their authentic counterparts cooked in the subcontinent. There is no better example of these differences than the two korma recipes overleaf.

When we think of the curry-restaurant korma, we picture in our minds a very mild curry, pale golden in colour and of thickish creamy texture, achieved mostly by the use of creamed coconut block. In India, *korma* refers to a cooking style, where only ghee or oil is used in the initial cooking. Water is introduced later, but this must be entirely evaporated during the cooking process, indicated at the end of cooking when the ghee or oil 'floats' on top of the cooked dish. There are many types of authentic korma, all of which are aromatic and awash with a mellow gravy, achieved in the north by using yoghurt and/or cream, and in the south with coconut milk. Korma does not necessarily mean mild; it is quite normal to add fresh chillies. In Kashmir, one famous dish, the Mirchwangan Korma, is red in colour and hot in taste from the prolific use of chillies. The recipe for this is on page 109.

The korma has been around for centuries but it was perfected by the Moghuls. It was said that if a chef could cook a korma he could cook for the court. If he could cook two dozen variations he would be 'king of the kitchens', and cook for the Emperor's table.

The first recipe overleaf produces the archetypal restaurant Chicken Korma (illustrated far left), using creamed coconut but nary a chilli in sight. The other recipe recreates a totally authentic classic North Indian Moghul lamb korma, using yoghurt and optional chilli, cooked in the traditional manner.

Coriander

Dhania

CORIANDRUM SATIVUM

Coriander is a member of the ubiquitous Umbelliferae family. It was native to India, but now grows worldwide as a herbaceous annual plant. Its seed and leaf are widely used, and its rather bitter root is also used in India and Thailand. Coriander leaves are mid-green and flat, with jagged edges, and are also important, some people say indispensable, in Indian cookery (see pages 20-21). However, the flavour of the leaves bears absolutely no resemblance to that of the seed, and not everyone enjoys their distinctive musky candle-waxy odour, also present in unripe seeds. Indeed, the word 'coriander' derives from the Greek word *koris*, a bug, supposedly because its foetid smell resembles that of bed bugs! That's as may be, but ripe dried coriander seed imparts a sweetish flavour, with a hint of orange. In terms of volume (but not value), coriander seed is the most important spice in Indian cookery. The country exports 80,000 tons a year.

There are many coriander species, giving minor variations to the appearance of coriander seed. Depicted in the photograph opposite are, top, a Middle Eastern variety with small, buff-coloured spheres (about 3-4 mm in diameter), and, below, the slightly larger, paler, more aromatic Indian, oval-shaped variety. The seeds are used whole or ground, forming the largest single ingredient in most masalas, and are delicious roasted – try them as a garnish.

Korma

Chicken korma restaurant style

SERVES 4

675 g (1½ lb) skinless chicken breast
3 tablespoons vegetable oil
1-3 teaspoons finely chopped garlic
200 g (7 oz) onions, finely chopped
150 ml (¼ pint) single cream
⅓ block (65 g) creamed coconut
1 tablespoon very finely chopped fresh
coriander leaves
2 teaspoons ground almonds
2-3 teaspoons garam masala (see page 30)
1 teaspoon white sugar
salt to taste

MASALA

2 teaspoons ground coriander
2 teaspoons curry masala (see page 31)
½ teaspoon ground cummin
½ teaspoon turmeric
½ teaspoon chilli powder

1. Cut the chicken into bite-sized pieces, discarding any unwanted matter.
2. Mix the masala spices with enough water to achieve an easily pourable paste.
3. Heat the oil in a karahi or wok until it is nearly smoking. Add the garlic and stir-fry briskly for 20-30 seconds. Add the spice paste and keep on stirring for about another minute.
4. Add the onion, reduce the heat, and stir-fry for at least 10 minutes, at most 20 minutes, until the mixture has thoroughly softened and caramelised.
5. Take the pan off the heat and purée the mixture in the pan using a hand-held electric blender.
6. Add the cream and coconut. When melted, add the chicken and simmer for 10-12 minutes, stirring occasionally, and adding just enough water to keep a thickish texture.
7. Add the remaining ingredients, including salt to taste, and continue cooking and stirring for a final 5 minutes or until the chicken is cooked. This is checked by cutting one of the largest pieces in half and ensuring it is white right through.

NOTE: The korma can be made in advance up to the end of stage 5, or can be made in larger batches up to this stage and frozen.

Classic Lamb Korma

Lamb in a mild creamy sauce

SERVES 4

675 g (1½ lb) fatless, boned lamb, cubed
2 teaspoons sugar
1 teaspoon salt
225 g (8 oz) natural yoghurt
4 tablespoons butter ghee or vegetable oil
½ teaspoon turmeric
2 teaspoons ground coriander
2 tablespoons finely chopped garlic
1 tablespoon finely chopped fresh ginger
8 tablespoons finely chopped onion
20-30 strands saffron
4 tablespoons ground almonds
2 teaspoons chopped fresh coriander
leaves
175 ml (6 fl oz) single cream
fragrant stock (see page 29) or water

MASALA

15 cm (6 inch) piece cassia bark
12 green cardamoms
10 cloves
8 bay leaves
1 teaspoon fennel seeds

GARNISH

toasted flaked almonds
edible silver leaf (vark)

1. In a non-metallic bowl, mix the sugar, salt, yoghurt, lamb and masala, and leave to marinate for 6-48 hours.
2. Preheat the oven to 190°C/375°F/Gas 5.
3. Heat the ghee or oil in a karahi or wok and stir-fry the turmeric and coriander for 30 seconds. Add the garlic, ginger and onion, and stir-fry for 10 minutes.
4. Combine the fried mixture with the marinated lamb, place in a casserole, cover and cook in the oven for 25 minutes.
5. Remove the casserole from the oven, inspect and stir, then mix in the saffron, ground almonds, coriander and cream. Return to the oven for 20 minutes more.

6. Remove the casserole from the oven again, inspect, and, if it looks too dry, add a little stock or water. Taste for tenderness, and judge how much more cooking it needs to reach complete tenderness. It will probably need at least 10 minutes more. The korma can be served straight away, garnished with the flaked almonds and silver leaf, or reheated next day (some people prefer that, saying it is more marinated), or it can be frozen.

MADRAS

I have to tell you that no matter how many times you visit Madras, you will never ever come across a Madras curry. It simply does not exist in that sun-drenched south-eastern Indian city. Madras was the creation of the British back in 1640, as their second fortress trading post in India. It grew rapidly from a tiny fishing village to India's fourth largest city. Being in the deep south, the locals are partial to a chilli or two in their otherwise typically south-Indian, mostly fish or vegetarian curries, some of which we meet on page 151. The early British traders quickly adapted to curry, as we saw in my introduction on page 9, and, finding it addictive, they soon started to build up a tolerance to Madrassi levels of chilli heat.

Eventually these early ex-pats retired back to England, but they wanted to take their newly acquired taste for hot curry back with them to Blighty. Someone unrecorded in the mists of time dreamed up the notion of curry powder, or as those early sahibs also called it, 'curry-stuff'. And so began a trade which has continued to this day. Being a spice-growing area, Madras was easily able to manufacture 'curry-stuff', and one extra-hot version became known as Madras curry powder.

Coming more up to date, we have seen that the earliest curry houses were operated by Punjabis, whose food style and homelands were over a thousand miles from south India. The early curry menu formula did not offer particularly hot curries, but in the early post-war days a demand began to emerge for them. In response, one of those wily restaurateurs dreamed up the notion of adding a teaspoon of chilli powder, tomato, ground almond and lemon juice to a standard Medium Curry, and calling it by a name he knew to be associated with chilli heat, and hey presto, the Madras curry was born. However, hotter curries were yet to come; see pages 107 and 119!

Cummin, white

Jeera or *Zeera Safed*

CUMINUM CYMINUM

Cummin, always spelt this way by the Raj, but 'cumin' by others, after its Latin name *cuminum*, is an ancient spice, native to Syria and Egypt, and found, intact, whole, and apparently still edible, in the tombs of the Pharaos, having been placed there some 4,000 years before. Cummin is mentioned in the Old Testament, and was so important to the Romans that it was used instead of salt as a seasoning, causing it to be very expensive. It also became synonymous with excess and greed, to the extent that the gluttonous Emperor Marcus Aurelius was nicknamed 'Cuminus'. It still predominates in Middle Eastern cooking, and has found a new role in the USA in Tex-Mex chilli con carne. Cummin has always played a major role in India, its use in volume being second only to coriander. Ground, it is a major component in curry powder.

Cummin grows on a smallish annual herb of the coriander family (Umbelliferae). Its thin seeds are about 5 mm (¼ inch) long. They are grey-brown to yellowy-green in colour, and have nine stripy longitudinal ridges and small stalks. Its oil, cuminaldehyde, gives it a distinctive, savoury taste with a slightly bitter overtone. Cummin is important in masalas and curries, and it is one of the five spices of panch phoran. The flavour of whole cummin seeds is greatly enhanced by 'roasting'.

Madras Curry Gravy

Here we adapt the basic curry gravy into a hot Madras base.

MAKES ABOUT 450 G (1 LB)

450 g (1 lb) curry masala gravy
(see page 32)
½ teaspoon turmeric
½ teaspoon ground cummin
1 teaspoon freshly ground black pepper
1 teaspoon chilli powder
3 tablespoons vegetable oil
4 plum tomatoes, fresh or drained if canned
½ Spanish onion, thinly sliced
2 teaspoons garam masala (see page 30)
½ teaspoon dried fenugreek leaves
2 tablespoons ground almonds
1 tablespoon fresh lemon juice
aromatic salt to taste (see page 29)

1. Add just enough water to the turmeric, cummin, pepper and chilli powder to make a paste.
2. Heat the oil in a karahi or wok, then add the paste and stir-fry for a minute or two, until the oil 'floats'.
3. Add the fresh or canned tomatoes. When simmering, add the remaining ingredients.
4. Continue to simmer on low heat, stirring from time to time, for around 10 minutes, until everything is cohesively cooked. The clue is that it will be darker and thicker. It is now ready to add to meat, chicken, fish, prawns or vegetables, according to the following recipes.

Meat Madras

SERVES 4

675 g (1½ lb) lean meat, weighed after removing all unwanted matter and cut into bite-sized cubes
450 g (1 lb) Madras curry gravy (see left)
2 tablespoons finely chopped fresh coriander leaves
salt to taste

1. Preheat the oven to 190°C/375°F/ Gas 5.
2. Thoroughly mix the meat and the gravy in a lidded casserole dish of 2.25-2.75 litre (4-5 pint) capacity. Cover and cook in the oven for 20 minutes.
3. Remove the dish from the oven and inspect. Stir and add a little water to the curry if it looks dry.
4. Repeat after a further 20 minutes, adding the coriander and a little more water if it needs loosening.
5. Repeat after a further 20 minutes, by which time the meat should be really tender. If it is not quite as tender as you would like, cook on until it is.
6. Add salt to taste and serve with rice and pickles.

Chicken Madras

SERVES 4

675 g (1½ lb) skinned chicken breast fillets
450 g (1 lb) Madras curry gravy (see above)
2 tablespoons finely chopped fresh coriander leaves
salt to taste

1. Cut the chicken breast into bite-sized chunks.
2. Thoroughly mix the chicken with the gravy in a large karahi or wok.
3. Put the pan on a medium heat, and stir as required until the contents are simmering.

4. Lower the heat to achieve a gentle simmer, and cook for about 12 minutes, stirring occasionally to prevent sticking.

5. Stir in the coriander and add a little water if the mixture needs loosening. Add salt to taste and cook for a couple of minutes more.

6. Check that the chicken is cooked by cutting a piece in half. It should be white right through. If it isn't, carry on cooking until it is.

VARIATIONS
Prawn Madras

Replace the chicken with 675 g (1½ lb) cooked peeled prawns, or king prawns, and mix with the gravy as above. Put the pan on a medium heat, and stir as required until the contents are simmering. Stir in the coriander and add a little water if the mixture needs loosening. Add salt to taste and cook for a couple of minutes more.

Vegetable Madras

Replace the chicken with 675 g (1½ lb) prepared vegetables, e.g. cauliflower, broccoli, beans, peas, carrots, tomatoes, sweetcorn, etc. Steam or microwave the vegetables to crisp tenderness, then mix them thoroughly with the gravy as above. Put the pan on a medium heat, and stir as required until the contents are simmering. Stir in the coriander and add a little water if the mixture needs loosening. Cook for a couple of minutes more.

Balti Madras

Make the following changes to the basic Madras Curry Gravy and use in any of the above recipes: Omit the turmeric and cummin and replace with 1 tablespoon Balti masala (see page 60) and 1 tablespoon garam masala (see page 30). When the ingredients are simmering in the pan, add 2 tablespoons chopped fresh basil leaves with the coriander.

Tikka Madras Curry

SERVES 4

675 g (1½ lb) cooked hot or cold Lamb Tikka or Chicken Tikka (see page 56)
1 tablespoon ghee
2–4 tablespoons chilli powder
2–3 garlic cloves, finely chopped
225 g (8 oz) Madras curry gravy (see left)
225 g (8 oz) tikka tandoori masala curry gravy (see page 116)
salt to taste
whole coriander leaves to garnish

1. Heat the ghee in a karahi or wok, and stir-fry the chilli powder for 30 seconds. Add the garlic and stir-fry for a further 30 seconds, then add the two gravies and bring to a simmer.

2. Add the meat or chicken and stir-fry briskly for about 2 minutes. Add salt to taste, and serve, garnished with coriander leaves.

MASALA

Masala simply means 'mixture of spices' in many of India's languages. Since, by definition, every curry contains a mixture of spices, then every curry can be described by this word 'masala'. Indeed, amongst the snobs, though you are unlikely to find the word 'curry', you will almost certainly find the word 'masala', giving a simple dish a more glamorous title. Masala Gosht translates to a rather ordinary Meat Curry. Chilli Masala is a curry enhanced with sliced fresh green chillies, and often 'House Specials' are elaborated with the word 'masala', as in Tandoori Fish Masala or Shahi Battar Masala (quails), to give just two examples. At the Indian restaurant, the straightforward masala has generally come to mean a curry which is a cross between a Bhoona and a Medium Curry. The restaurants generally elaborate on it by adding colourful red and green peppers and tomato, and perhaps some coconut. To make it that bit special they often serve their masala in an authentic karahi, as I have done with this Murgh Masala (Chicken Curry), here using a heavy black cast-iron version.

Overleaf is a recipe for the similarly named, though quite different, Murghi Masalam. You will often find this on the Indian restaurant menu (also called Kurzi Murgh), described as requiring '24 hours notice to make'. This is because a whole chicken must be marinated for at least 12 hours before being cooked, stuffed with rice, eggs and keema – not the sort of thing a restaurant can do on spec! The chicken should be fairly dry and crusty, and should taste spicy and tangy. It is quite superb.

Finally, overleaf, since we are dealing with chicken, this is as good a place as any to find a recipe for Andai Masala – Egg Curry!

Curry Leaf

Neem or *Kari Phulia* or *Kurri Patta*

CHALCAS KOENOGII

Native to South-West Asia, the neem tree grows to about 6 metres (25 feet) in height, and 1 metre (3 feet) in diameter. It is especially pre-velant in the foothills of the Himalayas and south India. The tree is greatly adored as a garden orna-mental, when it is much smaller. The young curry leaf is a small pale green, delicate thing, which grows up to 4 cm (1½ inches) in length. Leaves are widely used whole in southern Indian cooking, and impart a delicious flavour to dishes such as Rasam, Sambar, Masala Dosa and Lemon Rice. Despite its name, the leaf has a lemony fragrance, and no hint of 'curry'. This is because it is related to the lemon family. Ground curry leaf is used in many commercial curry powder blends. In addition, it is used as a tonic for stomach and kidney disorders.

Fresh curry leaves (see pages 20-21) are imported into the UK by air-freight from Kenya, but are hard to locate. Dried leaves (illustrated opposite) are readily available from Asian stores and make passable sub-stitutes. If you enjoy south Indian food, they are a 'must-have' spice.

Murgh Masala
Chicken curry

SERVES 4

675 g (1½ lb) skinned chicken breast fillets
2 tablespoons ghee
6 fresh or dried red chillies, chopped
2 teaspoons chilli powder
450 g (1 lb) medium curry gravy (see page 96)
2 tablespoons finely chopped fresh coriander leaves
1 large boiled potato, quartered
salt to taste

1. Cut the chicken breast into bite-sized chunks.
2. Heat the ghee in a large wok or karahi, and stir-fry the chillies and the chilli powder for about 2 minutes.
3. Add the chicken and the gravy, and heat, stirring as required, until the contents are sim-mering.
4. Lower the heat to achieve a gentle sim-mer, and cook, stirring occasionally to prevent sticking, for about 12 minutes.
5. Stir in the coriander and the potato, and add a little water if the pan contents need loosening. Add salt to taste and cook for a couple of minutes more.
6. Check that the chicken is cooked by cut-ting a piece in half. It should be white right through. If not, carry on cooking until it is.

Murghi Masalam (Kurzi Murgh)
Spiced whole roast chicken

SERVES 4

1.5–1.75 kg (3 lb 5 oz–3 lb 12 oz) roasting chicken
1 large onion, coarsely chopped
5 cm (2 inch) piece fresh ginger, coarsely chopped
110 ml (4 fl oz) natural yoghurt
1 tablespoon fresh lemon or lime juice
4 tablespoons ghee or vegetable oil
2 garlic cloves, finely chopped
salt to taste
2 tablespoons chopped fresh coriander
1 tomato, thinly sliced

STUFFING

225 g (8 oz) Keema curry (see page 76)
225 g (8 oz) plain cooked rice
2 tablespoons frozen peas, thawed
1 tablespoon prawns in brine (optional)

MASALA ONE

2 bay leaves
1 brown cardamom
2 cloves
4 peppercorns

MASALA TWO

½ teaspoon chilli powder
1 teaspoon ground coriander
½ teaspoon black cummin seeds
½ teaspoon turmeric

1. Make a paste of the onion, ginger, yoghurt and lemon or lime juice, adding just enough water to make it pourable.
2. Skin the chicken, keeping it whole, and gash the flesh a little. Rub it all over, inside and out, with the paste. Put in a bowl, cover and marinate overnight (or for a minimum of 12 hours).
3. Mix the stuffing ingredients and Masala One together.
4. Heat the ghee or oil in a karahi or wok.

Remove the chicken from the bowl and fry in the ghee or oil for about 15 minutes, turning carefully to brown all sides. Remove from the pan, leaving the ghee and any remaining marinade behind. When the chicken is cold enough, stuff with the stuffing mixture.

5. Preheat the oven to 200°C/400°F/Gas 6.
6. Add the garlic and Masala Two to the karahi or wok, with any remaining marinade and salt to taste. Simmer gently, and add 150 ml (¼ pint) water bit by bit over 10 minutes, stirring as the mixture thickens.
7. Put the chicken on its back in a large lidded casserole dish and pour the contents of the karahi or wok over it. Put the lid on and cook in the oven for about 1 hour, basting once or twice.
8. Sprinkle the fresh coriander over the chicken, and put the tomato slices on top. Continue cooking, uncovered, for a minimum of 10 minutes more. You'll probably need longer, and possibly an increase in oven temperature to crust and dry the chicken. Keep a close eye on it. Skim off any spare oil (keep for future use) and serve the 'gravy' over the chicken.

Andai Masala
Egg curry

SERVES 4

6 tablespoons vegetable oil
2 large Spanish onions, finely chopped
400 g (14 oz) canned tomatoes
2 tablespoons tomato purée
salt to taste
4-8 hard-boiled eggs (depending on size and appetite)

MASALA

1 teaspoon turmeric
1 teaspoon ground cummin
1 teaspoon garam masala (see page 30)
1 teaspoon ground coriander
½ teaspoon chilli powder

1. Heat the oil in a karahi or wok and fry the onions until golden.
2. Mix the Masala with enough water to make a paste, then add it to the onion. Cook for 10-15 minutes, stirring as needed.
3. Add a little water to prevent the mixture sticking, and then add the tomatoes and tomato purée.
4. Cook for a further 5-10 minutes, then add enough water to create the texture of sauce that you require. Salt to taste.
5. Add the shelled whole hard-boiled eggs, and cook until hot. Serve immediately.

VARIATION
Bombay Curry

This is restaurant nomenclature for a Bhoona, Korma or Medium Curry with eggs. Simply add 2 halved hard-boiled eggs to the standard recipes.

MEDIUM CURRY

In the early days of Indian restaurant trading in the West, it was thought best to indicate the heat strength of all the curries on the formula menu, since it was felt, correctly perhaps in the early days, that without simplistic labelling, the diner would be lost and venture into pastures too hot to handle. The menus from the early curry houses therefore used to describe each and every dish with a heat grading from 'mild' to 'very very hot', via 'medium'. Some went further and promised that every dish on the menu could be produced at any heat strength. It was easy enough to do. Start with a medium-strength curry base, made using half a teaspoon of chilli powder per portion. (You always need a little chilli powder in curry; it acts as a catalyst to the other spices, bringing out their best flavours – salt does the same.) The medium-hot curry base could be made milder by adding cream or coconut, or simply by adding starchy items such as potato. Add a teaspoon of chilli powder to the medium base and you had a Madras strength, or 'hot' curry. Two teaspoons of chilli powder gave you 'very hot' strength, suitable for Vindaloo, and a curry made using three teaspoons of chilli powder was labelled 'very very hot', and became known as a Phall curry (see page 107).

The heat-grading tradition survives today in a few outposts of red flock and in nearly every factory-produced curry at the supermarket. But most curry restaurateurs have long since realised that their customers are pretty expert on the subject of their favourite food, and more sophisticated names are utilised these days. Having said that, Medium Curry remains ubiquitous at the curry house, and it can be used to create many other curries, as shown overleaf.

The photograph shows a standard Medium Curry made with chicken drumsticks. Alongside are two cachumber chutneys and tandoori raita (see page 187).

Dill

Sowa or *Sova*

ANETHUM GRAVEOLENS

Dill, a member of the parsley family, grows as a hardy annual, to about 1 metre (3 feet) high, and its feathery leaves are used as a (non-Indian) herb. Its seed is an oval, rowing-boat shape, about 3.5 mm in length, with a narrow pale buff rim surrounding a grey-brown mass. It has three ridges on its convex inner side. It is sweetly aromatic with a slightly lemony taste, which is bitter in excess. Dill belongs to the same family as caraway and, like caraway, its volatile oils contain carvone and limonenes. It originated in Europe and the Mediterranean, and was well known to the ancient Egyptians, Greeks and Romans. Dill got its name from the old Norse word, 'dilla', meaning to lull. Medievals held it in high enough regard to use it as a 'magic' brew, strong enough to counter witchcraft.

Today, dill is especially popular in Scandinavia, Germany and Russia. The Indian version of dill seed is slightly longer and narrower than the European, but is similar enough in flavour to make either interchangeable. There, it is sometimes called soya, but it has nothing to do with soya beans.

Dill has much wider use in Indian medication than in cooking, though it is great in naan bread or rice dishes. In fact, it can stand in for caraway or fennel in any dish which calls for either of these.

Medium Curry Gravy

This recipe gives two methods for making Medium Curry Gravy. For the first, all the components are made from scratch, while the second is based on ready-made curry masala gravy.

MAKES ABOUT 450 G (1 LB); SERVES 4

METHOD ONE

2 tablespoons curry masala (see page 31)
2 tablespoons vegetable ghee
50 g (2 oz) garlic cloves, finely chopped
250 g (9 oz) Spanish onions, chopped
4 canned plum tomatoes, drained
200 ml (7 fl oz) water
2 tablespoons finely chopped green bell pepper
aromatic salt to taste (see page 29)

1.   Add just enough water to the masala to make a paste.
2.   Heat the ghee in a karahi or wok, then add the paste and stir-fry for 1–2 minutes or until the oil 'floats'.
3.   Add the garlic and stir-fry for 1 minute, then lower the heat, add the onions and stir-fry until they have all become browned and caramelised (the *tarka*).
4.   Add the tomatoes and the water, then mulch the mixture down in a blender, or in the pan using a hand-held blender, until you achieve a smooth purée.
5.   Return the purée to the pan if necessary, add the green pepper and continue to simmer on low heat, stirring from time to time, for around 10 minutes, until everything is well combined and cooked, and the gravy darker and thicker. Add salt to taste. The gravy is now ready to add to meat, chicken, fish, prawns or vegetables, according to the following recipes.

METHOD TWO

2 tablespoons vegetable ghee
4 canned plum tomatoes, drained
2–3 tablepoons curry masala paste (see page 31)
2 tablespoons chopped onion
2 tablespoons finely chopped green bell pepper
450 g (1 lb) curry masala gravy (see page 32)
aromatic salt to taste (see page 29)

1.   Heat the ghee in a karahi or wok, add the tomatoes and stir-fry for a couple of minutes. Add the curry paste and, when simmering, add the onion and pepper.
2.   Add the masala gravy and simmer on low heat, stirring from time to time, for around 10 minutes or until everything is well combined and cooked, and the gravy darker and thicker. Add salt to taste. The gravy is now ready to add to meat, chicken, fish, prawns or vegetables, according to the following recipes.

Medium Meat Curry

SERVES 4

675 g (1½ lb) lean meat, weighed after removing all unwanted matter
450 g (1 lb) medium curry gravy (see above)
2 tablespoons finely chopped fresh coriander leaves
salt to taste

1.   Preheat the oven to 190°C/375°F/Gas 5.
2.   Thoroughly mix the meat and the gravy in a lidded casserole dish of 2.25–2.75 litre (4–5 pint) capacity. Cover and put in the oven.
3.   After 20 minutes, remove the dish and inspect the curry. Stir, and add a little water if it looks dry.
4.   Repeat after a further 20 minutes, adding the coriander. Add a little more water if the contents of the dish need loosening.

5. Repeat after a further 20 minutes, by which time the meat should be really tender. If it is not quite as tender as you would like, cook on until it is.

6. Add salt to taste, and serve with rice and pickles.

Medium Chicken Curry

SERVES 4

675 g (1½ lb) chicken breast fillets, skinned
450 g (1 lb) medium curry gravy (see left)
2 tablespoons finely chopped fresh
coriander leaves
salt to taste

1. Cut the chicken breast into bite-sized chunks.

2. Thoroughly mix the chunks with the gravy in a large karahi or wok.

3. Put the pan over medium heat, and heat, stirring as required, until the contents are simmering.

4. Lower the heat to achieve a gentle simmer, and cook for about 12 minutes, stirring as required to prevent sticking.

5. Stir in the coriander, and add a little water if the contents of the pan need loosening. Cook for a couple of minutes more.

6. Check that the chicken is cooked by cutting a piece in half. It must be white right through. If it isn't, carry on cooking until it is.

Medium Fish or Prawn Curry

SERVES 4

675 g (1½ lb) cooked cod steaks, cut into
bite-sized pieces, or cooked peeled
prawns, or king prawns
450 g (1 lb) medium curry gravy (see left)
2 tablespoons finely chopped fresh
coriander leaves
salt to taste

1. Thoroughly mix the fish or prawns with the gravy in a large karahi, wok or saucepan.

2. Put the pan over medium heat, and heat, stirring as required, until the contents are simmering.

3. Stir in the coriander, and add a little water if the contents of the pan need loosening. Cook for a couple of minutes more. Add salt to taste.

Medium Vegetable Curry

SERVES 4

675 g (1½ lb) prepared mixed vegetables,
e.g. cauliflower, broccoli, beans, peas,
carrots, tomatoes, sweetcorn, etc.
450 g (1 lb) medium curry gravy (see left)
2 tablespoons finely chopped fresh
coriander

1. Blanch all the vegetables to crisp tenderness in boiling water, then drain well.

2. Thoroughly mix all the vegetables with the gravy in a large karahi, wok or saucepan.

3. Put the pan over medium heat, stirring as required until the contents are simmering.

4. Stir in the coriander, and add a little water if the contents of the pan need loosening. Cook for a couple of minutes more.

PASANDA

It is the custom in the subcontinent to eat with the fingers of the right hand in preference to cutlery. Even now, the middle classes, whilst quite conversant with knives and forks, are equally content to use their fingers. The once-all-powerful Shah of Persia said that *'eating with a knife and fork was like making love through an interpreter'*. It's a knack, of course, aided greatly by using your Indian bread as a type of spoon to mop up the food and carry it to your mouth. In truth it is a skill we Westerners have lost only as recently as Tudor times, when eating with the hand was the norm. Apart from items like chicken drumsticks, Indian food is always chopped up into bite-sized pieces.

Traditional Pasanda is a relatively sophisticated dish, developed for the Moghul emperors. Young meat, such as calf or kid, was always used, strips of tender leg fillet being gently beaten and marinated in spiced yoghurt. When the meat strips were cooked they were so tender that they were easy to break up with the fingers, thus avoiding the need for a knife.

Though Moslem, some of the Moghul emperors, including Babur, were not above enjoying alcoholic beverages. The Portuguese had introduced wine to the courts in the early sixteenth century. Jehangir in particular was an alcoholic, blessing the wine so as to convert it to 'holy water' and thus avoid the rules of Islam. My traditional recipe overleaf, therefore, makes no apology for using wine as the marinade catalyst.

The restaurant Pasanda has evolved rather differently. More often than not, it comes to the table made from unbeaten meat, and if beating is done at all, it is done to the precooked main ingredient (meat, chicken or even prawns) before its sauce is added. As is depicted in the photograph, the gravy surrounding the beaten meat is intense with creamed coconut, so it is very rich.

Fennel

Saunf, Sunf or *Soonf*

FOENICULUM VULGARE

Fennel, a European native, is a hardy perennial, which grows to about 2 metres (6 feet) in height. Its leaf and bulb were used by the Romans, both as a vegetable and medicinally. The great fifteenth-century spice explorers, the Portuguese, when probing the still uncharted Atlantic, literally followed their noses to the island of Madeira. The strong fragrance of fennel on the prevailing westerlies led them there, and they named the port Funchal, from their word *funcho*, fennel!

Today, fennel bulb and leaf are still relished in Europe, though not in India. What is important there is the small pale greenish-yellow stripy seed, slightly plump and greener than cummin, which grows to around 5 mm (¼ inch) in length. It is quite sweet and aromatic. Frequently confused in India with the smaller aniseed (see page 44), fennel seed is much more prevalent. Its slightly milder though similar flavour comes about because fennel shares with aniseed, and with star anise (see page168) its very distinctive essential oil, anethole. Fennel contains 70 per cent (compared with 90 per cent in aniseed), with a smaller amount of fenchone. This combination gives it a sweet and aromatic flavour, making it ideal for subtle dishes, garam masala and *pan* mixtures. It is unique in that it is the only spice to be common to both the five spice mixtures of India (panch phoran) and of China. Grown all over north India, the variety from Lucknow is the best quality. It is used medicinally as gripe water, and for eyesight, obesity and chest problems.

Meat Pasanda
A traditional recipe

SERVES 4

four 225 g (8 oz) pieces lean steak (fillet, sirloin or rump, etc.)
300 ml (½ pint) red wine
3 tablespoons butter ghee
225 g (8 oz) onions, roughly chopped
4 garlic cloves, roughly chopped
5 cm (2 inch) cube fresh ginger, roughly chopped
2 tablespoons chopped fresh coriander
1 tablespoon desiccated coconut
2 tablespoons ground almonds
1 tablespoon tomato purée
fragrant stock (see page 29) or water
20 whole almonds
1 teaspoon garam masala (see page 30)
aromatic salt to taste (see page 29)

MASALA

1 teaspoon turmeric
1 teaspoon ground cummin
1 teaspoon ground coriander
1 teaspoon paprika
1 teaspoon chilli powder
1 teaspoon poppy seeds

1. Beat the steak out to thin pieces, less than 5 mm (¼ inch) thick, with a wooden meat mallet. This is called the *pasanda*. Place the meat in a shallow bowl, cover with the wine and leave overnight.

2. Heat 1 tablespoon ghee in a karahi or wok, and stir-fry the onions, garlic and ginger until you have a golden *tarka* (see page 32). Cool a little, then purée in a blender with the coriander and coconut.

3. Add just enough water to the Masala to make a paste. Heat the remaining ghee in the karahi or wok and, when hot, add the paste. Stir-fry at quite a high temperature for about 2 minutes or until the oil 'floats'. Add the onion purée and stir-fry at a simmer for about 5 minutes. Mix in the ground almonds and the tomato purée, adding a little stock or water if the mixture is too dry.

4. Preheat the oven to 190°C/375°F/Gas 5. Put the meat, its marinade and the purée mixture in a lidded casserole dish, ensuring the meat is well covered, cover with the lid, and put in the oven.

5. After 30 minutes, inspect and stir, and add a little more stock or water if required. Replace in the oven.

6. After a second 30 minutes, again inspect and taste the casserole; the meat should be tender. Again add more stock or water if needed. Add the whole almonds, garam masala and salt to taste, return to the oven and turn off the heat. Serve after 10 minutes.

Murgh Badam Pasanda
Chicken Pasanda
A traditional recipe

SERVES 4

4 chicken breast fillets, skinned
3 tablespoons ghee
225 g (8 oz) onions, finely chopped
1 teaspoon garlic purée
50 g (2 oz) raw cashew nuts
6 cloves
4 green cardamoms
½ teaspoon turmeric
½ teaspoon freshly ground black pepper
225 ml (8 fl oz) fragrant stock (see page 29)
aromatic salt to taste (see page 29)

MARINADE

150 g (5 oz) natural yoghurt
1 teaspoon very finely chopped fresh ginger
1 teaspoon freshly ground allspice
¼ teaspoon ground green cardamom
½ teaspoon turmeric
1 teaspoon coriander seeds, roasted and ground
½ teaspoon aniseed, freshly ground

GARNISH

toasted almonds
chopped fresh coriander leaves

1. Combine the marinade ingredients, and brush liberally on the chicken. Cover and refrigerate for several hours.

2. Remove the chicken from the marinade and set the latter aside for later use.

3. Heat the ghee in a karahi or wok and sauté the chicken over medium heat for 3–4 minutes on each side, until golden brown. Remove from the pan and set aside.

4. Add the onions, garlic and cashews to the same pan and stir-fry for 3–4 minutes.

5. Take the pan off the heat and scrape the contents into a food processor or blender. Add the cloves, cardamom, turmeric, pepper and 50 ml (2 fl oz) stock to the blender or processor, and purée to a paste.

6. Return the paste to the karahi or wok, and simmer over medium heat for 5 minutes, stirring occasionally. Add the remaining stock and the chicken with the reserved marinade, and continue to simmer for a further 10–15 minutes or until the chicken is cooked. Test by cutting into a piece; it should be white right through. Add salt to taste.

7. Sprinkle with toasted almonds and coriander leaves, and serve.

Meat Pasanda Restaurant Style

SERVES 4

675 g (1½ lb) lean lamb
2 teaspoons curry masala (see page 31)
3 tablespoons vegetable oil
½ teaspoon turmeric
1–3 teaspoons finely chopped garlic
200 g (7 oz) onions, finely chopped
fragrant stock (see page 29) or water
⅓ block (65 g) creamed coconut
150 ml (5 fl oz) single cream
1 tablespoon very finely chopped fresh coriander leaves
2 teaspoons ground almonds
2–3 teaspoons garam masala (see page 30)
1 teaspoon white sugar
aromatic salt to taste (see page 29)

1. Trim the meat of any fat and gristle, and beat it out to thin pieces, less than 5 mm (¼ inch) thick, with a wooden meat mallet. Preheat the oven to 190°C/375°F/Gas 5.

2. Mix the masala with enough water to achieve an easily pourable paste.

3. Heat the oil in a karahi or wok until it is nearly smoking. Add the turmeric and garlic, and stir-fry briskly for 20–30 seconds. Add the spice paste and keep on stirring for about another minute.

4. Add the onions, reduce the heat, and stir-fry for 10–20 minutes or until the mixture has thoroughly softened and caramelised.

5. Take the pan off the heat, cool slightly, and purée the mixture in a blender, or in the pan using a hand-held blender.

6. Put the purée and the meat into a lidded casserole dish, cover with the lid, and put in the oven.

7. After 20 minutes, inspect, stir and taste, and add stock or water if required. Replace in the oven.

8. After a further 15 minutes, again inspect and taste the casserole. Stir in the coconut, and when it has dissolved, add the cream. Return the casserole to the oven.

9. Cook for a further 15 minutes, after which time the meat should be tender. Add the remaining ingredients, including salt to taste and more stock if necessary. Replace the casserole in the oven and turn off the heat. Serve after 10 minutes.

VARIATION

Chicken Pasanda Restaurant Style

Cut 675 g (1½ lb) skinless chicken breast into bite-sized pieces. Follow the meat recipe up to the end of stage 5, then return the purée to the pan with the coconut and cream. When the coconut has dissolved, add the chicken and cook for 10–12 minutes, adding water if necessary. Add the remaining ingredients and cook for a further 5 minutes or until the chicken is fully cooked.

PATIA

On page 67 I explained about the Parsees who escaped from Persia to India to avoid religious persecution. Their religion is Zoroastrianism, and was founded in about the sixth century BC by a Persian prophet. Islam was not founded for a further twelve hundred years, and did not reach Persia for some centuries after that, but when it did it left no room for ancient religions. Zoroastrianism is based on the struggle between light and dark, and good and evil, and the symbolism of earth, wind and fire is of paramount importance. Of equal importance is harmony and balance in Parsee food; sweet, sour, heat and savoury must all balance.

Parsees have no food taboos, and they love eggs, all meats and fish. Indeed, one of their favourite dishes is Patia (fish curry). There are numerous Parsee Patia recipes involving all kinds of fish. My favourite is Prawn Patia which works supremely well with peeled prawns in brine since their salty taste contributes greatly to the end result. As in the picture alongside, keep a few prawns uncurried to garnish the dish. It is served here with green rice (see page 173). Tamarind juice is a key ingredient for its essential sour taste which has no substitute. Lemon, vinegar and mango powder are all souring agents, but they will not do. Tamarind is pictured on page 29 and the all-important but easy recipe for extracting the purée from dried tamarind block appears on page 44. Sweetness comes ideally from jaggery (see page 112), but honey and brown sugar can be used instead. Tomato purée and ketchup, though not traditional, are used by a Parsee cook I know well, to contribute to both colour and taste, and red chillies are an optional but desirable extra.

The restaurant Patia is a pale imitation of the real thing. Not content with it being a fish or shellfish curry, the restaurants also make it available in meat, chicken or vegetable versions. Using a Madras base, they add tomato, sugar and lime.

Fenugreek, Dried Leaf

Tej Methi

TRIGONELLA
FOENUM-GRAECUM

Two parts of the fenugreek plant are used in Indian cookery, the seed (see page 108), and the leaf, which grows, grey-green in colour, on a clover-like annual herb, which produces pale triangular-shaped yellow flowers, hence its botanical name, *Trigonella*. Pronounced 'maytee' in Hindi, fenugreek leaf derives from the Latin, *foenum*, dried grass or hay ('Greek hay'); indeed the leaf is still used as cattle fodder.

Fenugreek is popular in north Indian and Punjabi cookery. The leaf is used fresh (see pages 20-21) in the same way as spinach, although it gives a strong bitter taste, disagreeable perhaps at first, but once acquired, adding a further interesting, delicious depth to Indian food, and least bitter when added late in the cooking. Fresh fenugreek is available at Asian greengrocers, but in its dried form it keeps like any other spice. A few notes of caution: After cropping, the leaves are spread out and dried in the sun on flat roofs. Consequently, it is imperative that you pick through them to remove grit and small stones. Unfortunately, you will also always find a lot of tough stalks, deliberately shown in the photograph opposite to assist with identification. These too should be discarded. Whilst doing this, you will notice how strongly the spice smells. It is a good idea to double pack it in an airtight container within a second airtight container. The leaf is rich in carotene, vitamin A, ascerbic acid, calcium and iron.

Prawn Patia with Peas

A modern-day Parsee recipe

SERVES 4

500 g (1 lb 2 oz) small cooked peeled prawns
3 tablespoons natural yoghurt
150 g (5½ oz) onions, roughly chopped
2 garlic cloves, chopped
2.5 cm (1 inch) cube fresh ginger, chopped
2 tablespoons mustard blend oil
2 tablespoons jaggery (palm sugar) or brown sugar
1 tablespoon white spirit vinegar
1 tablespoon tomato ketchup
2 tablespoons tamarind juice (see page 45)
200 g (7 oz) frozen peas, thawed
aromatic salt to taste (see page 29)

MASALA ONE

½ teaspoon mustard seeds
½ teaspoon fennel seeds
½ teaspoon cummin seeds
½ teaspoon fenugreek seeds

MASALA TWO

½ teaspoon turmeric
1 teaspoon ground coriander
½ teaspoon ground cummin
2 teaspoons paprika

1. Inspect the prawns and remove any veins from their backs with a sharp knife, then rinse and clean them.
2. Pound or blend the yoghurt, onions, garlic and ginger, plus 4 tablespoons water, to a paste.
3. Heat the oil in a karahi or wok, and fry Masala One for about 30 seconds or until the seeds start to pop. Add Masala Two and cook for a further minute. Add the yoghurt blend and fry for about 10 minutes or until golden.
4. Add the jaggery, vinegar, tomato ketchup and tamarind juice to the fried mixture, and simmer for 5 minutes more at most, until you have a thick, dark gravy.
5. Add the prawns and peas, and salt to taste. Simmer until hot right through, then serve with green rice, *chupattis* and chutneys.

Prawn Ballichow

This is a tasty pickle that is good on its own, or for cooking with. Properly bottled, it keeps indefinitely.

MAKES ABOUT 1.8 KG (4 LB)

1 litre (1¾ pints) distilled malt vinegar
1 litre (1¾ pints) vegetable oil
1 kg (2¼ lb) prawns in brine, drained
1.8 kg (4 lb) small hard tomatoes, chopped
1 tablespoon jaggery (palm sugar) or brown sugar
12 garlic cloves, finely chopped
6-8 fresh chillies, chopped

MASALA ONE

1 tablespoon turmeric
1½ tablespoons ground cummin
1½ tablespoons ground coriander
2 tablespoons paprika
1 tablespoon chilli powder
1 tablespoon mango powder

MASALA TWO

1 tablespoon mustard seeds
1 tablespoon cummin seeds

1. Add some of the vinegar to Masala One to make a paste. Let it stand for a few minutes. Meanwhile, heat 225 ml (8 fl oz) oil in a karahi or wok, and stir-fry Masala Two until the seeds pop.
2. Add the Masala One paste to the pan and fry for 10 minutes, stirring constantly and adding more oil as required to maintain a good paste-like texture.
3. Add the prawns, tomatoes, remaining vinegar and all the other ingredients, except the remaining oil, and stir-fry for 10 minutes. Preheat the oven to 190°C/375°F/Gas 5.
4. Put the pickle into a large lidded casserole dish, cover with the lid and put in the oven for 1 hour. Warm the preserving jars in or near the oven towards the end of the cooking time to dry them out completely.
5. Fill the warm jars to the brim with the warm pickle. Heat the remaining oil and pour

over the top of the pickle to form a liberal seal.

6. Cover each jar with greaseproof paper cut to size, and cap tightly. Leave for at least 4 weeks to mature before serving.

King Prawn Patia Restaurant Style

SERVES 4

675 g (1½ lb) cooked peeled king prawns
1 tablespoon ghee
3 garlic cloves, finely chopped
2 teaspoons paprika
1 teaspoon chilli powder
450 g (1 lb) curry masala gravy (see page 32)
1 tablespoon tomato purée
2–3 tomatoes, finely chopped
½ red bell pepper, very finely chopped
2 teaspoons brown sugar
1 tablespoon fresh lime juice
aromatic salt to taste (see page 29)

1. Heat the ghee in a karahi or wok, and stir-fry the garlic, paprika and chilli powder for 30 seconds. Add the curry gravy and stir-fry for a further minute, or until it is simmering.
2. Add the king prawns and the remaining ingredients, except the salt, and stir-fry briskly for about 5 minutes.
3. Salt to taste and garnish.

VARIATIONS
Meat Patia, Chicken Patia, Vegetable Patia

These variations on King Prawn Patia are all offered by restaurants. Use the recipe for king prawns, left, and follow the relevant recipe method for Medium Curry on pages 96–97 for meat, chicken or vegetables.

Tikka Patia Curry

Modify the King Prawn Patia recipe as follows:

1. Cook the king prawns by the tikka method on page 56.
2. Omit the curry masala gravy and replace it with 450 g (1 lb) tikka tandoori masala curry gravy (see page 116).

PHALL

The first thing to say about Phall is that it is unheard of in the India subcontinent, where *phall* means fruit. It is a creation of the British Indian restaurant as the hottest curry their cooks can create, some say to wreak vengeance on the lager-louts, whose Saturday-night bad behaviour and racist humour do anything but bring a smile to the lips of the unfortunate staff who have to serve them. These vermin arrive drunk in the late hours and demand a really hot curry to mop up their next ten pints. Though many a better restaurant refuses to admit such custom, or closes before pub throw-out time, others less fortunate simply have to stay open and take whatever trade they can get, no matter how painful the process. Their only revenge, it is said, is to administer a good dose of Phall, which it is hoped will punish 'evil' customers with painful torment next day! There are numerous other jokes about Phall. One celebrated London restaurateur, Praveen Rai, chef-owner of Chelsea's Nayab, despises it so much that he refuses to serve it. He even goes as far as telling his clients in his menu that: *'Phall comes from the Hindi phrase "Bhuna Phar" meaning "bottom ripping".'* Be that as it may, Phall is no punishment to those respectable curry aficionados who have built up a tolerance to any level of chilli heat. They adore it. I know because I am one of them. And let me tell you too that, contrary to popular belief, high heat levels do not block out all other tastes to a palate which is used to chilli heat.

Two final observations: one is that real heat lovers will not be satisfied unless they use extra-hot chilli powder and/or the hottest chillies – Scotch Bonnets or Habañeros (see page 23) or Bangladeshi Nagas; the second is a serious warning to those not used to heat – do not try this curry!

Fenugreek Seed

Methi

TRIGONELLA
FOENUM-GRAECUM

As well as leaves (see pages 104 and 105), the fenugreek plant yields bean-like pods, 10-15 cm (4-6 inches) long, which contain 10-20 miniature, hard, yellow ochre-brown, nugget-like, grooved seeds about 3 mm (⅛ inch) long.

Fenugreek seeds have been found in Egyptian tombs. To this day, the spice remains·very popular in the Middle East, where fenugreek predominates in a spicy dip called *hilbeh*. It also appears in Arab bread (*khoubiz*), and the Greeks enjoy it with honey. India produces over 20,000 tons of fenugreek seed a year, placing it in their top ten exported spices, the seed being a minor but important ingredient in curry powder, and one of the panch phoran five spices.

Though seeming to smell of curry, fenugreek seed is quite bitter, its main oil being coumarin. Used whole, split or ground, in moderation, it is an important flavouring in masalas. Light roasting gives the seed an interesting depth, and another way of using it is to soak it overnight. Incidentally, fenugreek seed can also be sprouted, like mung beans, for beansprouts, and they have a light curry flavour. Fenugreek has always been said to be good as a contraceptive and a hair tonic, and in Java it is used to counter baldness. It lowers blood pressure, but it contains steroids. This may be why it was used by harem women to enlarge their chests!

Chicken or King Prawn Phall
The restaurant's hottest curry

SERVES 4

675 g (1½ lb) skinned chicken breast fillet, cubed, or raw peeled king prawns
2 tablespoons ghee
4 teaspoons extra-hot chilli powder
3 garlic cloves, finely chopped
450 g (1 lb) medium curry gravy (see page 96)
175 g (6 oz) tomatoes, chopped
4-8 fresh red and green chillies, chopped
salt to taste

1. Heat the ghee in a karahi or wok, and stir-fry the chilli powder for 2 minutes or until the ghee 'floats'. Add the garlic and continue to stir-fry for 30 seconds.
2. Add the chicken or prawns and stir-fry briskly for about 3 minutes.
3. Add the medium curry gravy and bring to a simmer. Add the tomatoes, fresh chillies and salt to taste, and simmer for up to 15 minutes more, until cooked.

Meat Phall

SERVES 4

675 g (1½ lb) lean lamb, beef or pork
2 tablespoons ghee
4 teaspoons extra-hot chilli powder
3 garlic cloves, finely chopped
450 g (1 lb) medium curry gravy (see page 96)
175 g (6 oz) tomatoes, chopped
4-8 fresh red and green chillies, chopped
salt to taste

1. Heat the ghee in a lidded flameproof casserole dish of 2.25-2.75 litre (4-5 pint) capacity, and stir-fry the chilli powder for 2 minutes or until the ghee 'floats'. Add the garlic and continue to stir-fry for 30 seconds.
2. Trim the meat of any unwanted matter, and cut it into bite-sized cubes. Preheat the oven to 190°C/375°F/Gas 5.
3. Add the medium curry gravy and the meat to the casserole, put the lid on, and put it in the oven.
4. After 20 minutes, inspect, stir and taste. Add water if required, and replace in the oven.
5. Repeat 20 minutes later, this time adding the tomatoes and fresh chillies.
6. After a final 20 minutes, again inspect and taste. The meat should be tender. Add salt to taste, replace the casserole in the oven, and turn off the heat. Serve after 10 minutes.

Hare Mirchi Kari
Green chilli curry

SERVES 4

450 g (1 lb) fresh green cayenne chillies
2 tablespoons ghee
225 g (8 oz) onions, finely chopped
3 tablespoons curry masala paste (see page 31)
175 g (6 oz) green cabbage, shredded
salt to taste
extra-hot chilli powder to taste
freshly ground black pepper to taste

1. De-stalk the chillies, but keep them whole.
2. Heat the ghee in a karahi or wok, and stir-fry the onions for about 5 minutes. Add the curry paste, and mix well.
3. Bring the mixture to a simmer, then add the chillies and cabbage, and simmer slowly over a low heat for about 15 minutes, stirring from time to time. Add a little water if the mixture starts to stick. Add salt, chilli powder and/or pepper to taste.

Mirchwangan Korma

A traditional Kashmiri red hot chilli korma

As we saw on page 83, *korma* is a style of cooking, and does not necessarily mean mild, as this seriously hot dish from the Kashmir Maharajas firmly proves.

SERVES 4

675 g (1½ lb) lean boned leg of lamb
4 tablespoons butter ghee
4-6 flakes alkanet root (see page 36)
2-4 garlic cloves, finely chopped
225 g (8 oz) red onions, chopped
fragrant stock (see page 29) or water
1 teaspoon garam masala (see page 30)
aromatic salt to taste (see page 29)

MARINADE

1 tablespoon tomato purée
1 tablespoon paprika
110 ml (4 fl oz) red wine
25 ml (1 fl oz) bottled beetroot vinegar
1 bottled beetroot, about the size of a
ping-pong ball, drained and sliced
20 fresh red chillies, coarsely chopped
1 red bell pepper, coarsely chopped

MASALA

15 cm (6 inch) piece cassia bark
12 green cardamoms
10 cloves
8 bay leaves
1 teaspoon fennel seeds

1. Cut the meat into cubes about 4 cm (1½ inches) in size, remembering that they will shrink during cooking as the liquids come out.

2. Put all the marinade ingredients in a blender, and process to a loose paste.

3. Place the paste in a large non-metallic bowl with the meat, and mix well. Cover and refrigerate for 24-60 hours.

4. Preheat the oven to 190°C/375°F/Gas 5.

5. Heat the ghee in a karahi or wok and add the alkanet root, which will colour the ghee red in a few seconds. Strain, using a metal strainer, and keep the oil. Discard the alkanet.

6. Return the red ghee to the pan, reheat, and stir-fry the garlic for 1 minute, then add the Masala and onions, and stir-fry for about 5 minutes.

7. Put the fried ingredients and the meat and marinade into a 2.25-2.75 litre (4-5 pint) lidded casserole dish, put the lid on, and place it in the oven.

8. After 20 minutes, inspect and stir the korma, adding stock or water if it is becoming too dry.

9. Repeat 20 minutes later, this time adding the garam masala and salt to taste.

10. Cook for a further 20 minutes, then serve with plain rice.

NOTE: To make this dish even hotter, use only red Scotch Bonnet or Habañero chillies, and use 1 tablespoon extra-hot chilli powder instead of the paprika.

ROGHAN JOSH GOSHT

Like the classic Korma, the classic Roghan Josh Gosht is an astoundingly aromatic Moghul meat (*gosht*) dish, perfected in Kashmir centuries ago. There are two possible derivations of the word 'Roghan'. In the Kashmiri language, it means 'red'. However, in Persian, it means 'clarified butter'. I was told this by Dallas etymologist Kenneth Grisham, who traced its roots back into ancient Persia, where meat, he told me, was cooked in ghee. Camelia Punjabi, India's foremost food expert and founder of the Bombay Brasserie, agrees: '*The meat itself should be on the bone with enough fat to contribute to its own cooking oil.*' 'Josh', she says, means 'heat', which describes the intense but slow heat required to get the most from this dish. The alternative meaning for 'Josh' is 'juice'. The fact is that none of these meanings are incorrect. The dish did originate in Persia as a slow-cooked meat dish. Much later, when the Moghuls used the cool of the Kashmir Mountains to escape the heat of the summer, it acquired highly aromatic Kashmiri spices, such as brown cardamoms, saffron and fennel. It also became red with the use of alkanet root (see pages 36 and 40) and a strange indigenous plant called *maaval* which was called 'cockscomb' by the British because it resembles that bodily piece of the male chicken! In its unavailability, I use beetroot powder as a non-traditional but truly non-artificial colouring. Another important ingredient which helps with reddening is chilli and/or paprika if you do not like heat. The meat is marinated first in yoghurt which gives a creamy colour to the dish, so don't expect a bright red colour.

The restaurant version of Roghan Josh, illustrated far left, is frankly disappointing in comparison, being based on Medium Curry, to which is added nothing more than tomato and peppers.

Palm Sugar and Molasses

Jaggery and *Gur*

True jaggery is a fructose, coming from the sap of tropical palm trees, hence it is also called palm sugar. Its colour ranges from pale gold to dark brown, and it is toffee- or fudge-like in taste and texture. It is collected in *chattees* (earthenware pots) which are placed high up in the trees by specialists (whose nimble tree-climbing requires no tools). If left for more than a few hours, the sugar ferments to become toddy or *feni* (highly alcoholic brews), hence the tree-climbers are called toddy wallahs. Amongst jaggery aficionados, the very best jaggery comes from the city of Kolaphur.

However, there is another way to make jaggery or *gur*, which is more commonly available, and much cheaper. It does not have quite the same fudge-like flavour, and is a sucrose, which is more intense than sugar. Sugar cane is crushed to obtain a liquid (molasses) which is dehydrated and resembles jaggery in appearance, although it is less vibrant in colour. Visitors to India will have observed street vendors, whose trolleys have a kind of hand-operated mangle. This is the press, and a bit of vigorous turning yields sugar cane juice, which is sold there and then, as a street-side drink.

Various grades of jaggery or *gur* are available from Asian stores, but good-quality molasses or brown sugar make good substitutes.

Roghan Josh Gosht

Aromatic meat curry
A traditional Moghul recipe

SERVES 4

675 g (1½ lb) lean lamb, cubed
110 g (4 oz) natural yoghurt
225 g (8 oz) onions, roughly chopped
5 cm (2 inch) piece fresh ginger, roughly chopped
2 garlic cloves, finely chopped
400 g (14 oz) canned tomatoes, drained
4 tablespoons butter ghee
5–6 flakes alkanet root (see page 36), optional
milk for thinning
1 tablespoon chopped fresh coriander leaves
2 teaspoons garam masala (see page 30)
20–25 strands saffron
aromatic salt to taste (see page 29)

MASALA ONE

6 green cardamoms
1 brown cardamom
6 cloves
3–4 pieces cassia bark
4 bay leaves

MASALA TWO

2 teaspoons paprika
½ teaspoon chilli powder
1 teaspoon roasted and ground coriander
1 teaspoon freshly ground allspice
2 teaspoons beetroot powder

1.   Trim the lamb of any fat, gristle and other unwanted matter, and mix it with the yoghurt and Masala One in a non-metallic bowl. Cover and marinate in the fridge for 6–24 hours.

2.   Put the onions, ginger, garlic and tomatoes in a blender, and process to a purée.

3.   Heat the ghee in a karahi or wok. Add the alkanet root, if using, and, as soon as the ghee turns red, strain the oil though a metal sieve, discarding the alkanet and keeping the red ghee.

4.   Return the ghee to the pan and reheat. Add Masala Two with a spoon or two of water, and stir-fry for a couple of minutes, until the ghee 'floats'. Add the puréed onion mixture and continue to stir-fry for 3–4 minutes more.

5.   Preheat the oven to 190°C/375°F/Gas 5. Put the fried purée in a 2.25–2.75 litre (4–5 pint) casserole with a lid. Add the meat with its marinade, and mix well. Cover with the lid and put the casserole in the oven.

6.   After 20 minutes, inspect, stir and taste the curry. If, at any time, the curry gets too dry, add a little milk to thin it. Replace in the oven.

7.   Repeat after a further 20 minutes, this time adding the coriander, garam masala and saffron.

8.   After a final 20 minutes, again inspect and taste the casserole. The meat should be tender. Add more milk if needed, and salt to taste. Replace the casserole in the oven and turn off the heat. Serve after 10 minutes.

Roghan Josh Gosht Restaurant Style

SERVES 4

675 g (1½ lb) lean meat, weighed after
removing all unwanted matter
1 tablespoon ghee
110 g (4 oz) onions, sliced
450 g (1 lb) medium curry gravy (see
page 96)
2 tablespoons finely chopped fresh
coriander leaves
½ red bell pepper, chopped
½ green bell pepper, chopped
2 tomatoes, halved
salt to taste

1. Heat the ghee in a large karahi or wok
and stir-fry the onions for 3-4 minutes.

2. Preheat the oven to 190°C/375°F/Gas 5.

3. Thoroughly mix the meat and the gravy
in a lidded casserole dish of 2.25-2.75 (4-5
pint) capacity. Add the fried onion, cover with
the lid, and put the dish in the oven.

4. After 20 minutes, remove the casserole
and inspect. Stir and add a little water if the
mixture looks dry.

5. Repeat after a further 20 minutes, this
time adding the coriander, red and green pepper, and tomatoes. Add a little more water if
the contents of the casserole need loosening.

6. Repeat after a further 20 minutes, by
which time the meat should be really tender.
If it is not quite as tender as you would like,
cook on until it is.

7. Add salt to taste, and serve with rice and
pickles.

Roghan Josh Chicken Curry Restaurant Style

SERVES 4

675 g (1½ lb) chicken breast fillets, skinned
1 tablespoon ghee
110 g (4 oz) onions, sliced
450 g (1 lb) medium curry gravy (see
page 96)
2 tablespoons finely chopped fresh
coriander leaves
½ red bell pepper, chopped
2 tomatoes, halved
salt to taste

1. Cut the chicken breast into bite-sized
chunks.

2. Heat the ghee in a large karahi or wok,
and stir-fry the onions for 3-4 minutes.

3. Add the chicken chunks and the gravy,
and heat until the contents are simmering,
stirring as required.

4. Lower the heat to achieve a gentle simmer, and cook for about 12 minutes, stirring
occasionally to prevent sticking.

5. Stir in the coriander, red pepper and
tomatoes, and add a little water if the contents
of the pan need loosening. Add salt to taste,
and cook for about 5 minutes more.

6. Check that the chicken is cooked by cutting a piece in half; it must be white right
through. If not, carry on cooking until it is.

TIKKA MASALA

The concept of this dish is simple: make a tandoori or tikka meat, chicken or fish dish, and make a typical curry-house rich, creamy, tangy, mild gravy to go with it, but colour it red, with ingredients such as tandoori or tikka spices, tomato purée, tomatoes themselves and red peppers.

Remarkably, the concept was invented, not in India, but in the British Indian restaurant as recently as the 1980s. It caught on at once, and swept so rapidly round the restaurant circuit that within a couple of years it was a standard item at all curry houses. Almost certainly without knowing it, that ingenious restaurateur, identity unknown, had created the world's most popular curry. At the British Indian restaurant over 25 per cent of all orders are for Chicken Tikka Masala. Not only that, but it appears as a sandwich filler, as a potato crisp flavour, as a pizza topping, as a spaghetti sauce, as a flavour for mayonnaise, and in all manner of non-traditional guises. I would not be surprised if it one day appeared in chewing-gum, or as a perfume fragrance!

Equally remarkably, before that date it certainly never appeared in Pakistan, where tandoori and tikka originated, nor anywhere in the subcontinent. Now, however, following Britain in a 'coals-to-Newcastle' move, Tikka Masala is to be found on the menus of the better restaurants in Bombay, Delhi and elsewhere, and it is equally popular. True, there had been traditional forerunners, and you'll find more about them on page 131.

Lemon Grass

Takrai

CYMBOPOGON CITRATUS

Lemon grass is native to India and South-East Asia, and grows as a perennial grass plant, about 1 metre (3 feet) high. It is depicted fresh in the photograph on pages 20-21. Its actual grass blades are quite hard, and are discarded, as is the rhizome, or root base. It is the bulbous, lower end of the grass, measuring 10-15 cm (4-6 inches) in length, which contains its oil, citral aldehyde. This gives it that distinctive fragrance, so familiar in the world of cosmetics, and that unique flowery, slightly zesty, vaguely lemony, sweet and aromatic taste to Thai, Indonesian, Malaysian and Vietnamese cooking. Generally, the stalk is not actually soft enough to eat. You'll get more flavour if you cut the fresh stalk into tassels (witch's broom-style), which will give greater surface area. Only if the stalk is particulary fresh and soft, and it is 'cross-cut' into tiny half-moons, can it be eaten.

Lemon grass is not widely used in Indian cooking, though it grows extensively there, in the garden. It is used to flavour tea, and Parsee and Gujarati soups. The Raj also used it in their hybrid curries, such as their coconut-based Malaya curry. Fresh lemon grass is widely available, but if you adore its flavour, it is worth keeping it dried (shown in the picture opposite in tassels and cross-cut). Incidentally, lemon peel or zest is no substitute for lemon grass.

Tikka Tandoori Masala Curry Gravy

MAKES 450 G (1 LB) GRAVY

2 tablespoons vegetable oil
2 garlic cloves, finely chopped
110 g (4 oz) onions, very finely chopped
1 tablespoon curry masala paste (see page 31)
1 tablespoon red paste (see page 56)
4 canned plum tomatoes
1 tablespoon white spirit vinegar
1 tablespoon tomato ketchup
175 ml (6 fl oz) canned tomato soup
½ green bell pepper, chopped
4 fresh green chillies, chopped
2 tablespoons coconut milk powder
1 tablespoon garam masala (see page 30)
1 tablespoon dried fenugreek leaves
1 tablespoon chopped fresh coriander leaves
salt to taste

1. Heat the oil in a large karahi or wok, and stir-fry the garlic for 30 seconds. Add the onions and stir-fry for 8-10 minutes.
2. Add the pastes and stir-fry for a couple of minutes.
3. Add the tomatoes, vinegar, ketchup, soup, green pepper and chillies, bring to a simmer and stir-fry for about 5 minutes.
4. Add the remaining ingredients, and simmer for a further 5 minutes, adding water as necessary to maintain a gravy consistency.

Chicken Tikka Masala

SERVES 2-3

20-24 cooked chicken tikka pieces (see page 56)
2 tablespoons ghee
3 garlic cloves, finely chopped
225 g (8 oz) onions, very finely chopped
1½ tablespoons curry masala paste (see page 31)
1½ tablespoons red paste (see page 56)
6 canned plum tomatoes
1 tablespoon white spirit vinegar
1 tablespoon tomato ketchup
175 ml (6 fl oz) canned tomato soup
½ green bell pepper, chopped
4 fresh green chillies, chopped
100 ml (3½ fl oz) single cream
1 tablespoon garam masala (see page 30)
1 tablespoon chopped fresh coriander
salt to taste

1. Heat the ghee in a large karahi or wok, and stir-fry the garlic for 30 seconds. Add the onions and stir-fry for 8-10 minutes until golden brown.
2. Add the pastes and stir-fry for 2 minutes. Add the tomatoes, vinegar, ketchup, soup, green pepper and chillies, and stir-fry for about 5 minutes. Add the chicken, cream, garam masala and coriander, and simmer for a further 5 minutes, adding a little water if it needs it. Salt to taste and serve.

NOTE: You can speed up the above recipe by combining 450 g (1 lb) tikka tandoori masala curry gravy (see left) with the chicken tikka pieces. Serve when hot right through.

Meat Tikka Masala

Substitute 20-24 meat tikka pieces (see page 57) for the chicken, and follow the Chicken Tikka Masala recipe.

Balti Tikka Masala

Yes, some restaurants do offer this combination dish. To either Chicken or Meat Tikka Masala, add 2 tablespoons Balti masala (see page 60) at the early frying stage and omit the curry masala paste.

Fish Tikka Masala Curry

SERVES 4

675 g (1½ lb) raw cod fillet steaks, cut into cubes
450 g (1 lb) hot tikka tandoori masala curry gravy (see left)

Combine the cod chunks with the hot gravy. Simmer for 8-10 minutes, then serve with plain rice.

VINDALOO

This dish was brought to India by the Portuguese, when they first arrived in Goa in 1496. Called *vinha d'alhos*, it consisted of pork marinated in wine vinegar and garlic (*alho*), and is still found in Portugal today. The local Goanese Indians were soon converted to Christianity, so had no problems with consuming pork and wine. Not surprisingly, they found the dish to be bland, so they increased the garlic quantity, and added spices, notably plentiful quantities of chilli. Its name was simplified to Vin-*dar*-loo, with the emphasis on the second syllable, as in the Portuguese version. Unchanged to this day, the dish has become a Goanese classic (illustrated on the right of the photograph).

In another guise, Vindaloo has become the archetypal benchmark dish at the curry house. We saw on pages 87 and 107 that in the early days of the British curry house evolution, the original Punjabi restaurateurs found there was a demand for hot curries. Most Punjabis prefer highly flavoured but mild curries, but they had no problem making their standard 'medium' curry hotter – they just added chilli powder: one teaspoon for 'hot'; two for 'hotter'; and three for 'hottest'. They needed smart names for their dishes, and looked for inspiration to southern India, where the people like their curries hot. Madras and Phall became the hot and hottest curries. Vindaloo seemed like a well-named candidate for the heat-grade in between. But it was to bear no resemblance to its Goan namesake. Pork was out, so was wine, both being contentious for Moslems. Marination was too time-consuming for busy restaurants, and instead of using garlic, huge chunks of potato mistakenly became an integral part of the dish, *aloo* meaning potato in many Indian languages. Even the pronunciation of *Vin*-daloo evolved differently, with the emphasis on the first syllable.

Here are both versions, and the real thing is enhanced with a serving of Chilli Rice (recipe on page 173). And there is another delight for hot heads . . . a recipe, overleaf, for the hottest curry ever, Tindaloo.

Lovage

Ajwain or *Ajowan*

LIGISTICUM OFFICINALIS

Lovage is an annual, herbaceous plant, which grows up to 60 cm (2 feet) high, with feathery leaves and pretty vermilion flowers. It is a member of the prolific Umbelliferae family, which also includes aniseed, caraway, celery, coriander, cummin, dill and fennel. They all have a characteristic taste, which of course is a result of their having thymol in varying quantities as a component of their volatile oil. But, once again, this is a spice with a confusing nomenclature. In this case, *ajwain* is called 'carom' or, more commonly, 'lovage' (another relative), but it is not European lovage. *Ajwain* is indigenous to Egypt, Afghanistan and north India. Its seed is smaller than its European counterpart. In size, it closely resembles celery seed (see page 68), with its tiny, round, striped seed, about 1.5-2 mm in diameter. *Ajwain* is greyer in colour, but totally different in taste, being a little bitter, with a slightly musky, but quite distinctively intense flavour of thyme, which is an acquired taste. Once acquired, however, you'll enjoy this minor spice in Bombay mix, snacks and fish dishes.

Traditional Goan Pork Vindaloo

SERVES 4

675 g (1½ lb) lean leg of pork, cut into 4 cm (1½ inch) cubes
3 tablespoons ghee
6 garlic cloves, chopped
225 g (8 oz) onions, chopped
fragrant stock (see page 29) or water
2 tablespoons fresh lemon juice
1 tablespoon chopped fresh coriander leaves
4 fresh red cayenne chillies, finely chopped
aromatic salt to taste (see page 29)

MARINADE

200 ml (7 fl oz) red wine
2 tablespoons red wine vinegar
6 garlic cloves, crushed
3 tablespoons fresh chilli purée (see page 189)
1 teaspoon aromatic salt (see page 29)

MASALA

10 cloves
6 green cardamoms
5 cm (2 inch) piece cassia bark
1 teaspoon cummin seeds

1. In a large non-metallic bowl, mix the meat with the marinade. Cover and refrigerate for up to 60 hours.
2. Heat the ghee in a karahi or wok, and stir-fry the garlic and Masala for 1 minute. Add the onions and continue to stir-fry for 5 minutes.
3. Preheat the oven to 190°C/375°F/Gas 5.
4. Transfer the fried ingredients to a 2.25-2.75 litre (4-5 pint) lidded casserole dish and add the pork and its marinade. Combine well, cover with the lid and place in the oven.
5. After 20 minutes, inspect and stir, adding a little stock or water if the curry is becoming too dry.
6. Repeat 20 minutes later, adding the remaining ingredients.
7. Cook for a further 20 minutes or until cooked to your liking.

Harsha Tindaloo
The hottest duck curry

This is an authentic Bangladeshi recipe for the hottest curry I know, hotter even than Phall!

SERVES 4

675 g (1½ lb) duck breasts, weighed after removing all unwanted matter and cut into 4 cm (1½ inch) cubes
10 tablespoons butter ghee
6-8 garlic cloves, very finely chopped
225 g (8 oz) onions, very finely chopped
2-4 red Habañero, Scotch Bonnet or Nagar chillies, chopped
up to 225 ml (8 fl oz) fragrant stock (see page 29)
2 tablespoons chopped fresh coriander leaves
salt to taste

MASALA

2 teaspoons ground coriander
1 teaspoon ground cummin
1 teaspoon garam masala (see page 30)
1-3 teaspoons extra-hot chilli powder

GARNISH

toasted almonds
onion tarka (see page 32)
whole fresh coriander leaves

1. Preheat the oven to 190°C/375°F/Gas 5. Heat the ghee in a 2.25-2.75 litre (4-5 pint) flameproof casserole dish with a lid, add the Masala and stir-fry for 30 seconds. Add the garlic, lower the heat and cook for about 5 minutes to achieve a golden brown tarka.
2. Add the onions and continue stir-frying on a low heat for about 15 minutes to continue the tarka.
3. Add the duck and chillies, and continue to stir-fry for about 10 minutes, sealing the meat.
4. Put the lid on the casserole dish and put it in the oven.
5. After 20 minutes, remove from the oven, inspect and stir. The duck should not be shriv-

elling or drying out. We want it to be juicy, in a juicy gravy. Add just enough stock to ensure this, now and throughout the cooking as necessary. Return the casserole to the oven.

6. Inspect again after 20 minutes. Add the chopped coriander and salt to taste. Return to the oven for a final 10 minutes, by which time the duck should be really tender. If not, return to the oven.

7. Remove the casserole from the oven, stir and leave to rest for another 10 minutes. Spoon off the excess ghee and reserve for another time.

8. Garnish with the almonds, onion tarka and fresh coriander leaves.

Meat Vindaloo Restaurant Style

SERVES 4

675 g (1½ lb) lean meat, weighed after
removing all unwanted matter
2 tablespoons ghee
6 fresh or dried red chillies, chopped
2 teaspoons chilli powder
450 g (1 lb) medium curry gravy (see
page 96)
2 tablespoons finely chopped fresh
coriander leaves
1 large boiled potato, quartered
salt to taste

1. Preheat the oven to 190°C/375°F/Gas 5. Cut the meat into bite-sized cubes.

2. Heat the ghee in a karahi or wok, and stir-fry the chillies and chilli powder for about 2 minutes.

3. Thoroughly mix this stir-fry with the meat and the gravy in a lidded casserole dish of 2.25-2.75 (4-5 pint) capacity. Cover with the lid and put in the oven.

4. After 20 minutes, remove the dish from the oven and inspect. Stir, and add a little water if the curry looks dry.

5. Repeat after a further 20 minutes, adding

the coriander and add a little more water if the contents of the casserole need loosening.

6. Repeat after a final 20 minutes, by which time the meat should be really tender. If it is not quite as tender as you would like, cook on until it is. Switch the oven off. Add the potato and salt to taste, and return the casserole to the oven for a final 10 minutes.

VARIATIONS

Chicken, Prawn, Fish or Vegetable Vindaloo, Restaurant Style

Follow the recipe for the appropriate Medium Curry on page 97, adding two or more teaspoons chilli powder at the masala-frying stage, and a large chunk or two of cooked potato towards the end of cooking.

In this chapter, in alphabetical order, are sixteen favourite curries. Here are the first four (recipes overleaf).

Achari Murgh

Achar means 'pickle', and Achari Murgh means 'chicken curried in a pickle base'. Pictured top right, this curry is very simple in concept: the curry is cooked as a Jalfrezi (see page 72), the only difference being the addition of your chosen bottled pickle at the early spice-frying stage, giving the curry a very powerful taste.

Afghani Sabzi (vegetables)

Linking Iran and Pakistan, Afghanistan's rugged mountainous passes are home to fierce tribes who prefer warring to 'wokking'. Pulses, wheat and root vegetables are the staples they store for their hard winters. The restaurant Afghani curry interprets this by adding nuts and dried fruit to a Medium Curry. The rather more authentic recipe overleaf (illustrated top left) uses carrots, swedes, onion, courgette and leeks, with a typically light spicing using just *char masala* (four aromatic spices).

Bengali Beef

Before partition, there existed both West and East Bengal. The latter is now part of Bangladesh, but their food is still referred to as 'Bengali' and they love chicken and beef dishes. The Bengali style creates a dry curry (bottom left of the photograph), using a beef or lamb Medium Curry as the base, to which potato, tomato, sugar and chilli are added.

Ceylon Curry

The name Ceylon has not been used since 1947, and try as you may, you won't find this curry in Sri Lanka (see page 135). To curry restaurateurs, the Ceylon is a hot, creamy, tangy curry (bottom right of the photograph), adapted from the Bhoona by adding coconut milk, dried chillies and lemon.

Mace

Javitri

MYRISTICA FRAGRANS

Mace is unique, because it grows inseparably with another popular spice, nutmeg (see page 140). Their tree is a tall, tropical evergreen, which originally grew only on the tiny Indonesian island of Ambon. The Chinese knew of its location centuries before Christ, and their *dhows* took mace, nutmeg and clove back to China, from where it travelled the length of the spice route to the Middle East, and onwards to Europe. The Romans introduced such spices into Britain, and though many markups made spices very expensive, by Tudor times they were so much in demand that no effort was spared in finding their elusive sources. Ambon was eventually discovered by the Portuguese in 1512 and later taken by the Dutch, and fought over, but never occupied for long, by the British, who broke the monopoly by deviously obtaining nutmeg/mace and planting it in Sri Lanka, south India and Grenada, in the West Indies. Mace is very aromatic and oily, its volatile oil being eugenol, though it has less of this than nutmeg.

When cropped, it is pliable and easy to separate from its nutmeg and flatten, before it is dried in the sun. Grenada mace, shown opposite, is redder than others. Moluccan is yellow, though their flavours are indistinguishable. Its use in Indian cooking is minimal. Its subtle flavour goes well with lighter fish, vegetable and sweet dishes.

Achari Murgh
Chicken curried with pickle

SERVES 4

675 g (1½ lb) chicken breast fillets, skinned
4 tablespoons ghee or vegetable oil
½ teaspoon turmeric
1 teaspoon white cummin seeds
1 teaspoon mustard seeds
4 garlic cloves, finely chopped
5 cm (2 inch) piece fresh ginger, finely chopped (optional)
2 tablespoons curry masala (see page 31)
1 large Spanish onion, chopped
2 or more fresh green chillies, sliced
½ green bell pepper, coarsely chopped
½ red bell pepper, coarsely chopped
2 tablespoons chopped fresh coriander leaves
2–3 fresh tomatoes, chopped
2 tablespoons brinjal pickle, chopped
1 tablespoon lime pickle, chopped
2 teaspoons garam masala (see page 30)
salt to taste
lemon juice to serve

1. Cut the chicken into bite-sized pieces.
2. Heat the ghee or oil in a karahi or wok, and fry the turmeric and seeds for about 30 seconds. Add the garlic and ginger, if using, and stir-fry for about 30 seconds more, then add the masala, with just enough water to make a paste, and stir-fry for a further minute.
3. Add the chicken pieces and stir-fry for about 5 minutes.
4. Add the onion, chillies and peppers, and continue to stir-fry for about 5 minutes more.
5. Add the coriander, tomatoes, chopped pickles and garam masala, and stir-fry for about 5 minutes on medium heat. Add a little water if needed.
6. Test that the chicken is cooked by cutting a piece in half; it must be white right through. When it is, add salt to taste, and serve with a squeeze of lemon juice over the top.

VARIATION
Achari Gosht
(Meat curried with pickle)

Meat needs a much longer cooking time than chicken. Adapt the Medium Meat Curry recipe on page 96 by adding the pickle.

Afghani Sabzi
Vegetables in the Afghan style

SERVES 4

175 g (6 oz) carrots, chopped into batons
175 g (6 oz) swede, chopped into batons
175 g (6 oz) courgettes, sliced into discs
2 tablespoons vegetable oil
175 g (6 oz) onions, chopped into batons
175 g (6 oz) leeks, sliced into discs
20 shelled and peeled peanuts
6–8 walnuts
1 teaspoon aromatic salt (see page 29)

CHAR MASALA
(FOUR AROMATIC SPICES), ALL ROASTED AND GROUND (SEE PAGE 30)

½ teaspoon green cardamom seeds
½ teaspoon cummin seeds
1–2 pieces cassia bark
½ teaspoon cloves

1. Blanch the carrots, swede and courgettes in boiling water until tender, then drain.
2. Heat the oil in a karahi or wok. Stir-fry the onion and leeks for about 3–4 minutes, or until they become translucent.
3. Add the *char masala* and the nuts, and, when sizzling, add the blanched vegetables.
4. Stir-fry for just enough time to heat everything right through, then salt to taste and serve with bread or plain rice and/or another curry.

Bengali Beef Curry

SERVES 4

675 g (1½ lb) stewing steak, weighed after
removing all unwanted matter
2 teaspoons chilli powder
3-4 fresh red chillies, chopped
2 large raw potatoes, peeled and halved
350 g (12 oz) medium curry gravy (see
page 96)
2 fresh plum tomatoes
2 teaspoons jaggery (palm sugar) or
brown sugar
salt to taste

1. Preheat the oven to 190°C/375°F/Gas 5.
2. Thoroughly mix the meat, chilli powder, fresh chillies, potato and gravy in a lidded casserole dish of 2.25-2.75 litre (4-5 pint) capacity. Cover with the lid and put in the oven.
3. After 20 minutes, remove the dish from the oven and inspect the curry. Stir and add a little water if it looks dry, though you should expect it to be drier than a Medium Curry.
4. Repeat after a further 20 minutes, adding the tomatoes and sugar, and a little more water if the contents of the casserole need loosening.
5. Repeat after a final 20 minutes, by which time the meat should be really tender. If it is not quite as tender as you would like, cook on until it is.
6. Add salt to taste, replace the casserole in the oven and turn off the heat. Serve after 10 minutes, with plain rice.

Ceylon Pork

SERVES 4

675 g (1½ lb) lean pork, weighed after
removing all unwanted matter
3 tablespoons mustard blend oil
1-3 teaspoons very finely chopped garlic
200 g (7 oz) finely chopped onion
1-4 dried red chillies
6-10 fresh or dried curry leaves
⅓ block (65 g) creamed coconut, chopped
150 ml (5 fl oz) single cream
1 tablespoon fresh lemon juice
salt to taste

MASALA

2 teaspoons curry masala (see page 31)
1 teaspoon ground coriander
½ teaspoon turmeric

1. Cut the pork into bite-sized cubes.
2. Mix the Masala with enough water to achieve an easily pourable paste.
3. Heat the oil in a karahi or wok until it is nearly smoking. Add the garlic and paste, and stir-fry for 1 minute. Add the onion, reduce the heat, and stir-fry for at least 5 minutes.
4. Take the pan off the heat, cool slightly, then purée the mixture in a blender, or in the pan using a hand-held blender.
5. Preheat the oven to 190°C/375°F/Gas 5.
6. Put the chillies, curry leaves, pork and purée in a lidded casserole dish of 2.25-2.75 litre (4-5 pint) capacity, cover with the lid, and put in the oven.
7. After 20 minutes, inspect the curry. Stir and add a little water if it looks dry. Repeat after a further 20 minutes, adding the coconut and cream.
8. Repeat after a final 20 minutes, by which time the pork should be really tender. If it is not quite as tender as you would like, cook on until it is. Add the lemon juice. The sauce should be quite runny; add more water if it needs thinning.
9. Add salt to taste, replace the casserole in the oven, and turn off the heat. Serve after 10 minutes, with lemon rice.

Dopiaza

This is a north Indian dish. *Do* meaning 'two' and *piaza*, meaning 'onions', this curry is so called because two batches of onions are used in the cooking, one in the initial frying, and the other later in the cooking. Originating in Persia, it was a Moghul favourite. A 1590 book describing court life, says that it is *'a meat dish cooked with ghee, spices, yoghurt and a lot of onion'*. The recipe here (illustrated top right) uses veal, though any meat works equally well. The restaurant interpretation is to add ghee, fried onion and peppers to a Medium Curry base.

Jeera Chicken

This is the signature dish of a family of Kenyan Asian restaurateurs, the Anands, who settled in Southall in the 1970s and established the highly successful Brilliant and Madhu's Brilliant restaurants. It works as a starter, as well as a main course.

Karachi Karahi Curry

Illustrated top centre is a dish I met years ago at the Karachi Sheraton. It is an amazing mixture of tender lamb, curried with minced chicken and spinach, and topped with crumbled egg. At the Sheraton, incidentally, it was served in the karahi, the standard two-handled cooking wok, earning it the nifty title Karachi Karahi.

Kashmiri Curry

Kashmiri food is the most aromatic of all the food of the subcontinent, of which a good example is Roghan Josh. The curry house has its own interpretation, wide of the real Kashmiri mark, but popular in its own way. To Medium Curry is added canned lychees, pineapple, banana, cream and coconut. King Prawn Kashmiri Curry is shown here, top left. Also in the photograph are restaurant pullao rice and Tarka Dhal, which accompany this dish nicely.

Dried Mango

Am Chur or *Kachcha Am*

MANGIFERA INDICA

The mango (*am*) is India's most revered fruit. It has been cultivated there for over 6,000 years, and has earned itself the title 'Queen of Fruit', as well as substantial revenue as an export crop. Mango is also used as a vegetable, particularly for pickling, and some examples of fresh mangoes are illustrated on pages 24 and 25. Mangoes grow seasonally on a pretty tree, whose dark leaves spread out like a huge parasol. In Britain and the West, we are fortunate enough to be supplied with fresh mangoes virtually all year round, with imports from many countries. In India, this is not the case, and the mango season is a much-anticipated but rather short highlight of the year. One answer is to dry the fruit, but only sour unripened, stoned mangoes are used. The resultant spice, at the top in the photograph opposite, is exceedingly sour, but very distinctive. It is mostly used ground into a fine grey powder (see pages 16 and 17).

Mangosteen (bottom in the picture) is a Malaysian native, though it too grows in India, where it is known as Indian gooseberry (*amla*). Though it too is sour when dried, and it is used in pickles, and though it has a similar name to mango, it is not related, its oval bright green, stripy, smooth, gooseberry-like, six-seeded fruits growing only to a length of 1.5–2.5 cm (½–1 inch). Neither should it be confused with *kokum*, a plum-like, dark, purple-black souring agent depicted in the *daba* on page 15.

Dopiaza Veal
Veal curried with onion

SERVES 4

700 g (1lb 7 oz) lean veal, weighed after removing all unwanted matter
3 tablespoons ghee
225 g (8 oz) onions, thinly sliced
3 tablespoons mustard blend oil
3–4 garlic cloves, finely chopped
110 g (4 oz) onions, finely chopped
250 ml (9 fl oz) fragrant stock (see page 29) or water
2–3 fresh red chillies, shredded (optional)
2 tablespoons finely chopped fresh coriander leaves
2 teaspoons garam masala (see page 30)
salt to taste

MASALA

2 teaspoons coriander seeds, roasted and ground
½ teaspoon cummin seeds, roasted and ground
1 teaspoon turmeric
1 teaspoon chilli powder

1. Cut the veal into 4 cm (1½ inch) cubes. Preheat the oven to 190°C/375°F/Gas 5.
2. Heat the ghee in a karahi or wok on a lowish heat and stir-fry the sliced onions for at least 15 minutes or until they are brown (see page 32). Transfer the onions to a bowl and set aside.
3. Add just enough water to the Masala to make a thin paste.
4. Using the same karahi or wok, heat the mustard oil and stir-fry the garlic for 1 minute. Add the Masala paste and continue to stir-fry for another couple of minutes, until the oil 'floats'.
5. Put the contents of the karahi or wok into a casserole dish of 2.25–2.75 litre (4–5 pint) capacity with the veal. Cover with the lid and put in the oven.
6. After about 15 minutes, inspect the curry and add the chopped onions, stock or water, and optional chillies. Return to the oven for a further 20–25 minutes.

7. Inspect again, this time adding the fresh coriander and garam masala. Return to the oven for a final 20 minutes, or until the veal is perfectly tender and the liquid is reduced to a thick consistency, about half its original quantity.
8. Add the cooked, sliced onions and salt to taste, and return the casserole, lid off, to the oven. Switch off the heat and leave the curry for 10 minutes, before serving with Tarka Dhal and *parathas*.

Jeera Chicken
Chicken cooked with cummin

SERVES 4 AS A STARTER

450 g (1 lb) chicken breast fillets, skinned
50 g (2 oz) butter
1 tablespoon cummin seeds
2 tablespoons ground cummin
150 ml (5 fl oz) chicken stock or water
salt to taste

1. Cut the chicken into small chunks, about 2 cm (¾ inch) square.
2. Heat the butter in a karahi or wok to quite a high heat. Add the cummin seeds and stir-fry for about 30 seconds. Add the ground cummin and continue to stir-fry for a further 30 seconds, then add 3–4 tablespoons stock or water and stir-fry for 2–3 minutes more.
3. Add the chicken pieces and stir-fry briskly for about 2 minutes, then lower the heat a little and, over the next 5 minutes, add the remaining stock or water, stirring as necessary.
4. To finish off, turn up the heat and resume brisk stir-frying for about 5 minutes to reduce the remaining liquid to a dryish gravy and coating.
5. Check that the chicken is cooked by cutting a piece in half; it should be white right through. If not, continue stir-frying until it is. Add salt to taste and serve as a starter with chutneys or as a main course with *puris*.

Karachi Karahi Gosht

This is tender lamb curried with minced chicken and spinach, and topped with crumbled egg.

SERVES 4

350 g (12 oz) lean leg of lamb
2 tablespoons butter ghee
350 g (12 oz) minced chicken breast
225 g (8 oz) medium curry gravy (see page 96)
1 tablespoon dried fenugreek
300 g (10 oz) fresh spinach leaves
aromatic salt to taste (see page 29)
crumbled hard-boiled egg to garnish

1. Trim the meat of any unwanted matter and cut into bite-sized cubes. Preheat the oven to 190°C/375°F/Gas 5.

2. Heat the ghee in a flameproof casserole dish of 2.25-2.75 litres (4-5 pint) capacity, and stir-fry the meat for about 5 minutes. Add the chicken and the gravy, cover with the lid, and put in the oven.

3. After 15 minutes, inspect the curry and stir. The curry should be fairly dry, but add a little water if required. Replace in the oven.

4. After a further 20 minutes, repeat and add the fenugreek.

5. After a final 20 minutes, taste the dish. The meat should be tender, but dry. Add a little more water if needed. Mix in the spinach leaves and salt to taste. Replace the casserole in the oven and turn off the heat.

6. After 10 minutes, remove the curry from the oven, garnish with the egg, and serve with rice and bread.

Kashmiri Curry

For this fragrant Kashmiri dish, canned lychees, pineapple, banana, cream and coconut are added to the restaurant Korma.

SERVES 4

675 g (1½ lb) cooked peeled king prawns
1 tablespoon ghee
2-3 garlic cloves, finely chopped
3-4 tablespoons finely sliced onions
225 g (8 oz) medium curry gravy (see page 96)
½ tablespoon each finely chopped red and green bell pepper
4 pineapple cubes (optional)
4 canned lychees (optional)
¼ block (50 g) creamed coconut
50 ml (2 fl oz) double cream
2 tablespoons juice from the lychee can
1 tablespoon dark muscovado sugar
aromatic salt to taste (see page 29)
sliced banana to garnish

1. Heat the ghee in a karahi or wok, and stir-fry the garlic for 30 seconds. Add the onions and stir-fry for a further 2-3 minutes.

2. Over about 5 minutes, gradually add the gravy to the pan, stir-frying briskly so that it thickens.

3. Add the remaining ingredients (except the banana), including salt to taste, and simmer until it is hot right through.

4. Garnish with the banana and serve with pullao rice.

Makhani Chicken

On page 114 we found that the world's most famous curry does have traditional roots. Makhani, Masalador or Makhanwalla are variations on the same theme. Chicken, meat or seafood is marinated in spiced yoghurt, then cooked in ghee or butter with an aromatic sauce containing tomatoes and cream. Delicious though these dishes are, they do not involve the *tandoor*, so their flavour is quite different from the curry house interpretation. Here, bottom right, is one such version, where tandoori chicken leg is served in a rich pink sauce.

Malai King Prawn

Whenever you see a Malai curry in India, you know it will be a rich, mild dish. A celebrated favourite is Malai Kofta, where spherical meat, fish or vegetable rissoles are served in a light, creamy sauce (see page 81). Here, top left, in this restaurant favourite, the sauce can be milder and richer even than Korma, unless you add the optional dried chillies.

Malaya Fish Curry

Malayan curries show their Indian, Chinese and Thai influences. Thinner fragrant gravies, often based on coconut milk, also contain chillies, ginger and lemon grass, as shown here, bottom left. The British curry house interprets its Malaya Curry as very mild, rich and based on the Korma, with the addition of creamed coconut, milk, double cream, pineapple and/or other fruit.

Methi Gosht

Methi (fenugreek) Gosht (meat) is robust, very savoury and very spicy, though not chilli hot. It comes originally from the pungent Punjab and so was one of the original dishes on offer at the early British curry houses. To this day, it has changed little, if at all, from its traditional ancestor. The fenugreek (*methi*) in question is dried, and is an acquired taste.

Mint

Podina

MENTHA SPICATA

Mint grows prolifically as a herbaceous perennial, its bushy shrub growing up to 1 metre (3 feet) in height. Mint cross fertilises, and therefore hybridises easily with other mints, making true identification of species and varieties a subject of debate. One authority believes there to be as many as 40 species of mint worldwide. Be that as it may, the most popular mint is spearmint. Like all mints, it is native to Europe, and was particularly popular with the Greeks and Romans, who distributed it throughout their empires.

Spearmint's distinctive flavour comes from its volatile oil, consisting predominantly of menthol, with lesser amounts of carvone and limonene. Other popular mint species are applemint and peppermint. These, in common with all other mints, have less powerful aromatics (and less menthol) than spearmint, though all have interesting characteristics of their own. Lemon mint and chocolate mint, for example, are as subtley redolent of their namesakes as of mint.

Fresh mint grows in India, but is little used in cooking, appearing here and there in chutneys and certain dishes, such as Podina Gosht and Balti. Dried mint is a useful storecupboard item. The traditional way to dry mint in India is to hang bundles of it in the shade for a couple of days, after which it is a mere 25 per cent of its original weight. Freeze-dried mint not only retains a lovely colour, as depicted opposite, but it has an intensity of flavour almost as good as fresh.

Makhani Chicken

SERVES 4

4 chicken legs and 4 chicken breast pieces
1 medium onion, roughly chopped
2 garlic cloves, roughly chopped
5 cm (2 inch) piece fresh ginger, roughly chopped
6 tablespoons ghee or butter
2-3 tomatoes, skinned, de-seeded and very finely chopped
1 tablespoon tomato purée
100 ml (3½ fl oz) single cream
2 tablespoons chopped fresh coriander
salt to taste

MARINADE

175 g (6 oz) natural yoghurt
1½ teaspoons paprika
1½ teaspoons ground coriander
1 teaspoon chilli powder
1 teaspoon garlic powder
½ teaspoon red food colouring powder

MASALA

2 teaspoons paprika
1 teaspoon garam masala (see page 30)
1 teaspoon ground coriander
¼ teaspoon yellow food colouring powder (optional)
1 teaspoon garlic powder

1. Skin the chicken pieces and lightly prick or gash the flesh.

2. Mix the marinade ingredients together in a non-metallic bowl. Add the chicken and mix well. Cover and place in the fridge for 24-60 hours.

3. Preheat the oven to 190°C/375°F/Gas 5. Remove the chicken from the marinade, shaking off and keeping any excess, but ensuring that there is a liberal coating left on each piece. Place the chicken on an oven tray and bake in the oven for 20 minutes, then remove and keep warm. Strain the liquid off the oven tray and reserve.

4. Meanwhile, purée the remaining marinade with the onion, garlic and ginger in a food processor or blender, adding just enough water to keep it pourable.

5. Mix the Masala with just enough water to make a paste.

6. Heat the ghee or butter in a karahi or wok and fry the Masala paste for about 2 minutes, or until the oil 'floats'. Add the purée and simmer for 10 minutes.

7. Add the tomatoes, tomato purée, cream, fresh coriander and the oven tray liquid, and simmer for the few minutes it takes for it to start to change colour and go orangey. Salt to taste. Add the warm cooked chicken to the gravy, and serve with pullao rice.

Malai King Prawn Curry

SERVES 4

675 g (1½ lb) cooked king prawns, peeled but tails left on
3 tablespoons vegetable oil
2-3 garlic cloves, finely chopped
225 g (8 oz) onions, very finely chopped
1 tablespoon finely chopped green bell pepper
1 red bell pepper, coarsely chopped
110 ml (4 fl oz) single cream
aromatic salt to taste (see page 29)

MASALA

1 tablespoon curry masala (see page 31)
½ teaspoon coarsely ground black pepper
½ teaspoon turmeric
¼ teaspoon asafoetida

1. Mix the Masala with just enough water to make a paste.

2. Heat the oil in a karahi or wok and stir-fry the garlic for 30 seconds. Add the masala paste and stir-fry for a couple of minutes or until the oil 'floats'.

3. Add the onions and green pepper, and stir-fry briskly for about 5 minutes.

4. Add the red pepper and the cream, and bring to a simmer. Add the king prawns, and simmer until hot right through. Add salt to taste, and serve with rice and breads.

Malaya Fish Curry

SERVES 4

675 g (1½ lb) white fish, skinned and boned
4 tablespoons mustard blend oil
200 g (7 oz) onions, chopped
1 garlic clove, finely chopped
1 teaspoon yellow mustard seeds
1 teaspoon black mustard seeds
4 dried red chillies
300 ml (½ pint) canned coconut milk
2 stalks lemon grass
10-12 curry leaves
2 fresh green chillies, chopped
salt to taste
fresh lemon juice
8-12 cubes pineapple

1. Heat half the oil in a saucepan or small wok and stir-fry the onions and garlic to make a golden tarka (see page 32), then set aside.
2. Heat the remaining oil in a karahi or wok and stir-fry the mustard seeds for a few seconds or until they pop. Add the dried chillies, coconut milk, lemon grass and curry leaves, and bring to a simmer, then add the fish and green chillies.
3. Cook for 10-15 minutes until the fish is tender, keeping the sauce fairly thick but fluid while cooking by adding a little water as required.
4. Add salt to taste and sprinkle with lemon juice. Garnish with pineapple and serve with lemon rice.

Methi Gosht
Punjabi-style fenugreek-flavoured meat curry

SERVES 4

675 g (1½ lb) lean lamb
4 tablespoons butter ghee
2 teaspoons ground coriander
450 g (1 lb) medium curry gravy (see page 96)
4 tablespoons dried fenugreek or 110 g (4 oz) fresh fenugreek leaves, chopped
2 teaspoons garam masala (see page 30)
2 tablespoons chopped fresh coriander leaves
salt to taste

1. Trim the meat of any unwanted matter and cut into bite-sized cubes. Preheat the oven to 190°C/375°F/Gas 5.
2. Heat the ghee in a lidded flameproof casserole dish of 2.25-2.75 (4-5 pint) capacity, and stir-fry the ground coriander for 3 minutes, then add the gravy and simmer for about 5 minutes more to thicken it a little.
3. Add the meat to the casserole, put the lid on and place in the oven.
4. After 20 minutes, inspect, stir and taste the curry. Add a little water if required, then replace in the oven.
5. After a further 20 minutes, inspect again. Add the fenugreek, garam masala and fresh coriander, and return to the oven.
6. After a final 20 minutes, taste the dish. The meat should be tender. Add more water if the contents of the dish need loosening. Add salt to taste, then replace the casserole in the oven and turn off the heat. Serve after 10 minutes with Lachadar Parathas and Raita.

Nepalese Rajma Maahn

With hard winters, Nepal depends on dried ingredients such as beans, pulses, rice and root vegetables. The colourful curry illustrated, bottom left, is a typical nutritious winter curry. *Rajma* (red kidney beans) are combined with *urid dhal* (whole black lentils) and spiced with ginger, garam masala and dried chillies.

Bangladeshi Rezala

Richer even than Korma, the traditional Bangladeshi Rezala, top left, must contain no red colours. The recipe illustrated is made using saffron and turmeric; fresh green chilli is mandatory. The richness comes from canned evaporated milk, and meat or chicken is used. For a change, try turkey. You can omit the sugar and raisins, a taste beloved by Bangladeshis, but do use top-quality rose water for a gorgeous fragrance.

Sri Lankan Shellfish Curry

Fishing is one of Sri Lanka's primary industries. Amongst thousands of species caught are all types of shellfish, and this results in many traditional national dishes. The one illustrated is a luscious crab and king prawn curry, laced with a hot, watery, red chilli sauce and coconut.

Green Thai Pork Curry

Thai food is fragrant and very hot. The Thai curry, of which this one, pictured top right, is typical, is totally unlike the Indian curry. The sauce is always runny; in this case it is coconut-based. The main ingredients are stir-fried. Lemon grass, lime leaf and basil give it its aromatics, and tiny chillies its heat.

Mustard Seed

Rai or *Kalee Sarson*

BRASSICA: JUNCEA, ALBA AND NIGRA

Mustard could be the world's oldest cultivated spice. Its branched annual plant is a member of the cabbage family. There are three varieties of mustard seed: brown (*juncea*) from India, with spherical seeds around 1 mm in diameter (top of the photograph); white (*alba*), which is yellow ochre in colour; and black (*nigra*). Both white and black mustard seeds are around 2 mm in diameter (bottom) and are native to the Mediterranean. They are both used to manufacture mustard and cress, and the familiar bright yellow powder or paste, although black is cropped less frequently these days. The seeds are de-husked, then milled. Flour, and turmeric for colour, are also added. If you taste mustard powder, you find that it is not at first hot; its heat develops when the seeds are crushed or milled, and cold water is added. This causes a chemical reaction when its components, including its volatile oil, isothiocyanate, react and develop a pungent heat. Indeed, mustard gets its name from the Latin *mustum ardens*, meaning 'a burning must'.

Brown Indian mustard seeds are not as pungent as the others; in fact, tasted raw, they are unappealing and bitter. When cooked, however, they become sweet and appetising, and are not as hot as you might expect. They are immensely popular in Bengal, where they are one of the five spices in panch phoran, and in southern India, where they appear in many recipes roasted or fried, or as a garnish.

Nepalese Rajma Maahn

Whole black lentils and red kidney beans

SERVES 4

225 g (8 oz) whole *urid dhal* (black lentils)
40 g (1½ oz) fresh ginger, finely chopped
1 tablespoon ghee or vegetable oil
225 g (8 oz) red onion, finely chopped
75 g (3 oz) canned red kidney beans, drained and rinsed
salt to taste

MASALA

½ teaspoon chilli powder
¾ teaspoon coriander seeds, roasted and ground
1 teaspoon cummin seeds, roasted and ground
2 teaspoons garam masala

1. Check through the *urid dhal* for grit. Rinse in warm water three or four times to remove dust.
2. Fill a large saucepan with water (about three times the volume of the lentils), bring to the boil and add the lentils and half the ginger. Boil for 10 minutes, then reduce the heat and simmer for a further 20–25 minutes, stirring from time to time.
3. Meanwhile, heat the ghee or oil in a karahi or wok, and stir-fry the onion for about 3 minutes.
4. Add the remaining ginger and the Masala to the wok with a spoonful or two of water, and stir-fry for a couple more minutes.
5. Add this fried mix to the lentils after the 20–25 minutes of cooking, and stir well. Cook on for a further 15 minutes.
6. To test for readiness, mash a few lentils with the back of a spoon against the side of the pan, and, if soft, they are ready. Add the kidney beans, and when they are hot, add salt to taste. The dish should not be too dry (add a little water during cooking if necessary). Stir and serve.

Bangladeshi Rezala

Creamy turkey and mushroom curry

SERVES 4

500 g (1 lb 2 oz) skinned turkey meat, weighed after removing unwanted matter
4 tablespoons butter ghee
1 teaspoon turmeric
10 garlic cloves, very finely chopped
225 g (8 oz) onions, very finely chopped
3–4 fresh green chillies, sliced lengthways
450 g (1 lb) canned evaporated milk
20–30 strands saffron (optional)
1 tablespoon raisins (optional)
2 teaspoons white granulated sugar
2 tablespoons chopped pistachio nuts
1 tablespoon ground almonds
200 g (7 oz) button mushrooms
1 teaspoon garam masala (see page 30)
salt to taste
1 tablespoon rose water

MASALA

12 green cardamoms, crushed
three or four 5 cm (2 inch) pieces cassia bark
2 teaspoons panch phoran (see page 29)

1. Cut the turkey into bite-sized cubes.
2. Heat the ghee in a large karahi or wok, add the Masala and stir-fry for 30 seconds. Lower the heat, add the turmeric and garlic, and stir-fry for about 2 minutes to obtain a golden tarka (see note below).
3. Add the onions and continue stir-frying on a low heat (just sizzling) for about 15 minutes to continue the tarka.
4. Add the turkey and the chillies and, when sizzling, add the milk and the saffron. Simmer for about 15 minutes, then add the remaining ingredients, except the salt and rose water.
5. Simmer for a further 5 minutes, then check that the turkey is cooked evenly right through. Add salt to taste and the rose water, and serve with plain rice.

Sri Lankan Shellfish Curry

SERVES 4

four 450 g (1 lb) cooked crabs in their shells
8 cooked king prawns, each weighing about 50 g (2 oz), shell on
1 tablespoon mustard blend oil
2 tablespoons sesame oil
1 teaspoon mustard seeds
1 teaspoon sesame seeds
4-5 spring onions, bulbs and leaves, choppedslivers of fresh red and green chilli
salt to taste
lightly fried red and white onion tarka (see page 32) and coconut flakes to garnish

PASTE

2-4 garlic cloves, crushed
1-3 fresh red chillies, chopped
75 g (2½ oz) fresh coconut flesh
2 tablespoons coconut milk powder
½-2 teaspoons chilli powder

1. Put the paste ingredients in a food processor and mulch, using enough water to achieve an easily pourable paste.
2. Extract all the meat you can from the crabs. Wash the shells and keep them for later.
3. Heat the oils in a karahi or wok, and stir-fry the seeds for 20 seconds, then add the spring onions and the chilli slivers, and stir-fry for 2-3 minutes. Add the paste, and stir-fry for a further 5 minutes.
4. Add the crab meat and king prawns to the pan, with sufficient water to prevent the mixture sticking. When simmering and hot right through, add salt to taste.
5. Remove the king prawns and strain the curry, keeping the juice. Fill each crab shell with curry. Place the remaining curry in a serving bowl, and place the filled crab shells and the prawns decoratively on top.
6. Pour the spare liquid into the bowl. Garnish with onion tarka and coconut.

Green Thai Pork Curry

SERVES 4

675 g (1½ lb) lean boned leg of pork, weighed after removing all unwanted matter
3 tablespoons sunflower or soya oil
1 teaspoon finely chopped garlic
1 tablespoon finely chopped fresh ginger
2 teaspoons Thai green curry paste
400 ml (14 fl oz) canned coconut milk
1 stalk lemon grass, finely chopped
2-3 fresh lime leaves, shredded
1 teaspoon Thai fish sauce (nam pla), optional
3-4 tablespoons very finely chopped fresh sweet basil
1 teaspoon very finely chopped fresh coriander leaves
4-6 spring onions, leaves and bulbs, chopped
2 tablespoons chopped green bell pepper
75 g (2½ oz) frozen garden peas, thawed or cooked pea aubergines (see page 27)

1. Cut the pork into thin strips.
2. Heat the oil in a wok, add the garlic, ginger and curry paste, and stir-fry for about 1 minute.
3. Add the coconut milk, lemon grass and lime leaves to the pan, and simmer for about 2 minutes, stirring occasionally.
4. Add the pork and cook for 15 minutes, stirring from time to time. If the curry becomes too thick, add water as required.
5. Add the remaining ingredients. Continue to cook for about 5 minutes more, then test that the pork is fully cooked by cutting one piece in half; the meat should be an even colour right through.

'House Specials' appear on the menu at most restaurants. The actual selection varies from house to house, allowing chefs the chance to offer unusual dishes. Here are four Indian themes, Moghul, Maharajah, Raj and south Indian, each offering a super choice of 'specials'. See page 200 for more information about each theme.

Moghul Raan

A leg of lamb or beef is pared of fat, marinated in spicy yoghurt for hours, then slow-roasted until tender. Now you know why at the restaurant this dish, alternatively called Kurzi, requires the legendary '24 hours notice and a deposit'.

Moghlai Lobster

The curry house Moghlai or Muglai dish uses cream and coconut gravy with almonds and aromatic spices to create a rich dish. Any main ingredient is acceptable, but what better than something even the land-loving Moghuls probably never had – lobster.

Handi Vegetables

The *handi* is a traditional, round-bottomed cooking pot which sits directly on a bed of coals, and slowly simmers its curry contents until tender. It can be made of cast iron, steel, earthenware, pottery or, as shown here, to the right, of tinned, hand-beaten copper, which is pretty enough to serve at table.

Murghi Dum

Dum means cooking by steaming, a style developed for the Nawabs, the rich royals of Lucknow. A *handi* was filled with ingredients and the lid was sealed with dough, which hardened early during the slow cooking process, preventing the steam from escaping. We can replicate this by using a heavy lidded casserole dish in the oven.

Nutmeg

Jaifal

MYRISTICA FRAGRANS

Nutmeg needs no introduction. It is mace's other half, and on page 124 we saw where it grows. As to how it grows, mace forms an arril or blade, which surrounds the inner seed, the nutmeg, in a tendril-like net. Both are enclosed in a pithy, inedible, bright green case (resembling a smooth horse-chestnut casing). When the green case is first opened, the mace is a delightful bright colour, crimson in Grenada, and yellow in India and the Moluccas, through which peeps the shiny red-brown nutmeg. As it dries, the nutmeg turns rather greyer in colour. All but one of the nutmegs illustrated opposite are Grenadan. The odd nutmeg out is a rich brown Moluccan example, with some of its yellow mace still surrounding it.

Nutmeg, with its very aromatic eugenol flavour, has always been popular in Britain, the little hard, egg-shaped nuts offering their magic when grated into puddings and cake mixes, and over hot chocolate drinks and mashed potato. Indeed, the familiar little grater (see page 15) was a seventeenth-century British invention. Indian cooking does not call for nutmeg often as an individual spice, but it is excellent grated over desserts, and it is an ingredient of garam masala.

Moghul Raan

This dish of marinated roast leg of lamb is also known as Kurzi Gosht.

1.5–1.8 kg (about 3½ lb) leg of lamb on the bone
about 110 ml (4 fl oz) milk

MARINADE

150 g (5½ oz) natural yoghurt
2 tablespoons sunflower oil
2 tablespoons fresh lemon juice
3–4 garlic cloves, chopped
2.5 cm (1 inch) cube fresh ginger, chopped
2–3 fresh red chillies, chopped
1 tablespoon chopped fresh coriander leaves
4 tablespoons dried onion flakes
2 tablespoons ground almonds
½ teaspoon aromatic salt (see page 29)

MASALA

2 tablespoons coriander seeds
1 tablespoon allspice
1 teaspoon green cardamom pods
1 teaspoon fennel seeds

1. Roast and grind the Masala ingredients (see page 30).
2. Put the marinade ingredients and the ground masala in a blender or food processor and pulse to a purée which is easy to pour, gradually adding the milk.
3. Pare away all the fat and skin membrane from the meat. Stab it all over with a small sharp knife and put in a non-metallic bowl. Pour over the marinade, cover and put in the fridge for 24–60 hours.
4. Preheat the oven to 180°C/350°F/Gas 4. Transfer the lamb and marinade to a roasting tin and slow-roast in the oven for about 3 hours. When really tender, the flesh should literally fall off the bone. Prior to serving, let the Raan rest for 30 minutes in a low oven.

VARIATION
Kurzi Murghi

Festive chicken

A large whole chicken can be treated in a similar way. Skin the whole chicken and stuff with Keema and/or rice, then coat it with the marinade as above. Bake in the oven at 180°C/350°F/Gas 4 for an initial 40 minutes plus 20 minutes per pound weight (450 g) of the stuffed bird.

Moghlai Lobster

SERVES 4

2 whole cooked lobsters, each weighing 1 kg (2¼ lb)
4 tablespoons ghee
1 tablespoon white cummin seeds
2 garlic cloves, finely chopped
200 g (7 oz) onions, finely chopped
1–2 fresh red chillies, chopped
4 fresh tomatoes, chopped
1 tablespoon tomato purée
1 tablespoon chopped fresh coriander
150 ml (5 fl oz) single cream
110 ml (4 fl oz) canned coconut milk
½ teaspoon freshly ground black pepper
aromatic salt to taste (see page 29)

MASALA

1 tablespoon coriander seeds, roasted and ground (see page 30)
1 teaspoon cummin seeds, roasted and ground
6–8 cloves, roasted and ground
3–4 brown cardamoms, roasted and ground
1 teaspoon garam masala
1 teaspoon paprika

1. Halve the lobster shells and remove the meat from the shells, claws, etc. Chop the meat into small pieces.
2. Heat the ghee in a karahi or wok, and

stir-fry the cummin seeds for 1 minute, then add the garlic and Masala and stir-fry for 1 minute. Add the onions and stir-fry for 3 minutes.

3.   Add the chillies, tomatoes, tomato purée and coriander, and continue cooking until the mixture is quite dry.

4.   Add the lobster pieces, cream, coconut and pepper, and salt to taste. Simmer until hot, then serve with saffron rice.

Handi Vegetables

SERVES 4

110 g (4 oz) carrots, sliced into discs
110 g (4 oz) broccoli florets
110 g (4 oz) cauliflower florets
110 g (4 oz) mangetout
3 tablespoons vegetable ghee
2 teaspoons curry masala (see page 31)
2 garlic cloves, finely chopped
50 g (2 oz) spring onions, leaves and bulbs, chopped
1 tablespoon chopped red bell pepper
2 teaspoons brinjal pickle, chopped
2 teaspoons chopped fresh coriander leaves
½ teaspoon garam masala
salt to taste

1.   Steam the vegetables or cook in boiling water until tender.

2.   Heat the ghee in a karahi or wok, add the curry masala and stir-fry for 30 seconds. Add the garlic and continue stir-frying for another 30 seconds. Add 1-2 tablespoons of water to keep things mobile, then add the spring onions and pepper. Stir-fry for 3 minutes.

3.   Add the pickle, vegetables, coriander and garam masala, and stir-fry until the mixture starts to sizzle. Add just enough water to create a dryish curry consistency, and simmer for 4 minutes. Add salt to taste, and serve.

Murghi Dum
Pot-cooked chicken

SERVES 4

1 spring or broiling chicken, weighing about 1.5 kg (3 lb 5 oz)
4 garlic cloves
200 g (7 oz) onions, cut into strips
1 tablespoon ginger pickle (optional)
2-3 fresh green chillies, cut into strips
1 tablespoon jaggery (palm sugar) or brown sugar
1 teaspoon Worcestershire sauce
425 ml (¾ pint) fragrant stock (see page 29) or water
1 green bell pepper, cut into strips
110 g (4 oz) frozen peas, thawed
110 g (4 oz) runner beans, sliced
2 tablespoons finely chopped fresh coriander leaves
2 teaspoons garam masala (see page 30)
aromatic salt to taste (see page 29)

MASALA

2 teaspoons coriander seeds
1 teaspoon cummin seeds
5 cm (2 inch) piece cassia bark
6 cloves
1 teaspoon fennel seeds

1.   Skin the chicken and cut it into four pairs of joints, i.e. two drumsticks, two thighs, the back (halved) and two wings.

2.   Preheat the oven 190°C/375°F/ Gas 5.

3.   Roast and grind the Masala ingredients (see page 30).

4.   Combine the chicken pieces with the whole garlic cloves, onion, ginger pickle, chillies, jaggery, Worcestershire sauce and Masala in a 2.25-2.75 litre (4-5 pint) lidded casserole dish. Mix well, then add the stock or water. Cover the lid and cook in the oven for 40 minutes.

5.   Inspect the curry and stir in the green pepper, peas, beans, coriander and garam masala. Continue to cook for a further 20 minutes.

6.   Add salt to taste, and serve.

MAHARAJAS

The theme of these four dishes is Maharajas (great kings), who ruled India for centuries. Hunting was one of their pastimes, and so was good eating, the legacy of which is a range of outstanding game dishes.

Podina Wild Boar

Fresh wild boar is available at game butchers, and has a wonderful flavour, different from pork. You can, of course, substitute pork, or any meat, and it works with chicken too. *Podina* (mint) is added to the dish towards the end of its cooking, and imparts a truly unusual taste to it. Shown at the front of the photograph, the dish is quite rich, with its combination of yoghurt and cream.

Elaichi Duck

This dish is redolent with *elaichi* (cardamoms). The restaurant interpretation is to add cardamoms, cassia bark, garlic and ginger to a Bhoona, adding, perhaps, a tomato for colour. The version illustrated on the far left, is made with wild duckling, and is an authentic, very aromatic version.

Tandoori-Stuffed Quail

The secret of this delightful dish is to use boned quails. The quails are steeped in tandoori marinade, then filled with cooked rice, and reshaped to be quail-shaped again. The quails are then baked and finally glazed with spicy honey.

Karahi Venison

A very gamy meat such as venison has to have suitably matched spices. The dish illustrated uses tarka onions, garam masala, roasted cummin and coriander seeds to enhance the intense flavour and dark look of the meat, though the recipe works equally well with beef or lamb.

Pepper

Mirch

PIPER NIGRUM

Pepper, India's major spice revenue-earner for thousands of years, is justifiably called 'King of Spice'. The Romans brought it to England, where it was used as money. In the thirteenth century you could buy a sheep for a handful of pepper! Foreign ships entering London paid a levy of pepper, and it paid debts, such as (peppercorn) rent. Until chilli was discovered in the sixteenth century, pepper was the main heat-giving agent in cooking, its heat coming from the alkaloid piperine.

Peppercorns grow on a climbing vine which thrives in monsoon forests. Its heart-shaped leaf (*pan*), is used in digestives (see page 14). The vine flowers, then it produces berries, called spikes, in long clusters. Green peppercorns (see page 22) are immature when picked, and to retain their colour, they are immediately bottled, air-dried or, as shown opposite, freeze-dried. To obtain black peppercorns, the spikes are picked when they start changing colour to yellow. They are sun-dried, and soon become black and shrivelled (see page 158). To harvest white pepper, the spikes are left on the vine until they turn red. The outer red skin is removed by soaking it off, revealing an inner white berry which is then dried. Pink pepper is obtained in the same way, from a specific variety of vine, and it is immediately air-dried, to prevent it turning white. The red peppercorn, shown right, is not true pepper. It is from a South American shrub, whose reddy-brown berry is aromatic, and a little bitter, but not hot.

Elaichi Duck

Duckling cooked with brown and green cardamoms

SERVES 4

1 duckling, weighing about 1.5 kg (3 lb 5 oz)
2 garlic cloves, finely chopped
200 g (7 oz) onions, cut into long strips
12–16 green cardamoms
4 brown cardamoms
1 teaspoon allspice
¼ teaspoon caraway seeds
425 ml (¾ pint) fragrant stock (see page 29)
1 green bell pepper, cut into small squares
5 cm (2 inch) piece cucumber, cut into strips
2 tablespoons finely chopped fresh coriander leaves
1 tablespoon finely chopped fresh mint leaves
2 teaspoons garam masala (see page 30)
aromatic salt to taste (see page 29)

1. Skin the duckling, removing as much fat as possible, and cut it into four pairs of joints, i.e. two drumsticks, two thighs, the back (halved) and two wings.
2. Preheat the oven 190°C/375°F/ Gas 5.
3. Combine the duck pieces with the garlic, onions, cardamoms, allspice and caraway in a 2.25–2.75 litre (4–5 pint) lidded casserole dish. Mix well, then add the stock. Cover with the lid and cook in the oven for 40 minutes.
4. Inspect the curry and stir in the pepper, cucumber, coriander, mint and garam masala. Continue to cook for a further 20 minutes.
5. Add salt to taste, and serve.

Tandoori-Stuffed Quail

SERVES 4 AS A STARTER

4 boned, prepared quails, with skin on
4–6 tablespoons cold cooked rice
4 tablespoons clear honey
2 teaspoons Worcestershire sauce

MARINADE

110 g (4 oz) natural yoghurt
3 teaspoons tandoori masala (see page 31)
1 teaspoon dried mint
1 teaspoon garlic powder

1. Put the quails and the marinade together in a non-metallic bowl. Turn the quails in the marinade, then cover and place in the fridge for 24–60 hours.
2. Preheat the oven to 190°C/375°F/Gas 5.
3. Remove the quails from the marinade, reserving the marinade. Open out the quails and spread on a work surface.
4. Mix a small amount of spare marinade into the cold cooked rice to make it a little sticky. Take 1–1½ tablespoons rice, compress it, and gently fold a quail around it. Tuck in the skin flaps and the legs, and gently squeeze the quail into shape, so that it resumes its round quail shape. Repeat with the others.
5. Place the quails, top-side up, on a foil-lined oven tray. They don't need trussing providing you have got firm, shapely quails. Pour any remaining marinade over the quails.
6. Place the oven tray in the oven, and bake for 12 minutes.
7. About 2 minutes before taking them out of the oven, mix the honey and Worcestershire sauce in a small pan and heat to make a glaze.
8. Take the quails from the oven, and pour the glaze carefully over them, ensuring it covers all exposed flesh.
9. Return the quails to the oven for 1–2 minutes to finish off. Serve hot or cold.

Podina Wild Boar

SERVES 4

675 g (1½ lb) lean wild boar leg meat
150 g (5½ oz) natural yoghurt
1 tablespoon bottled minced coriander
4 tablespoons butter ghee
6 tablespoons de-stalked and chopped
fresh spearmint
2 tablespoons finely chopped fresh
coriander leaves
2 teaspoons garam masala (see page 30)
100 ml (3½ fl oz) single cream
aromatic salt to taste (see page 29)

MASALA

1 tablespoon coriander seeds
1 teaspoon green cardamom pods
1 teaspoon aniseed

1. Roast and grind the Masala ingredients
(see page 30).
2. Trim the meat of any unwanted matter
and cut into bite-sized cubes. Put it in a large
non-metallic bowl with the yoghurt, bottled
coriander and ground masala and mix well.
Cover and marinate in the fridge for up to 24
hours.
3. Preheat the oven to 190°C/375°F/Gas 5.
4. Heat the ghee in a lidded flameproof
casserole dish of 2.25–2.75 litre (4–5 pint)
capacity, add the marinated meat and stir-fry
it for about 5 minutes. Cover with the lid and
put in the oven.
5. After 20 minutes, inspect, stir and taste the
curry. Add a little water if required, then
replace in the oven.
6. After a second 20 minutes, inspect again
and this time add the mint, fresh coriander
and the garam masala. Replace in the oven.
7. After a final 20 minutes, taste the curry.
The meat should be tender. Add the cream
and salt to taste. Replace the casserole in the
oven and turn off the heat. Serve after 10
minutes.

Karahi Venison

SERVES 4

675 g (1½ lb) best lean venison meat, cut
into bite-sized pieces
3 tablespoons butter ghee
4–6 garlic cloves, very finely chopped
2.5 cm (1 inch) cube fresh ginger, chopped
250 g (9 oz) onions, chopped
400 g (14 oz) canned tomatoes
slivers of fresh red chilli
1 tablespoon small squares of red pepper
1 tablespoon chopped coriander leaves
aromatic salt to taste (see page 29)

MASALA ONE

1 teaspoon chilli powder
3 teaspoons ground coriander
½ teaspoon ground cummin
½ teaspoon turmeric

MASALA TWO

1 teaspoon garam masala
1 teaspoon coriander seeds
1 teaspoon allspice
1 teaspoon dried fenugreek leaf
⅓ teaspoon lovage seeds
3–4 brown cardamoms

1. Heat the ghee in a karahi and stir-fry the
garlic for 1 minute. Add the ginger and continue to stir-fry for a further minute. Add the
onions and Masala One, and stir-fry at a low
simmer for at least 15 minutes.
2. Preheat the oven to 190°C/375°F/Gas 5.
3. Put the venison and Masala Two in a lidded flameproof casserole of 2.25–2.75 litre (4–
5 pint) capacity, and heat over a medium-high
heat for 10 minutes to seal.
4. Add the *tarka* and the tomatoes to the
meat. Cover the casserole with the lid, and
cook in the oven for 40 minutes. Check from
time to time, stirring, and add sufficient water
to keep it creamy and fluid, not dry.
5. After 40 minutes, add the chilli, pepper
and coriander, and stir well, then cook for a
further 15 minutes or until the meat is
cooked. Add salt to taste, leave for 10 minutes,
then serve.

RAJ

Amongst the many good things Britain gained from India, was a taste for spicy food. Apart from curry, a whole new cuisine evolved, called Anglo-Indian food. Here are four interesting Raj dishes, which appear on the menus of some of our Indian restaurants.

Mulligatawny Soup

Originally a fiery Tamil vegetable consommé, with the name Muligu (pepper) Tunni (water), Raj cooks transformed it into a thick potage to spice up, and use up, leftover cooked meat. It became so popular that Heinz even canned it.

Country Captain

Until the coming of the railways, the quickest way for the Raj to travel round India, was on small Indian coastal vessels. This dish, neither a curry nor English, often appeared at the captain's table and was made from veal, kid or, as illustrated here (bottom left), chicken. It was saved from blandness by the addition of garlic, onion, cummin and turmeric.

Patrani Machli

It was not uncommon to have Parsee cooks, and with them came this dish. It suited the Raj palate well, because it is not over spicy. A filleted white fish, such as pomfret, cod or plaice, is coated with a ground green paste, wrapped in foil, and baked.

Stuffed Bell Peppers

Stuffing things was something Raj cooks enjoyed doing, and did often. Bell peppers make good colourful subjects. The red pepper contains mashed potato curry, the green one Keema and the yellow one *sag* (spinach).

Pomegranate

Anardana

PUNICA GRANATUM

Pomegranate grows on a deciduous tree, up to 7 metres (23 feet) high, native to the Himalayas, Afghanistan and Iran, with deep green leaves and vermilion flowers. Its fruit is about the size, colour and shape of the average apple. Indeed, its name derives from the Latin, *poma granata*, the apple of Carthage. There, though, the resemblance ends. Cut the pomegranate open, and its remarkable secret is revealed, in the form of a neat package of translucent, bright crimson flesh, encasing numerous seeds (see page 24). Once dried, the seeds become a very attractive deep, reddy-brown colour. They are sticky, with a unique taste combination of astringent, sour, bitter and sweet. Pomegranate is an ancient fruit, and was certainly used in pre-biblical times. More intriguingly, it is widely believed to be none other than Adam's forbidden 'apple' in the Old Testament. Owning pomegranate was also considered to be a symbol of prosperity in ancient times.

Today, pomegranate grows in Africa, the Mediterranean and the USA. It is an ingredient in the syrup grenadine. It is highly prized in its native country, Iran, where it is eaten raw and is used in cooking, especially in the Iranian national dish, *Faisanjan*, an exotic duck concoction. And, of course, it is used in specialist north Indian dishes, contributing both colour and taste to salads and raitas, Moghul curries, and Punjabi *chanas* and *chaats*.

Mulligatawny Soup

SERVES 4

1 litre (1¾ pints) vegetable or meat stock
2 tablespoons mustard blend oil
1 teaspoon mustard seeds
½ teaspoon crushed black peppercorns
2 teaspoons curry masala (see page 31)
2–3 garlic cloves, finely chopped
110 g (4 oz) onions, finely chopped
1–2 fresh red and/or green chillies, shredded
1 tablespoon basmati rice
1 tablespoon *massoor dhal* (polished split red lentils)
2 tablespoons tamarind purée
2 tablespoons chopped coriander leaves
fresh or dried curry leaves
salt to taste
halved onion rings to garnish

1.   Bring the stock to a simmer in a 3 litre (5¼ pint) saucepan.
2.   Meanwhile, heat the oil in a karahi or wok, and stir-fry the seeds, black pepper and masala for 30 seconds. Add the garlic, onions, chillies, rice and lentils, and stir-fry for a further 3–4 minutes.
3.   Add the fried items to the simmering stock, stirring at first to ensure that nothing sticks to the bottom of the pan.
4.   Simmer for 20 minutes, then add the tamarind purée and the coriander and curry leaves.
5.   Give the soup a final 3 minutes simmering, then add salt to taste. Serve in shallow soup bowls, garnished with the onion.

Country Captain

SERVES 4

700 g (1 lb 9 oz) skinned chicken breast fillets
4 tablespoons ghee
2 teaspoons celery seeds, roasted
½ teaspoon turmeric
4 garlic cloves, finely chopped
225 g (8 oz) onions, cut in long strips
2 fresh red chillies, in long strips
½ red bell pepper, chopped
½ green bell pepper, chopped
4 cherry tomatoes, halved
2 tablespoons chopped fresh coriander leaves
4 tablespoons single cream
salt to taste
1 lemon

1.   Remove any unwanted matter from the chicken and cut into bite-sized pieces.
2.   Heat the ghee in a karahi or wok, and stir-fry the seeds and turmeric for 1 minute.
3.   Add the garlic and stir-fry for a further minute.
4.   Add the onions and chillies, and continue stir-frying for 5 minutes.
5.   Add the chicken and fry for 10 minutes, turning the pieces of chicken over from time to time.
6.   Meanwhile, chop the peppers, tomatoes and coriander leaves, and add these and the cream to the stir-fry after 10 minutes.
7.   Simmer for a further 5–10 minutes. The dish should be fairly dry, but not sticking, so add a little water if needed. Add salt to taste, and serve with a squeeze of lemon juice.

Patrani Machli
Coriander-baked fish

SERVES 4

4 pieces filleted cod steak, each weighing
about 225 g (8 oz)
3 tablespoons mustard blend oil
2 tablespoons white spirit vinegar
desiccated coconut and lemon wedges
to garnish

COATING

200 g (7 oz) onions, coarsely chopped
2 bunches fresh coriander, leaves and
tender stalks, chopped
1 tablespoon bottled minced coriander
1-4 fresh green chillies, coarsely chopped
2 garlic cloves, chopped
1 tablespoon coconut milk powder
1 teaspoon sugar
½ teaspoon salt
1 teaspoon ground cummin
juice of 1 lemon

1. Preheat the oven to 190°C/375°F/Gas 5.
2. Purée all the coating ingredients together
in a blender or food processor. The paste
should be of a thick porridge-like consistency. If it is too thin, transfer it to a sieve to
drain; if too thick add a little water.
3. Lay each piece of fish on a large piece of
foil, then cover completely with the paste,
using up all the paste. Wrap the fish pieces
tightly in the foil.
4. Put the oil and vinegar in an a roasting tin
and put in the oven. When the oil and vinegar is hot, put the foiled fish into the tin and
bake for 20 minutes.
5. To serve, carefully unwrap the fish, discarding the foil. The coating should have
adhered to the fish and it should be quite
moist. Pour all or some of the liquid in the
pan over the fish. Garnish with coconut and
lemon wedges.

Stuffed Bell Peppers

SERVES 4

4 medium, firm bell peppers, any colour

FILLINGS

Use one or more of the following
samosa fillings (see page 41):
Vegetable
Meat
Sag Paneer

1. Cut the stalk ends off the peppers and
remove the seeds and pith. Preheat the oven
to 160°C/325°F/Gas 3.
2. Blanch the peppers in boiling water for 2
minutes.
3. Fill each pepper with the filling of your
choice, and place in a foil-lined oven dish in a
manner which enables the peppers to stand
upright without falling over.
4. Bake in the oven for 15-20 minutes.

SOUTH INDIAN

South Indian curries are quite different from those of the north. The main ingredients are coconut, mustard, curry leaves, pepper, turmeric and chilli. The food is rice-based, with no wheat. The inedible banana leaf is traditionally used to serve the meal on, in lieu of crockery, and all courses are served together, without cutlery. Here is a typical full-course meal, consisting of papadoms, coconut rice, *dhal*, coconut and chilli chutneys, lime pickle and Indian sweets. The main dishes are:

Masala Dosa

At the front are Dosa, pancakes made from rice and *urid dhal* flour batter, which is allowed to ferment, causing the bubbles in the finished pancakes. The 'masala' in the name of the dish refers to mashed potato curry which is rolled up in the Dosa.

Sajjar Avial

In the largest coconut shell is Avial, or mixed vegetable curry, with, in this case, drumsticks (*sajjar*) as the major ingredient.

Sambar

Sambar is eaten at any time of day. Being a cross between soup and *dhal*, it can be as thick or watery as you please.

Rasam

This is a savoury, hot and sour consommé-style soup which must contain, amongst other things, garlic, dried red chilli and tamarind purée. In south India it accompanies the meal, but it is great as a starter on its own.

Poppy Seed

Cuscus

PAPAVER SOMNIFERUM

The familiar European red poppy is a pretty wild flower, native to Europe and north Asia. Unfamiliar in the West is the Asian poppy, with its white, pink or purple flowers. Both produce seeds which have culinary use, but the Asian poppy has a further by-product: opium.

Poppy is the world's most minuscule spice seed, being a minute 0.6 mm at the longest part of its kidney shape, and taking one million to weigh 450 g (1 lb). The European poppy has a further unique attribute: its seeds are blue, which makes the spice truly lovely to look at, as can be seen, and popular as a contrasting colour in baking. This variety, called *nigrum*, also grows in India, but its blue spice is not used there. What is used from the Asian poppy is the creamy-white (*alba*) seed, which is the same size and shape, and has the same neutral, nutty, slightly sweet taste as the blue seed. It is a minor spice, used to thicken curries, and to decorate breads and sweets. As to opium, it is made by extracting a sticky white sap from the unripe seed capsule of the Asian poppy. Once dried, it is ground to a powder. Opium contains morphine, heroin and codeine, essential in medication as a pain killer, reflected in its Latin name, *somniferum*.

Unfortunately, because poppy seed, which incidentally contains no narcotic traces, is so easy to grow, it is equally easy, and far more profitable for the grower, to produce illegal opium, which is difficult for respective governments to detect, let alone prevent.

Masala Dosa

Rice and lentil flour pancakes

MAKES 4

DOSAS

225 g (8 oz) finely ground rice flour
50 g (2 oz) finely ground *urid dhal* flour
1 teaspoon dried yeast powder
vegetable oil

FILLING

2 tablespoons mustard blend oil
1 teaspoon cummin seeds
1 teaspoon mustard seeds
8–12 fresh or dried curry leaves, chopped
1 large onion, thinly sliced
1½ teaspoons turmeric
4 large potatoes, boiled and mashed
2 fresh green chillies, chopped
1 teaspoon salt

1. Make the batter first by blending the rice and dhal flours and the yeast with enough warm water to make a creamy batter. Leave to stand for at least 4 hours in a warm place to ferment. This gives it its distinctive flavour and texture.

2. To make the filling, heat the oil in a karahi or wok. Add the seeds and leaves, and when the seeds start popping, add the onion and turmeric and stir-fry for about 5 minutes or until translucent.

3. Mix in the potato, chillies, salt and a little water. Heat through, then put to one side.

4. Now for the dosas (or *dosai*). Think of them as pancakes and it's easy. The batter should be nicely bubbling from its fermentation, but in all other respects it should be like a normal pancake batter – quite runny, but not too thin.

5. Dab some absorbent kitchen paper with oil and wipe it around a hot non-stick frying pan. Ladle in a little batter, spreading it rapidly and as thinly as possible. The dosa should be about 15-20 cm (6-8 inches) in diameter. The real thing is somewhat larger, up to 45 cm (18 inches), but it is easier to stay small!

6. Cook until the batter has set and the underside is flecked with brown, then turn and cook the second side. Remove from the frying pan and spoon a quarter of the potato curry on to the dosa. Roll it up, around the filling, and store in a warm oven.

7. Repeat stages 5 and 6 to make three more filled dosas. Serve with other south Indian dishes.

Sambar

South Indian lentils and vegetables

SERVES 4

350 g (12 oz) yellow oily *toovar* lentils, split and polished
6 tablespoons mustard blend oil
110 g (4 oz) onions, thinly sliced
1-3 tablespoons tamarind purée (see page 43)
4 tablespoons grated fresh coconut
25 g (1 oz) aubergine, cut into small cubes and blanched
25 g (1 oz) green beans, sliced and blanched
25 g (1 oz) potato, boiled and cubed
25 g (1 oz) white radish, cubed and blanched
25 g (1 oz) drumstick pieces (see page 24)
salt or black salt to taste

MASALA ONE

1 teaspoon ground coriander
1 teaspoon turmeric
1 teaspoon chilli powder
¼ teaspoon asafoetida

MASALA TWO

1 teaspoon mustard seeds
¼ teaspoon fenugreek seeds
6 fresh or dried curry leaves

1. Pick through the lentils to remove any grit or impurities, and rinse them several times, then soak in ample water for 24 hours.

2. Drain, then rinse the lentils, then boil

with Masala One in twice their volume of water. Simmer for about 45 minutes or until the lentils become soft. They might need a little mashing, and a little more water to prevent the texture becoming too dry.

3. Towards the end of stage 2, heat the oil in a karahi or wok and fry Masala Two for 1 minute, then add the onions and fry for 5 minutes or until browning.

4. Add the tamarind purée and coconut to the lentils, along with enough water to give a thick sauce consistency. Bring to a simmer, then mix in the fried items and vegetables. The dish should be quite runny, so add enough water to achieve the consistency you require. Add salt to taste and serve when piping hot.

Rasam

Hot and sour soup

SERVES 4

4 tablespoons red lentils (*massoor dhal*)
2 tablespoons mustard blend oil
4–6 large garlic cloves, halved
110 g (4 oz) onions, sliced
½ teaspoon turmeric
25 g (1 oz) carrot, finely grated
2–3 tablespoons tamarind purée (see page 45)
1–2 green cayenne chillies, shredded
8–12 fresh or dried curry leaves
salt or black salt to taste
fresh coriander leaves to garnish

MASALA

2–4 dried red chillies, roasted
1 teaspoon cummin seeds, roasted
1 teaspoon polished *moong dhal*, roasted
½ teaspoon black peppercorns, roasted and crushed
½ teaspoon mustard seeds, roasted

1. Pick through the lentils to remove any grit or impurities, and rinse several times.

2. Heat the oil in a 2.75 litre (5 pint) saucepan, and stir-fry the garlic and onions for 2 minutes. Stir in the turmeric and, when sizzling nicely, add 800 ml (27 fl oz) water and all the other ingredients, except the salt, coriander and Masala.

3. Bring to the boil, then simmer for about 30 minutes.

4. Add the Masala and salt, and simmer for 5–10 minutes more. Garnish with the coriander.

Sajjar Avial

Drumstick curry

SERVES 4

400 g can drumsticks in brine (see page 24)
400 g can sliced lotus in brine
flesh and water of ½ fresh coconut
2–4 fresh green chillies, roughly chopped
2 garlic cloves
1 small sour mango, skinned, stoned and chopped
50 g (2 oz) natural yoghurt
4 tablespoons coconut oil
2 teaspoons mustard seeds
½ teaspoon cummin seeds
1 teaspoon turmeric
10 curry leaves
salt to taste

1. Strain the drumsticks and the lotus, reserving the liquid.

2. Put the coconut flesh and water, the chillies, garlic, mango flesh and yoghurt in a blender and process to a paste. Add a little of the drumstick/lotus liquid if the paste is too dry.

3. Heat the oil in a karahi or wok. Add the seeds and turmeric, and stir-fry for about 30 seconds. Add the curry leaves and, almost at once, the paste. Stir-fry for about 3 minutes, then add just enough drumstick liquid to keep things mobile. You can make the dish runnier by adding water as required. Add salt to taste, and serve.

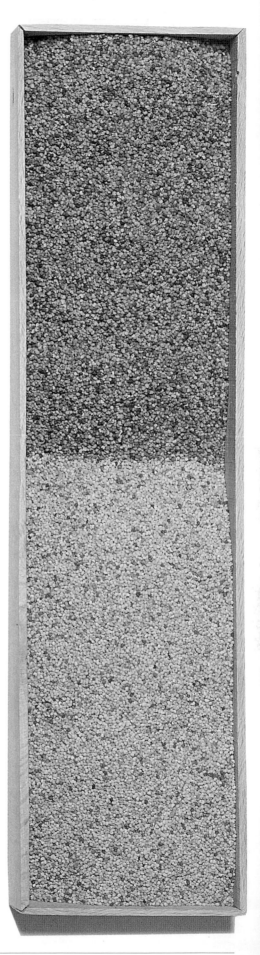

In this chapter, I present the 12 most popular restaurant vegetable dishes, plus four lentil dishes. They are crunchy, full of flavour, lightly spiced, and truly delicious.

Aloo Gobi Methi

Aloo is 'potato' and *Gobi* is 'cauliflower', and these two make a fine curry combination. The trick is to cook the vegetables first, then add them to a Bhajee or Bhoona curry base, adding peppers and tomato for colour and dried fenugreek leaves (*methi*) for flavour.

Bhajee

Not to be confused with the misnamed Onion Bhaji on page 38 (where *bhajia* or *bhaja* means to fry), the proper Bhajee or Bhaji means, literally in Bengali, 'a dryish vegetable curry'. Any vegetables can be cooked this way; here they are made into the restaurant classic, Mixed Vegetable Bhajee.

Bindi Bhajee

Okra (*bindi*), also known as 'ladies' fingers' are appalling if cooked badly, when they ooze an unpleasantly sticky, though tasteless, sap. This can easily be prevented by cooking them in the briefest possible time, without cutting them, and immediately prior to serving them. This way they are deliciously Indian.

Bombay Potato

The tomato and the potato were ignored by the Moghuls, Indian and British alike, until American missionaries brought them to India in the nineteenth century. Consequently, there are no traditional potato dishes. Fortunately, the potato is now fully accepted in India, but this explains why this one, which is now a curry-house classic, is yet another British restaurant invention.

Saffron

Zafron or *Kesar*

CROCUS SATIVUS

Native to Greece, the saffron crocus is a different species from the spring-time, orange- and purple-petalled, flowering garden plant. Throughout history, saffron has been used in medicine, dyeing, cosmetics and food. Once it was cropped in Saffron Walden, Essex. Today, the main saffron-producing areas are La Mancha, Spain, China (where it is called *safalan*), Kashmir (*kesar*) and Iran (*zafran*). It flowers there in October. The edible part is the golden stigma (a kind of stamen). Only three stigmas grow in each crocus flower, which must be picked on the very day the stigmas are ready. The stigmas are then carefully hand-plucked and dried. Once dried, it requires a remarkable 70,000 individual crocuses, or 200,000 stigma to weigh 450 g (1 lb) of saffron worth over £1,000. This places it not far behind gold (currently £3,600 per lb), which is why it is called 'liquid gold'.

There is no substitute for saffron, and because of its price many attempts are made to pass off imitation saffron. The caveat is to buy a reputable brand, and remember, there is no such thing as 'cheap' saffron. Beware the tasteless, cheap, similar-coloured, but feathery safflower (bastard saffron). And do not use turmeric, even when it is called Indian saffron. Too much saffron is poisonous. Fortunately, we need well under danger level, with no more than 4–6 saffron stigmas per person (which weigh less than 50 mg) imparting amazing colour, flavour and fragrance to savoury and sweet dishes alike.

Aloo Gobi Methi
Fenugreek-flavoured potato and cauliflower curry

SERVES 4

225 g (8 oz) cauliflower florets, blanched
2 large potatoes, peeled, cooked and quartered
4 tablespoons vegetable ghee
110 g (4 oz) onions, sliced
2 garlic cloves, finely sliced
2.5 cm (1 inch) piece fresh ginger, finely sliced
2–3 fresh tomatoes, halved
½ each green and yellow bell pepper, chunkily cut
1 fresh green chilli, chopped
1 tablespoon cashew nuts, crushed
1 tablespoon pistachio nuts, crushed
1 teaspoon sultanas (optional)
1 tablespoon coconut milk powder
1 tablespoon chopped fresh coriander
salt to taste

MASALA

1 teaspoon cummin seeds
1 teaspoon curry masala (see page 31)
½ teaspoon turmeric
½ teaspoon chilli powder
½ teaspoon garam masala (see page 30)

1. Heat the ghee in a karahi or wok, and stir-fry the onions, garlic and ginger for about 3 minutes.
2. Add the Masala with 1–2 tablespoons water, and continue stir-frying for a couple more minutes.
3. Add the tomatoes, peppers and chilli, and stir-fry for 5 minutes.
4. Add the cauliflower florets, and just enough water to keep things mobile, and simmer for about 5 minutes, or until the florets are tender.
5. Add the potatoes, nuts, sultanas if using, coconut powder, coriander and salt to taste. Mix well, heat through, and serve.

Bhajee
Mixed vegetable curry

SERVES 4

3 tablespoons sunflower oil
225 g (8 oz) onions, thinly sliced
4 garlic cloves, finely chopped
2–3 fresh green cayenne chillies, chopped
2 tablespoons chopped green bell pepper
4 large potatoes, peeled, cooked and quartered
4 large carrots, cooked and sliced into discs
110 g (4 oz) frozen peas, thawed
110 g (4 oz) frozen French beans, thawed
2 tomatoes, chopped
1 tablespoon sugar
2 teaspoons garam masala (see page 30)
1 tablespoon fresh lemon juice
salt to taste

MASALA

½ teaspoon turmeric
½ teaspoon ground coriander
4 cloves, crushed
1 piece cassia bark
2 green cardamom pods, crushed

1. Heat the oil in a karahi or wok, and stir-fry the Masala for about 1 minute. Add the onion, garlic, chillies and green pepper, and continue to stir-fry for about 3 minutes. Add the potatoes, and continue to stir-fry for a couple of minutes to coat them with the mixture.
2. Add the carrots, peas, beans and tomatoes, and stir in enough water to keep things mobile. Simmer for 2 minutes more.
3. Add the sugar and garam masala, and stir and simmer for a final minute.
4. Stir in the lemon juice, add salt to taste, and serve.

Bindi Bhajee
Stir-fried okra curry

SERVES 4

450 g (1 lb) okra
6 tablespoons mustard blend oil
2 teaspoons black mustard seeds
½ teaspoon black cummin seeds
4 tablespoons chopped pink onion
2 tomatoes, finely chopped
1 tablespoon green bell pepper strips
2-3 fresh green chillies, sliced longways
1 tablespoon sugar
juice of 1 lemon
1 tablespoon chopped fresh coriander
leaves
salt to taste

MASALA

½ teaspoon turmeric
1 teaspoon cummin seeds, ground
1 teaspoon coriander seeds, ground
½ teaspoon chilli powder
1 teaspoon cassia bark, ground
½ teaspoon green cardamom seeds,
ground

1.   Carefully wash the okra.
2.   Heat the oil in a karahi or wok, and stir-fry the seeds for 30 seconds, then add the Masala and onion and stir-fry for 5 minutes.
3.   Add the tomatoes, green pepper, chillies and sugar, and stir-fry for 5 minutes.
4.   Add the uncut okra to the pan and stir-fry for 5 minutes. Stir gently; if the okra gets bruised or cut it will go very sappy. Add water by the spoonful to keep things mobile.
5.   Add the lemon juice and the chopped coriander leaves, and stir-fry for 5 minutes more. If the okra were tender to start with, they will now be perfectly cooked. Add salt to taste and serve at once.

NOTE: Do not refrigerate or freeze this dish; it will go sappy and mushy.

Bombay Potato

SERVES 4

500 g (1 lb 2 oz) new potatoes, cooked
4 tablespoons sunflower oil
150 g (5½ oz) onions, thinly sliced
1 tablespoon finely chopped yellow
bell pepper
8 tablespoons curry masala gravy (see
page 32)
2 tomatoes, roughly chopped
1 tablespoon chopped fresh coriander
leaves
salt to taste

MASALA

½ teaspoon turmeric
½ teaspoon chilli powder
¼ teaspoon mango powder
¼ teaspoon wild onion seeds (nigella)

1.   Heat the oil in a karahi or wok, and stir-fry the Masala for 30 seconds. Add the onions and yellow pepper, and continue to stir-fry for a further 3 minutes.
2.   Add the curry gravy and stir-fry for 2 minutes, then add the tomatoes and coriander leaves and simmer for 5 minutes.
3.   Add the cooked potatoes and simmer until hot. Add salt to taste, and serve.

Brinjal Bhajee

A number of traditional Indian dishes use aubergine. One, Baigan Burtha, literally means mashed or puréed aubergine. Its distinction comes because the aubergine is first slightly charred by grilling or baking. This not only helps in the removal of the skin, but it greatly enhances the flavour. Chillies and peppers are treated in the same way. Because of the work involved, you are unlikely to get this dish done in this way at the average curry house. You will, however, find Brinjal Bhajee, for which the pre-cooked aubergine is chopped and mixed with curry sauce. The recipe overleaf is a mixture of the two methods.

Gobi Bhajee

Cauliflower, *gobi* or *phoolgobi*, makes a good subject for currying. It grows robustly in the harsher climates of the north of the subcontinent, where it will be found in dishes from Pakistan, Kashmir, Nepal and Bhutan. The dish illustrated (recipe overleaf) comes from Darjeeling and uses a subtle mix of spices, plus some tomato and peppercorns.

Mattar Valor

This is a light curry of peas and beans. It is important to maintain the natural bright green colour of these gorgeous vegetables. Though it does not affect texture, too prolonged an immersion in curry gravy turns them a dull, uninspiring colour, and this is a criticism of many a curry restaurant. It does not matter if you use frozen peas and beans.

Khoombi Bhoona Bhajee

The Mushroom Bhajee at the restaurant is made by adding mushrooms to a Bhoona or Medium Curry, with peppers and tomato added for colour. Mushrooms are good curry subjects providing they are not stewed by prolonged cooking.

Salt

Namak, Kala Namak or Saindhar

Salt is the most important taste additive, or seasoning, in the world, as well as the most ancient. It is an inorganic mineral, whose taste comes from sodium chloride, and it is essential to life. References to salt appear throughout history. For example, it was so important to the Romans that they paid their troops and officials part of their remuneration with salt, hence the word 'salary'.

Illustrated are two of the most interesting salts. The black lumps, resembling coal, at the top of the photograph, are black rock salt, or Halite. It is found underground, inland, at sites which are now-dried-out prehistoric lakes or seas. In India, the main source for black salt (*kala namak*) is in the Ganges district of central India. Ground, this salt is a pretty pink colour. Other mines give grey, or even blue salt. It has an acquired, distinctive taste, essential to *chaat masala*.

Sea salt, or bay salt, is manufactured differently from rock salt, being obtained by a process of evaporating seawater. It has a fine flavour. However, the best tasting white salt, shown here, is again a top-quality rock salt. Its natural, translucent, gleaming white crystals have a superb flavour, unmatched by ordinary commercial free-flowing table salt, to which phosphates, magnesium carbonate and starch are added to assist flow and inhibit moisture.

Gobi Bhajee
Cauliflower curry

SERVES 4

400 g (14 oz) cauliflower florets
1 tablespoon sunflower oil
½ teaspoon caraway seeds
1 teaspoon allspice
1 medium onion, cut into long thin strips
1 garlic clove, finely chopped
2.5 cm (1 inch) piece fresh ginger, finely chopped
200 g (7 oz) curry masala gravy (see page 32)
400 g (14 oz) cherry tomatoes, halved
½ each red and green bell pepper, chopped
salt to taste

1. Parboil or steam the cauliflower for about 8 minutes or until half-cooked.
2. Heat the oil in a saucepan, and fry the seeds and allspice for 30 seconds. Add the onion, garlic and ginger, and stir-fry for about 5 minutes more, then add the masala gravy.
3. When simmering, add the cauliflower florets, tomatoes and pepper, cover and cook for about 4 minutes more. Add a little water as it starts to dry up, but do not over-cook; keep the vegetables crisp. Salt to taste, and serve.

Mattar Valor
Peas and runner beans

SERVES 4

225 g (8 oz) fresh *valor* or kenyan (runner or French) beans, chopped
225 g (8 oz) fresh shelled peas
2 tablespoons sunflower oil
1 teaspoon celery seeds
1 tablespoon sweet mango chutney, chopped
aromatic salt to taste (see page 29)
onion tarka (see page 32) to garnish

1. Steam, microwave or boil the beans and peas until cooked.
2. Heat the oil in a karahi or wok, and stir-fry the seeds for 20 seconds. Add the beans and peas, and stir-fry gently to mix. Add the mango chutney and salt to taste, and serve garnished with the onion tarka.

Khoombi Bhoona Bhajee

Dry mushroom curry

SERVES 4

600 g (1¼ lb) mushrooms, washed and
thinly sliced
3 tablespoons vegetable ghee
2 teaspoons finely chopped garlic
6–8 green cardamoms
salt to taste
1 tablespoon finely chopped fresh chives

MASALA

2 teaspoons paprika
1 teaspoon garlic powder
½ teaspoon chilli powder

1. Heat the ghee in a karahi or wok and fry
the garlic and cardamoms over quite a high
heat for just 1 minute. Add the Masala, with
just enough water to make a paste in the pan,
and stir-fry for a couple more minutes.
2. Add the mushrooms and briskly but carefully, so as not to break them, stir them around
just to coat them. Add salt to taste, and serve
garnished with chives.

Brinjal Bhajee

SERVES 4

225 g (8 oz) aubergine, chopped and
blanched
4 tablespoons mustard blend oil
1 teaspoon panch phoran (see page 29)
½ teaspoon celery seeds
2 bay leaves
200 g (7 oz) onion tarka (see page 32)
2 tablespoons curry masala paste (see
page 31)
110 g (4 oz) celery, finely chopped
110 g (4 oz) spring onions, finely
chopped
1–2 fresh red chillies, chopped
1 tablespoon chopped red bell pepper
½ tablespoon chopped green bell pepper
½ tablespoon chopped yellow bell pepper
1 tablespoon finely chopped fresh
coriander leaf
1 teaspoon jaggery (palm sugar) or
brown sugar
juice of 1 lemon
aromatic salt to taste (see page 29)

1. Heat the oil in a karahi or wok, and stir-
fry the panch phoran, celery seeds and bay
leaves for 30 seconds.
2. Add the onion tarka and the masala paste,
and stir-fry for about 2 minutes.
3. Add about 175 ml (6 fl oz) water, and
bring to a simmer, stirring. Add the celery,
spring onions, chillies and peppers, plus the
aubergine, and simmer for about 6 minutes.
4. Add the coriander, sugar and lemon juice,
and simmer for a while longer. Add salt to
taste, and serve at once.

One really authentic way to present Indian food is to use the *thali*, a large tray, which holds a complete meal or main course, the wetter items being served in varying-sized, smaller, matching bowls called *katori*. Here is a vegetarian *thali*, with Niramish, shown centre left of the *thali*, and clockwise: Sag Paneer, Mattar Paneer, Patra and Kulcha Naan (see page 185). The sizzler (see page 165) contains a Vegetable Kebab and Tandoori Paneer on the skewers.

Paneer

Paneer can be crumbled, as in Sag or Palak (spinach) Paneer. Paneer cubes can be served without further cooking or they can be fried like french fries, here accompanying peas (*mattar*). Equally interesting is Tandoori Paneer, which is marinated, then grilled on skewers.

Niramish

This Bengali vegan curry, containing no dairy products, garlic or onions, gets its interesting flavour from five spice mixture (panch phoran) fried in mustard blend oil, here with celery, courgette, sweetcorn and mangetout.

Patra

Patra is the fleshy green leaf from a tuber called taro, colocassi, dasheen, or kocchu. In the vegetarian state of Gujarat, a dish known as Patra is made by spreading the leaf with a spicy gram-flour paste. It is then rolled into cylinders, swiss roll-style, steamed, cooled and shallow pan-fried. If all that sounds like hard work, Patra is available in cans at the Asian store. All you have to do is slice it and fry it.

Sabzi Kebab

Sabzi simply means 'vegetables'. Shown here in the sizzler, these vegetarian 'kebabs' are in fact very tasty rissoles.

Sesame

Til

SESAMUM INDICUM

Sesame is a tropical, herbaceous, annual plant growing up to 2 metres (6 feet) in height, native to India and China, and now found in Africa, where it is known as *benne*, Asia and America. Its capsules contain a large amount of tiny, buff, disc-shaped seeds, which grow to around 3 mm (⅛ inch) in diameter. They are shown unhulled at the top of the photograph, and below is the seed after polishing, following which it becomes creamy-white in colour. Sesame is very ancient, and a further contender to being the first cultivated spice. It was used to make a flour by the ancient Egyptians. It was also a main source of oil. To this day, it is still more popular in the Middle East than elsewhere. There, it is made into a basic paste called tahini, fundamental to the chick pea purée, humous, both of which were popular with the Romans.

The manufacture of sesame cooking oil remains a major industry, and is a role which suits the seed well, since it is already very oily, with 60 per cent of its content made up of oleic and linoeic volatile oils. Though sesame is a minor spice in Indian cooking, it is an important export crop there. It has a somewhat neutral, nutty taste and it is used to texture delicate cooking, and in Indian bread and confectionery. It is also used as a garnish. As with many spices, sesame improves greatly with a little 'roasting'. As a cooking oil, the nutty flavour of sesame is delightful, but wasted in anything other than subtle dishes.

Mattar Paneer
Pea curry with Indian cheese

SERVES 4

1 quantity paneer, cut into cubes
(see page 33)
oil for deep-frying

PEA CURRY

3 tablespoons butter ghee
225 g (8 oz) onions, finely chopped
2 garlic cloves, finely chopped
6-8 tablespoons curry masala gravy
(see page 32)
200 g (7 oz) canned chopped tomatoes
450 g (1 lb) frozen peas, thawed
2 tablespoons chopped fresh coriander
leaves
salt to taste

MASALA

1 teaspoon ground coriander
1 teaspoon ground cummin
1 teaspoon turmeric
½ teaspoon chilli powder

1. Heat the ghee in a karahi or wok, and fry the onions and garlic until golden. Add the Masala and fry the mixture on a gentle heat for 3 minutes.
2. Add the gravy and tomatoes, and simmer for 10 minutes, then add the peas and coriander and simmer for a few minutes longer. Add salt to taste.
3. While the curry sauce is simmering, preheat the oil in a deep-fryer to 190°C/375°F, and deep-fry the cubes of cheese until golden brown. Put them into the oil rapidly, one piece at a time. This prevents them sticking together, and maintains the oil at the correct temperature. To serve, place the cheese on top of the pea curry. This shows off the colour contrast effectively as well as helping to keep the cheese crisp.

Sag Paneer
Spinach with Indian cheese

SERVES 4

450 g (1 lb) frozen spinach
1 quantity paneer, crumbled (see page 33)
2 tablespoons ghee
½ teaspoon caraway seeds
1 tablespoon finely chopped garlic
4 tablespoons finely sliced onion
1 tablespoon curry masala paste (see page 32)
2 tablespoons natural yoghurt
1 teaspoon garam masala (see page 30)
aromatic salt to taste (see page 29)

1. Thaw the spinach in a sieve over a bowl.
2. Heat the ghee in a karahi or wok, and stir-fry the seeds for 30 seconds. Add the garlic and stir-fry for 30 seconds, then add the onion. Stir-fry for a further 3 minutes, adding splashes of water to prevent sticking.
3. Add the curry paste and, when simmering, add the spinach. Add the paneer and stir-fry until it is hot. Add the yoghurt and garam masala, and salt to taste.

Tandoori Paneer

SERVES 4

16 large cubes paneer (see page 33)
200 g (7 oz) red marinade (see page 56)
1 lemon, cut into wedges

1. In a non-metallic bowl, combine the marinade with the paneer cubes. Cover and refrigerate for 6 hours.
2. Preheat the grill to medium. Arrange four pieces of paneer on a bamboo skewer. Repeat with three more skewers.
3. Place the skewers on a rack over a foil-lined grill tray. Cook in the midway position under the grill for 2-3 minutes.
4. Turn the skewers, and cook for a further 2 minutes. Serve with lemon and salad.

Niramish
Stir-Fried Mixed Vegetables

150 g (5½ oz) each celery, mange tout,
courgettes
150 g canned sweetcorn
2 tablespoons mustard blend oil
1 teaspoon of panch phoran (see page 29)
aromatic salt to taste (see page 29)

1. Wash and chop the vegetables into bite-sized pieces, suitable for stir-frying. Strain the sweetcorn, keeping the liquid.
2. Heat the oil. Stir-fry the panch phoran for 30 seconds. Then add the vegetables. Stir-fry for about 4 or 5 minutes, adding the sweetcorn liquid bit by bit.
3. Salt to taste. Serve hot.

Patra
Cabbage roll

SERVES 4

400 g can of Patra
oil for frying

Simply open the can at both ends, and push out the Patra. Cut it into slices, and fry it until hot, turning once.

Sabzi Kebab

MAKES 8

225 g (8 oz) fresh peas, cooked, or frozen
peas, thawed, partly mashed
225 g (8 oz) mashed cooked potato
1 teaspoon aromatic salt (see page 29)
2 fresh green chillies, finely chopped
2 eggs, beaten
breadcrumbs
vegetable oil for deep-frying

MASALA

1 teaspoon ground cummin
1 teaspoon ground coriander
1 teaspoon garam masala (see page 30)
½ teaspoon lovage seeds
1 teaspoon chilli powder

1. Mix the peas, potato, salt, chillies and masala together to create a mouldable mixture.
2. Divide the mixture into eight equal-sized portions, and mould them into sausage-shapes.
3. Dip each kebab into beaten egg, and then roll in breadcrumbs.
4. Heat some oil in a large shallow frying pan, and fry the kebabs for about 10 minutes. Serve hot with chutney.

Sizzlers

Tandoori and kebab dishes can be served at the table, very hot, smoking and still sizzling. This is a restaurant technique, and to do it you'll need to buy special heavy, cast-iron 'sizzlers'. There are two types – a flat oval tray and a small two-handled karahi dish, each made of cast iron, and each with a wooden base. They make an attractive presentation, but be careful not to burn yourself or your guests with the excruciatingly fire-hot dishes, nor to splutter hot oil over their clothes.

1. The food is cooked to readiness in a separate pan.
2. Just prior to serving, place the dry cast-iron dish directly on the stove over a ring at its hottest. Let the dish get as hot as it can. It takes at least 5 minutes.
3. Turn off the heat (to prevent the oil catching fire) and add 1-2 teaspoons ghee or oil to the pan.
4. Carefully add ½ teaspoon water or lime juice. Take care, because the hot oil and water will splutter and steam. Add the food at once. Do not overload.
5. Warn the other diners, then take the sizzler to the table, still hissing, using good oven gloves and table mats.

DHAL

Kabli Chana (Chole)

Chick peas are one of nature's most satisfying products. They are nutritiously full of protein and starch, and, like all lentils, are the perfect substitute for meat. Canned chick peas are fine, though it is cheaper to use whole dried ones. They need a long soak, during which time they almost double in size, as you can see in the photograph.

Lobhia (Black-eyed Beans)

Again the beans can come from a can, as here. The spicing is light and the peppers and tomato are added for colour.

Maharani Dhal

This classic north Indian dish is held in such respect that its name means 'lentil queen'. The cooked dish, top right in the wooden dish, obtains its gorgeous dark golden brown colour from the split *urid*. Butter ghee and cream are added to the *dhal*, and you can purée to as creamy and smooth a texture as you wish. Also illustrated, in the same dish, are *urid* lentils that have been cooked, but not yet puréed, the split lentils uncooked, and whole *urid* lentils.

Tarka Dhal

This is the easiest dish to cook. Split and polished red lentils (*massoor*) are simply simmered in a measured quantity of water. It is finished off with salt, spices, plentiful garlic and browned onion *tarka*. The making of the *tarka* is described on page 32.

Star Anise

Anasphal

ILLICIUM VERUM

Star anise grows on a small, evergreen tree of the magnolia family, native to China, the Philippines and Indo-China. It flowers with single, yellow-green petals, followed by the seed, which develops into a green star, the average size of which is around 2.5 cm (1 inch) in diameter. It has eight regularly spaced arms (star points) radiating from the centre. When cropped, the still-closed star is dried, after which it becomes red-brown in colour. At this stage, some of the arms may open slightly, each revealing one gleaming seed. A whole specimen of star anise is arguably the prettiest spice on earth, but it is fragile, and the arms can easily break off.

Although it has no relationship at all to aniseed (see page 44), star anise gets its name from the fact that it smells and tastes of aniseed, because it has the same volatile oil, anethole.

Star anise has been used since ancient times in Japanese cooking, and as one of the spices in Chinese five spices. Yet despite the fact that clove, nutmeg and mace were traded in great volume from China, via the spice route, in Roman times, there is no evidence that star anise was sold to them, the Arabs or to India, so there is no traditional Indian use of the spice, even in Moghul times. Equally, there is no record of star anise use in Europe until the seventeenth century, when the Dutch used it to flavour their tea. Modern Indian masterchefs have discovered the attributes of star anise. It is astounding, for example, used in pullao rice as much for its shape as its colour.

Kabli Chana (Chole)
Chick pea curry

SERVES 4

225 g (8 oz) chick peas
2 tablespoons mustard blend oil
2-4 garlic cloves, chopped
225 g (8 oz) onions, chopped
2 tablespoons ghee
75 g (3 oz) grated fresh coconut
2-4 fresh red chillies, shredded
200 ml (7 fl oz) canned coconut milk
1 tablespoon chopped fresh coriander leaves
aromatic salt to taste (see page 29)
1 tablespoon onion tarka to garnish (see page 32)

MASALA

1½ teaspoons mustard seeds
6-10 fresh or dried curry leaves
1 teaspoon sesame seeds
½ teaspoon caraway seeds

1.   Check that the chick peas are free of grit, rinse them well, then soak them in twice their volume of water for 6-24 hours.
2.   Drain the chick peas, rinse with cold water, then simmer in ample water for 40-45 minutes or until tender. Omit these stages if using canned chick peas.
3.   About 5 minutes before the chick peas are ready, heat the oil in a karahi or wok. Stir-fry the Masala for 30 seconds, then add the garlic and stir-fry for 30 seconds more. Add the onions and stir-fry for about 10 minutes or until the onions and garlic are golden.
4.   Add the fried mixture to the chick peas.
5.   Heat the ghee in a pan and stir-fry the grated coconut for 2 minutes. Add the chillies and, when simmering, add the coconut milk and fresh coriander.
6.   Add this mixture to the chick peas and return the saucepan to the stove to heat up, stirring continuously to prevent sticking. Add aromatic salt to taste, and serve garnished with onion tarka.

Lobhia

SERVES 4

225 g (8 oz) canned *lobhia* (black-eyed) beans, drained
4 tablespoons ghee
several flakes alkanet root (see page 36)
1 teaspoon chilli powder
4 garlic cloves, crushed
2.5 cm (1 inch) cube fresh ginger, chopped
1-3 fresh cayenne chillies, chopped
1 teaspoon green peppercorns in brine, drained
110 g (4 oz) onions, chopped
2-3 canned plum tomatoes, chopped
aromatic salt to taste (see page 29)
chopped red and green bell pepper to garnish

1.   Heat the ghee in a karahi or wok. Add the alkanet and stir it around for the few seconds it takes to colour the ghee red. Strain the ghee through a metal sieve and discard the alkanet.
2.   Return the red ghee to the pan and reheat. Add the chilli powder, garlic and ginger, and stir-fry for 1 minute, then add the chillies, peppercorns and onions, and continue to stir-fry for 5 minutes.
3.   Add the beans and tomatoes, and, when hot right through, add salt to taste. Garnish with red and green bell pepper.

Masala Dhal
(Tarka Dhal)
Spiced lentils

SERVES 4

225 g (8 oz) *massoor dhal* (split and
polished red lentils)
4 tablespoons vegetable ghee
1 teaspoon cummin seeds
½ teaspoon turmeric
6 garlic cloves, finely chopped
175 g (6 oz) onion tarka (see page 32)
1½ tablespoons curry masala paste
(see page 31)
2 teaspoons garam masala (see page 30)
aromatic salt to taste (see page 29)

1. Pick through the lentils to remove any
grit. Rinse them several times and drain, then
soak them in ample water for 4 hours.
2. Drain and rinse the lentils, then measure
an amount of water twice the volume of the
drained lentils into a 2.25 litre (4 pint)
saucepan. Bring to the boil, put in the lentils
and simmer for 30 minutes, stirring as the
water is absorbed. The texture should be
pourable, not too thick and not too thin.
3. Meanwhile, heat the ghee in a karahi
or wok, and stir-fry the seeds and turmeric
for about 30 seconds. Add the garlic and
continue to stir-fry for a further minute. Add
most of the tarka and the masala paste, and,
when simmering, turn off the heat.
4. When the lentils are cooked, add the
stir-fry, garam masala, and salt to taste. Serve
garnished with the remaining tarka.

Maharani Dhal
Queen's lentils

SERVES 4

225 g (8 oz) black *urid* lentils, split, skin on
1 tablespoon curry masala paste (see
page 32)
100 ml (3½ fl oz) double cream
1 teaspoon cummin seeds, roasted
1 teaspoon garam masala
50 g (2 oz) butter ghee
aromatic salt to taste (see page 29)
a curl of cream and some coriander
leaves to garnish

1. Pick through the lentils to remove any
grit. Rinse them several times and then drain,
then soak them in ample water for 4 hours.
2. Drain and rinse the lentils, then measure
an amount of water twice the volume of the
drained lentils into a 2.25 litre (4 pint)
saucepan. Bring to the boil, add the lentils,
and simmer for about 45 minutes or until
cooked.
3. When the lentils are cooked, mix in all
the remaining ingredients, except the salt and
garnishes. Optionally mash the lentils or even
purée them in a blender, or in the pan using a
hand-held blender, to achieve the smoothest
texture. Add salt to taste, and serve with a
garnish of cream and coriander leaves.

RICE

Rice has many natural colours and even more 'man-made' ones. Here we see some examples. The five cooked rices in the large pan are (clockwise from centre left): Thai black rice, plain boiled basmati rice, red Sri Lankan rice, American wild rice, and Brown Rice. Only the latter has been flavoured and coloured. It is plain rice to which caramelised onions and dark spices have been added, and it traditionally accompanies Dhansak (see page 66). The other four are simply boiled, and what you see are their attractive natural colours. Sri Lankan red rice is small-grained, with a good texture. Thai black rice retains its husk, so it takes quite a while longer to cook than de-husked rice. The result is delicious in texture and nutty in flavour. American wild rice is not native to India, nor is it a true rice, but it can be added to white rice to give it a really interesting, if untraditional, look. Its grains grow very long when cooked, and it too is satisfactorily nutty and chewy.

Far left is multi-coloured rice as often encountered at the curry house. The random colouring of the rice grains – red, yellow and green – is achieved by the use of food colouring powders, including tartrazine. How this is done is graphically illustrated in the dish at top left. A few dry grains of each powder are sprinkled on to the rice while it is still hot. It is then left for over half an hour during which time the colour seeps into the top layer of the rice. It is then gently forked around, spreading the coloured grains amongst the white. The much less startling result is shown in the dish below.

Bottom right is Lemon Rice, from south India. Turmeric is incorporated at the beginning of the cooking to give the requisite lemon colour, and mustard seeds, coconut and curry leaves make up the spicing. Top right is Fragrant Saffron Rice, beloved of the north. Here, aromatic spices are fried in ghee, imparting their flavour to the dish. Saffron is added after cooking to achieve the subtle colour.

Rice

Chawal

ORYZA SATIVA

Rice was domesticated in India 9,000 years ago, in irrigated 'paddy' fields. The plant is a slender grass, whose grain forms in thin 'ears'. Tamils called this grain *arisi*, derived from their word to 'separate', referring to the process of splitting the grain from the husk to produce 'brown rice' (which must not be confused with the cooked Parsee dish of that name, Brown Rice). This is further hulled to remove its brown bran, thus producing the familiar white polished grain. That Tamil word *arisi* became the derivation for the ancient Persian *w'rijza'h*, the Latin *oryza*, and the modern Italian *riso*.

Today, there are over 7,000 varieties of rice, and it is the staple of over two-thirds of the world's population. Paramount in Indian cooking is basmati, which grows mainly in the foothills of the Himalayas, and the best of which is from Derha Dun. Unhulled basmati is in the centre of the picture opposite, with polished above it. Basmati rice has an unparalleled flavour. Once cooked, it elongates enormously to create fluffy, superb-textured grains, especially if the grain is aged. And a great tip is to 'lay down' basmati rice, like fine wine. Keep it in an airtight container for one or more years (ten is not unheard of). Watch out for dirty rice (washed in muddy rivers), and 'cheap' brands, with broken grain or grit. Remember, you get what you pay for. The rice at the bottom of the photograph is from south India, where the grain is rounder and flatter, and not as fluffy when cooked.

Plain Boiled Rice

Use the lower quantity for smaller appetites, and the higher for larger appetites.

> ### SERVES 4
>
> 225–350 g (8–12 oz) basmati rice
> 1.25–1.75 litres (2–3 pints) water

1. Pick through the rice to remove any grit and impurities.
2. Put the water in a saucepan and bring to the boil (it is not necessary to salt it).
3. Meanwhile, rinse the rice briskly with fresh cold water until most of the starch is washed off. Run boiling kettle water through the rice for its final rinse. Drain it, and add it immediately to the boiling water, put the lid on and start timing.
4. When the water returns to the boil, remove the lid and stir frequently. After 6 minutes, remove and taste a few grains. If the centre is no longer brittle, but has a good *al dente* bite to it, remove from the stove and drain, shaking off excess water. The rice should seem slightly undercooked.
5. Transfer the rice to a warmed serving dish and place it in a warming drawer or in a low oven for at least 30 minutes to dry and separate. Stir gently once during this time to aerate and loosen the rice.

Plain Rice by Absorption

For easy measuring, 300 g (10 oz) is 2 teacups dry rice and 600 ml (20 fl oz) water is about 1⅓ times the volume of rice. This ratio of 1 : 2 (300 : 600/10 : 20) is easy to remember, but do step up or down the quantities in proportion, as required.

For four small appetites, use 225 g (8 oz) rice : 450 ml (16 fl oz) water; for four large appetites, use 350 g (12 oz) rice : 700 ml (24 fl oz) water.

The following is my foolproof method for cooking enough rice by the absorption method for four 'average' appetites.

> ### SERVES 4
>
> 300 g (10 oz) basmati rice
> 600 ml (20 fl oz) water
> 1 tablespoon butter ghee

1. Soak the rice in cold water for at least 10 minutes, at most 20 minutes.
2. Rinse the rice until the water is more or less clear, then drain.
3. Measure the water into a saucepan and bring it to the boil.
4. Choose a saucepan or a flameproof casserole dish with a lid, with a capacity of at least twice the volume of the drained rice.
5. Heat the ghee in your chosen pan.
6. Add the rice and stir-fry, ensuring the oil coats the rice, and it heats up.
7. Add the boiling water and stir well.
8. As soon as the water starts bubbling, put the lid on the pan and reduce the heat to under half. Leave well alone for 6 minutes, but turn the heat off after all the water has disappeared, which, to save you looking, is after 3 minutes or so.
9. After 6 minutes, inspect. Has the liquid on top of the rice been absorbed? If not, replace the lid and leave for 2 minutes. When the liquid has been absorbed, stir the rice well, ensuring that it is not sticking to the bottom. Now taste. It should not be brittle in the middle but should have a good *al dente* bite to it. If it is still brittle, add a little more boiling water, return to high heat and cook until the rice is ready.
10. Place the saucepan or casserole, lid on, in a warming drawer or oven preheated to its very lowest setting. This should be no lower than 80°C/175°F and no higher than 100°C/210°F/Gas ⅛. You can serve the rice at once, but the longer you leave it, the more separate the grains will be. Thirty minutes is fine, but it will be quite safe and happy left for up to 90 minutes.

Pullao Rice by Absorption

You can omit some of these spices if you don't have them to hand, and if you don't like chewy spices, omit or remove the cloves, bay, cassia, etc. Saffron can be optionally added, after the rice has been stir-fried, as in the photograph on page 171, to make Fragrant Saffron Rice.

SERVES 4

300 g (10 oz) basmati rice
600 ml (20 fl oz) water
1 tablespoon butter ghee
25-30 strands saffron (optional)

MASALA

4 green cardamoms
4 cloves
5 cm (2 inch) piece cassia bark
2 bay leaves
1 teaspoon fennel seeds
½ teaspoon black cummin seeds
1 brown cardamom
2 star anise

1. Follow the recipe for cooking rice by absorption, adding the Masala at stage 5, and stir-frying it for 30 seconds.
2. Proceed with the rest of the recipe, adding saffron, if using, at the end of stage 6. Alternatively, bury the saffron strands in the cooked rice before covering the pan in stage 10.

Flavoured Plain Rice

The following recipes are spice flavourings for plain rice, cooked either way. They are very quick to make and the method is the same for each variation.

1. Heat the ghee or oil and stir-fry the relevant Masala for 30 seconds.
2. Add the fried Masala and other ingredients to the plain rice, and stir until hot. Serve at once.

Lemon Rice

In this case, the turmeric must be boiled with the rice water to give an overall colouring.

SERVES 4

1 quantity cooked plain rice
½ teaspoon turmeric (see above)
2 teaspoons mustard blend oil
2 tablespoons fried cashew nuts
1 tablespoon coconut milk powder
juice of 2 lemons

MASALA

1 teaspoon mustard seeds
1 teaspoon sesame seeds
6 fresh or dried curry leaves

Brown Rice

SERVES 4

Add 225 g (8 oz) onion tarka (see page 32) and 1 teaspoon ground allspice to 1 quantity plain boiled rice.

Green Rice

Add green food colouring to 1 quantity cooked plain rice, as described above.

Tengai Sadam
Coconut rice

SERVES 4

1 quantity cooked plain rice
flesh of 1 coconut, chopped into 5 mm
(¼ inch) pieces
2 tablespoons coconut oil

MASALA

1 tablespoon black *urid* lentils
1 teaspoon mustard seeds
1 teaspoon chopped dried red chilli

Pullao

Iran invented the *pollou* thousands of years ago. It evolved into Turkey's *pilav*, Greek *pilafi*, Spanish *paella* and India's *pullao*. Rice and almost any main ingredient can be used in Pullao. Everything cooks together in a large pan, the water being absorbed, and the other flavours amalgamating as the contents of the pan are stirred. The curry-house Pullao is a simpler affair. There is not time to make huge pots of Pullao the real way, and the restaurateurs say they may be left with unordered waste. So the main ingredient (here, on the far left, it is pre-cooked curried chicken) is merely stirred into cooked rice, along with peppers and tomato, just before serving.

Biriani

The name of this dish also originated in Iran. The Persian word *berenji* is a type of rice. It was the Moghuls, themselves of Persian ancestry, who developed the dish into a classic. A main ingredient, such as meat, is par-cooked and strained, its stock reserved. Rice is washed, then fried with spices. A layer is spread inside a shallow baking dish. A layer of meat follows, then more rice. This is repeated until the ingredients are used up, but rice must be on top. The stock is poured in. The dish is sealed and slowly oven-cooked for an hour or more. The result (shown on the right of the photograph) is a myriad of taste and flavour.

The Indian restaurant interpretation of this dish is much the same as their Pullao. The difference is that some curry gravy is incorporated, and sometimes a *tarka* of onion and spices too. The whole dish will come to the table garnished with cucumber, salad, onion, almonds, tomato, sultanas and omelette or fried egg. Almost certainly a curry gravy will be served in its own bowl, and it is a meal in its own right.

Rice

Chawal

ORYZA SATIVA

India's most popular rice is basmati. Another major variety is Patna. It is considerably cheaper than basmati, so it is widely used as the day to day rice in many households, with basmati rice reserved for special occasions. Patna is named after a city in north-eastern India, but the rice is used all over the country. It is shown in the centre of the photograph opposite, in its de-husked, unpolished form, and it can be seen that the grain is fatter and more pointed than basmati, but it is still a long-grained rice, when compared to south Indian, or the red-grained Sri Lankan rice depicted on page 170. Like basmati, Patna benefits from an airtight ageing process, although six months is sufficient. All unpolished rice takes considerably longer to cook, and is much chewier and nuttier in taste than the more refined polished versions.

Illustrated at the bottom of the photograph, Thai black rice is also unpolished, and takes quite a while to cook. The result is delicious in texture and nutty in flavour. Though not Indian, it makes a very interesting, if untraditional, presentation, to cook separately, a small amount of black rice, mixing it (say, 6:1) with white rice before serving. The universally available American wild rice (shown at the top) can perform the same function. It is not native to India, nor is it a true rice, and though it too takes a while to cook, its grains grow really long, and it is satisfactorily nutty and chewy.

Biriani Gosht

Rice cooked with meat in the time-honoured, traditional way.

SERVES 4

1 kg (2¼ lb) lean leg of lamb, on the bone (see stage 1, below)
6 tablespoons butter ghee
4 large garlic cloves, chopped
300 g (10 oz) onions, finely chopped
300 g (10 oz) basmati rice
600 ml (1 pint) fragrant stock (see page 29)
30 strands saffron, infused in 50 ml (2 fl oz) warm milk
aromatic salt to taste (see page 29)
1 tablespoon onion tarka (see page 32)

MEAT MASALA

2 brown cardamoms
6 whole cloves
1 teaspoon cummin seeds, roasted
1 teaspoon coriander seeds, roasted
¼ teaspoon chilli powder

RICE MASALA

½ teaspoon turmeric
4–6 bay leaves
4–6 green cardamoms
4–6 cloves
5 cm (2 inch) piece cassia bark
1 teaspoon fennel seeds
2 star anise

1. Get the butcher to divest the lamb of fat and outer membranes, then, more importantly, to cut it, bone and all, into large bite-sized pieces. It is not a normal cut for the British butcher, but is almost impossible to do at home. Alternatively, simply use 750 g (1 lb 10 oz) diced lamb, off the bone.
2. Preheat the oven to 190°C/375°F/Gas 5.
3. Heat 4 tablespoons ghee in a lidded flameproof casserole dish of 2.25–2.75 litre (4–5 pint) capacity. Add the garlic and onion, and fry until golden (see *tarka* method, page 32), then add the Meat Masala, stirring well for a further minute.

4. Add the meat, cover the dish with the lid, and put it in the oven. Leave it undisturbed for 40 minutes.
5. Meanwhile, rinse and drain the rice. Heat the remaining ghee in a lidded saucepan. Add the Rice Masala and, when sizzling, add the rice and stir-fry for the few seconds it takes to absorb the ghee. Add the stock, and let it cook into the rice, with the lid on, for just 3 minutes. Remove from the heat and set aside, lid on.
6. When the meat has been cooking for 40 minutes, remove it and any meat gravy from the casserole. Lower the oven heat to 180°C/350°F/Gas 4.
7. Place a layer of rice in the same casserole dish (no need to clean it). Add a layer of meat, then add more rice and the infused saffron, then more meat, ending with a layer of rice. Add any meat gravy.
8. Cook in the oven for 30 minutes, lid on, then turn off the heat, leaving the rice undisturbed for at least a further 10 minutes.
9. Fluff up and add salt to taste before serving garnished with onion tarka.

VARIATION
Keema and Chicken Biriani

This recipe works equally well with minced meat or a skinned chicken, cut into eight joints.

Restaurant-Style Biriani

Using Bhoona Meat, Chicken, Prawn or Vegetable, this is a meal in its own right.

SERVES 4

6 tablespoons onion tarka (see page 32)
225 g (8 oz) pre-cooked Bhoona curry (see page 64)
450 g (1 lb) pre-cooked Pullao Rice (see page 172)
salt to taste
450 g (1 lb) curry masala gravy (see page 32)

GARNISH

sliced cucumber
salad leaves
onion rings
flaked almonds
tomato wedges
sultanas
desiccated coconut
omelette or fried egg

1. Mix the tarka with the Bhoona in a large karahi or wok, and stir-fry until simmering, then add the rice. Mix well, stirring gently so as not to break the rice grains.
2. Add salt to taste and serve when hot, or keep in a warmer until you are ready. Garnish with cucumber, salad, onion, nuts, tomato, sultanas, desiccated coconut and omelette or fried egg. Divide the curry gravy between four individual bowls, and serve with the Biriani.

Chicken Pullao

The main difference between the restaurant Biriani and the Pullao is that the latter is drier, and is served as one dish amongst several, rather than being a meal in itself. As with Biriani, any main ingredient can accompany Pullao, and, providing everything is pre-cooked, it is quickly put together at the restaurant. At home, therefore, it is an ideal way to use up leftover curries. This version, illustrated on page 174, combines pullao rice with Chicken Jalfrezi. Chicken Tikka is equally good.

SERVES 4

250 g (9 oz) pre-cooked Chicken Jalfrezi (see page 72)
350 g (12 oz) pre-cooked Pullao Rice (see page 172)
salt to taste
tomato and bell pepper to garnish

1. Put the Jalfrezi into a large karahi or wok, and stir-fry until simmering, then add the rice. Mix well, stirring gently so as not to break the rice grains.
2. Add salt to taste and serve when hot, or keep in a warmer or low oven until you are ready. Garnish with tomato and pepper, and serve.

VARIATIONS
Tikka Pullao

Use 250 g (9 oz) pre-cooked Chicken or Meat Tikka (see pages 56-57) in place of the Jalfrezi.

Kebab Pullao

Use 250 g (9 oz) chopped pre-cooked kebabs (any type, see page 52) in place of the Jalfrezi.

BREAD
Unleavened Breads

Unleavened dough has no raising agent, so cannot ferment to become aerated. Indian wholemeal flour (*ata*), comes from a harder, more glutinous grain than that of the West, and is finer ground, creating a more elastic dough. That, and skilful rolling and cooking, creates very light bread. Each type of bread can also be made with plain flour (*maida*), gram (*besan*), maize (*makkhi*), millet (*bajra*), barley (*koda*), and rice (*chaval*) flours. Further variations are created by spicing and stuffing.

Chupatti

Dry-cooked in a *tava*, a flat griddle pan, or even directly on a flame, the chupatti cooks fast, puffing up slightly and obtaining distinctive scorch marks.

Puri

Puris are rolled into thin discs, then deep-fried. They should puff up, as shown in the illustration. Eat at once, before they deflate.

Matthi

Matthis are crisp biscuits which can be stored in an airtight container for weeks.

Paratha

Dough is combined with ghee, thinly rolled out and folded over itself to create a layered disc, like puff pastry. It is pan-fried to create a crispy, yet soft bread. An alternative way to achieve layering is to make a long rope from the dough. It is coiled into a cone, then rolled into a disc. Shown on the board, it is called Lachadar (rope or snake) Paratha. Aloo Paratha is stuffed with spicy potato.

Wheat

Ata or *aata* or *atta*

Wheat is a grass plant, which grows in temperate areas. Its grain seeds grow in clusters, or 'ears'. When ripe, the ears are harvested, and the grain is separated from the chaff by threshing. The wheat grain, or kernel, pictured in the centre of the photograph opposite, is composed of starch and proteins, called gluten. The harder the grain, the more gluten it contains. About 83 per cent of the grain is endosperm, which makes white flour, 14 per cent is bran, and 2 per cent is the wheatgerm. The job of the miller is to separate these components and to make different types of flour. The process is complex. Grain is first sorted to remove unwanted items. It is then soaked and dried, to harden it. Then it is 'winnowed', or cracked open, between grooved rollers. Sieving separates the endosperm. Now called semolina, the endosperm is ground again through various stages of fine rolling. It is now plain white flour (shown at the bottom of the photograph). It is often bleached by the millers to make it whiter. The addition of a raising agent creates self-raising flour. Strong white flour is milled from one of the hard varieties of wheat grain, which has more gluten, and thus creates a more elastic dough, good for bread.

The separated bran is ground and blended into white flour, producing coarser, browner wholemeal flour. The Indian version of this, *ata*, pictured at the top, is similar to British wholemeal flour, but is finer ground, from a harder, more glutinous grain.

Basic Unleavened Dough

Before we get down to the individual breads, it is important to study basic dough-making techniques. Once you have mastered the method, you will confidently produce perfect bread. The principal secret lies in the first kneading, or mixing of the basic ingredients, flour and water. This requires patient and steady mixing, either by hand or by machine, transforming the tacky mass of flour and water into a dough. It should be elastic without being sticky, and should feel satisfying to handle. It should also be pliable, springy and soft.

1. Choose a large ceramic or glass bowl and put in the flour.
2. Add warm water little by little and work it into the flour with your fingers. Soon it will become a lump.
3. Remove it from the bowl and knead it with your hands on a floured board until the lump is cohesive and well combined.
4. Return the dough to the bowl and leave it to rest for 10 minutes, then briefly knead it once more. It is now ready.

Chupattis

Dry unleavened bread discs

MAKES 8

450 g (1 lb) *ata* or plain wholemeal flour
warm water

1. Make the unleavened dough as described above.
2. Divide the dough into eight equal parts and shape each one into a ball.
3. On a floured board, roll each ball into a thin disc about 15 cm (6 inches) in diameter.
4. Heat a *tava* or heavy frying pan until very hot. Place one chupatti on the *tava*, and after a minute or two turn and cook the other side.
5. Repeat with the other chupattis. Serve immediately.

Puris

Deep-fried unleavened bread discs

MAKES 16 PURIS

450 g (1 lb) *ata* or plain wholemeal flour
warm water
2 tablespoons butter ghee
vegetable oil for deep-frying

1. Make the unleavened dough as described left, but adding the ghee during stage 2.
2. Divide the dough into four, then divide each four into four, making 16 similar-sized pieces.
3. Shape each into a ball, then roll out to 10 cm (4 inch) discs.
4. Preheat the oil in a deep-fryer to 190°C/375°F and immerse one disc in the oil. It should sink to the bottom and rise to the top immediately, and it should puff up. Remove after 30 seconds. Repeat with the other puris, one at a time. Serve at once before they deflate.

Paratha

MAKES 4

450 g (1 lb) *ata* or plain wholemeal flour
warm water
110 g (4 oz) butter ghee
4 tablespoons ghee, to fry the parathas

1. Make the unleavened dough as described above, but adding the ghee during stage 2.
2. Divide the dough into four balls and roll each ball as thinly as you can. Flour it, then fold over and over, like puff pastry. Roll out again to four discs 20 cm (8 inches) in diameter.
3. Melt 1 tablespoon ghee in a frying pan. Fry one paratha on one side and then the other, until golden brown. Remove from the pan, shaking off excess oil, and keep hot while cooking the remaining parathas, one at a time. Serve hot and crispy.

Stuffed Parathas

1. Mix all the filling ingredients together.
2. Divide the paratha dough into eight balls. Roll out to eight thin discs, each about 15 cm (6 inches) in diameter. You will need two discs for each paratha.
3. Lightly spread 2 tablespoons filling on to one disc, leaving the perimeter, 2.5 cm (1 inch) clear. Brush the perimeter with melted ghee, place another disc on top and press the two discs together to seal. Make three more stuffed parathas in the same way.
4. Sprinkle the parathas with flour and roll out lightly to discs of about 20 cm (8 inches) in diameter.
5. Heat 1 tablespoon ghee in a frying pan. Fry one paratha on one side and then the other, until golden brown. Remove from the pan, shaking off excess oil, and keep hot while cooking the remaining parathas, one at a time. Serve hot and crispy.

Lachadar Parathas

1. Divide the paratha dough into four. Mixing in the melted ghee, roll each portion into a strip like a long thin sausage, at least 38 cm (15 inches) long.
2. Coil the strips around themselves into cone shapes (see picture on page 178). Lightly press down on each with the palm of your hand to make a disc.
3. Roll out to discs of about 18 cm (7 inches) in diameter.
4. Heat 1 tablespoon ghee in a *tava* or heavy frying pan, and gently fry one paratha until it is golden brown, then turn and fry the other side. Remove from the pan and keep hot while frying the remaining parathas, one at a time. Serve hot.

Matthi
Savoury biscuits

1. Mix the flour, seeds, salt and oil together. Add enough water to create a smooth-textured dough, and knead for 15-20 minutes. The dough should be quite stiff.
2. Divide the dough into 4 cm (1½ inch) diameter balls, then roll each ball into a 7.5 cm (3 inch) flat disc. Prick them to prevent them from puffing during cooking.
3. Heat the oil in a deep-fryer to just below smoking point, and fry the biscuits until light gold (not brown), turning as necessary.
4. Allow to cool on absorbent kitchen paper. Like biscuits, matthis can be stored for several weeks in an airtight container.

Leavened Breads

It is 4,000 years since the Egyptians discovered how to ferment dough by adding yeast, causing it to aerate with tiny bubbles, and rise. Called leavening, the dough in the photograph demonstrates it perfectly. The Egyptians also invented the side-opening clay oven, the *tonir*, and baking began. In ancient Persia, the oven was called the *tanoor* and the bread, *nane lavash*. It was the forerunner to India's *tandoor*, although we do not know how or when it turned into an upright sphere with a narrow-necked opening at the top. *Nane* evolved into *naan*, dough cooked by sticking a disc inside the tandoor neck. Gravity makes them go teardrop-shaped. At home we must 'cheat' by pre-shaping them, and grilling them.

Plain Naan

The following raising agents can be used: fresh yeast, though rarely used at the restaurant, is the most effective, though it gives a slightly sour taste; dried yeast powder is weaker, but acts faster; yoghurt does work, but it must be home-made (factory-made culture is too weak); self-raising flour with bicarbonate of soda is a common restaurant mixture. Milk is said to make the dough tastier, with or without water, and sugar can be added to make it sweeter. *Kalonji* (wild onion seeds or nigella) and/or sesame seeds are traditionally added to the dough. *Ata* (wholemeal) flour makes an interesting alternative naan.

Popular stuffed naans include Peshawari Naan (bottom left of the photograph) and Tandoori Keema Naan (bottom right).

Karak Naan

Also called *Kharri*, *Jandala*, Family Naan, or Elephant Ear, this is naan made as large as you can. The one shown here is about 45 cm (18 inches) long. At the Birmingham Balti House, where they compete to produce the largest Karaks, they can be twice that length.

183

Millet and Gram

Bajra and *Besan*

Wheat is not the only bread-making staple used in India. Millet (*bajra*), second from the top in the photograph opposite, is grown primarily in north and west India for flour. Long, thin, delicate corn-like ears are grown to about 15 x 1 cm (6 x ½ inch), and contain thousands of tiny seeds, the millet itself. The seeds are smooth spheres, about 1-1.5 mm in diameter, their colour a warm, stone-grey with a hint of yellow. Its flour, shown above the seeds, is finely ground into a silvery-grey flour, which is widely available. It can be substituted for all the wheat flour (*ata*) recipes here. Minor modifications will produce your authentic breads. A Gujarati speciality is called Bajra Rotla or Bhakri, a chupatti decorated with a series of depressions made with fingertips. Batlou is a square chupatti. Debra incorporates spinach and chilli. Talipeeth is more akin to a pan-fried paratha with turmeric, chilli and chopped fresh coriander leaves being incorporated into the dough.

Bengalis, in the north-east of India, adore gram flour (*besan*), so much so that one of its names is 'Bengal Gram'. It is, of course, the only flour to use in pakoras or onion bhaji, and is made, not from chick peas, as some cookbook writers insist, but from chana dhal, which gives the flour its gorgeous, blond colour, and its unique flavour. Both are pictured opposite. A Bengali speciality bread is Radha Bollobi, a gram flour puri. A gram flour bread, stuffed with onion, garlic and tomato is called Besan Ki Roti, and a *besan*-stuffed paratha is called Bihari.

Basic Leavened Dough

25 g (1 oz) fresh yeast
450 g (1 lb) strong white flour
warm water

1.   Dissolve the fresh yeast in a little luke-warm water in a small bowl.
2.   Choose a large ceramic or glass bowl at room temperature, and put in the flour.
3.   Make a well in the centre of the flour and pour in the yeast and sufficient warm water to combine the mixture into a dough.
4.   Turn the dough out on to a floured board and knead with the heel of your hand.
5.   Return the dough to the bowl and leave in a warm, draught-free place to ferment and rise (this is called proving). This can take an hour or so, after which time the dough should double in size. It should be bubbly, stringy and elastic, as shown in the photograph on the previous page.
6.   Turn out the dough and knock back to its original size by re-kneading it. Use fairly soon, or it will prove again.

Plain Naan

MAKES 4

1 quantity leavened dough (see left)
2 teaspoons sesame seeds
½ teaspoon wild onion seeds (nigella or *kalonji*)
1 tablespoon melted ghee

1.   Make the leavened dough as described above, adding the seeds during the first kneading.
2.   Divide the dough into four equal parts.
3.   On a floured work surface, roll out each piece into a teardrop shape at least 5 mm (¼ inch) thick.
4.   Preheat the grill to three-quarters heat, cover the rack with foil, put the naan on to it, and place in the midway position.
5.   Watch it cook (it can easily burn). As soon as the first side develops brown patches, remove it from the grill.
6.   Turn it over and brush the uncooked side with a little melted ghee. Return it to the grill and cook until sizzling, then remove and keep warm.
7.   Repeat with the other three *naans*, then serve at once.

VARIATION
Karak Naan

MAKES 2

Make the bread dough exactly as for Plain Naan, but divide into two equal parts instead of four. You will need a large baking sheet, and the dough will be hard to handle, but cook under the grill, as above. If it will not fit in one go, grill one half, then rotate it and grill the other half. Turn it over and repeat.

Peshawari Naan

This is Naan made sweet and rich by adding sultanas and almond flakes to the dough.

MAKES 4

1 quantity leavened dough (see left)
2-3 tablespoons flaked almonds
1-2 tablespoons sultanas
2 tablespoons melted ghee

1. Follow the Plain Naan recipe to the end of stage 2.
2. Roll each piece of dough to a disc about 7.5 cm (3 inches) in diameter and place a quarter of the almonds and sultanas in the centre of each. For each disc in turn, pick up the outside edges and bring them together in the centre, over the fruit and nuts. Press firmly, making a 'pattie'. Flour the patties and roll out to 20 cm (8 inch) rounds.
3. Complete the Plain Naan recipe from stage 4 to the end.

Tandoori Keema Naan

The easiest way to make this is to chop a cooked Sheek Kebab (see page 53) and to add it to the dough. It is shown on page 183 on an Indian bread-making press, the lazy way to 'roll out' bread.

MAKES 4

1 quantity leavened dough (see left)
175 g (6 oz) cooked Sheek Kebab, chopped (see page 53)
3-4 tablespoons melted ghee

Follow the Peshawari Naan recipe, left, replacing the almonds and sultanas with the kebab.

Kulcha Naan
Illustrated on page 162

MAKES 4

1 quantity leavened dough (see left)
½ teaspoon white cummin seeds
4 tablespoons fried onions
3-4 tablespoons melted ghee

Follow the Peshawari Naan recipe, left, replacing the almonds and sultanas with the seeds and onions.

VARIATIONS

Other types of stuffed savoury naan include Bhare Naan (stuffed with anything, e.g. mashed potato, vegetables, egg, etc.), and Lassan (garlic) Naan.

Ananas Naan

MAKES 4

1 quantity leavened dough (see left)
110 g (4 oz) pineapple chunks, fresh or canned, drained and coarsely chopped
3-4 tablespoons melted ghee

Follow the Peshawari Naan recipe, left, replacing the almonds and sultanas with the pineapple.

CHUTNEYS AND RAITAS

Chutneys split into two types, one which is cooked and preserved, often in a sugar syrup, such as mango chutney, and another which is freshly prepared and must be eaten that day. Raitas are always fresh, simple mixtures with yoghurt. Pickles are always cooked in oil with little or no sugar, and are usually spicy and salty, and they keep in the bottle.

The recipes overleaf give you a wide choice. And it may inspire you to make up your own items. Of the twenty-one items in this photograph, the nine marked ★ are factory-bottled.

Top row, left to right:

Onion Raita, Beetroot Raita, Sweet Mango Chutney★, Lemon Pickle★, Sweet Tomato Chutney★, and Mango Pickle★.

Second row:

Decorative Cucumber Raita (on the large plate), Green Mint Raita, Garam Masala Raita, and Cachumber Salad.

Third row:

Tamarind and Carrot Chutney, Imli, Date and Tomato Chutney★, Podina, and Garlic Pickle★.

Bottom row:

Yellow Tandoori Raita, Fruit and Nut Chutney★, Chilli Pickle★, Coriander and Coconut Chutney, Lime Pickle★, and Fresh Green Chilli Purée.

Pictured elsewhere in this book: Fresh Red Chilli Purée, page 42; Prawn Ballichow, page 46; Chilli Jeera Raita, page 54; Orange Capsicum Cachumber, page 62; Coconut Chutney, page 150; Red Cabbage Raita, page 154; Brinjal Pickle★, Ginger pickle★, and Cauliflower and Carrot Pickle★, page 162.

Tamala Leaf

Tej Patta

CINNAMOMUM TAMALA

If proof is needed that bay leaf is quite different from *tej patta*, please compare the photograph opposite with that on page 53. Bay's Latin name, *laurus nobilis*, gives us the clue that it is a member of the laurel family. So is *tej patta*, but its Latin name, *cinnamomum tamala*, gives us a different clue. Other varieties reinforce this. *Cinnamomum obtusifolium*, *cinnamomum zeylancium*, and *cassia lignea*, are similar leaves, all called *tej patta*. They are from cinnamon and cassia trees respectively, the latter being illustrated here. The *cinnamomum tamala* variety is typical, though it prefers a slightly cooler climate than the others. It is an evergreen, growing up to 8 meters (25 feet) high, in sub-tropical northern areas in India and the Sylhet district of Bangladesh, thriving in altitudes as high as 8,000 feet. The deeply veined, dark green leaves are not harvested until the tree reaches ten years old. After that each tree yields 13 kg (30 lb) per annum, for a century. Once dried in the sun, in bunches, the leaves become a pale silvery-green colour, and are used in curries and rice dishes in exactly the same way as bay leaf. *Tej patta*'s flavour is, however, totally different. Its volatile oil contains eugenol, with some cinnamic aldehyde, which gives the typical aromatic, sweet taste of cinnamon, with clove undertones. Cassia buds resemble cloves in appearance, and though they are a little paler in colour, and not as powerful in taste, they are occasionally used in place of clove in India.

Raita (Dahi)

Yoghurt chutney

225 g (8 oz) natural Greek yoghurt
salt or black salt to taste
½ teaspoon chilli powder (optional)
½ teaspoon garam masala (optional)

Mix together all the ingredients, and serve chilled.

VARIATIONS

Almost anything savoury can be mixed into the plain Raita above. Here are some suggestions:

Cucumber: Add cucumer cut into matchsticks, or make a decorative display on a flat plate as shown on the preceeding page.

Mixed Raita: Add chopped cucumber, onion, tomato and fresh coriander.

Green Mint Chutney: Add 1 teaspoon sugar, 1 teaspoon bottled mint sauce, ¼ teaspoon mango powder, and a little green food colouring (optional).

Onion: Add thinly sliced red and/or white onion.

Beetroot: Add some chopped bottled beetroot, with a little vinegar from the bottle.

Garam Masala: Add 1-2 teaspoons garam masala mixed in well. Sprinkle a bit more on top before serving.

Chilli Jeera: Add 1 teaspoon each chilli powder and ground cummin, plus some roasted cummin seeds.

Red Cabbage: Add some thinly sliced red cabbage.

Yellow Tandoori Raita: Mix together the following ingredients, cover and leave to marinate in the fridge for a minimum of 24 hours:

200 g (7 oz) natural yoghurt
2 tablespoons finely chopped fresh mint
100 ml (3½ fl oz) mango juice
2 tablespoons pineapple juice
1 tablespoon sugar
1 fresh green chilli, finely chopped
1 teaspoon finely chopped fresh ginger
1 teaspoon very finely chopped garlic
½ teaspoon salt
¼ teaspoon yellow food colouring

Cachumber Salad

1 large red or white onion, thinly sliced
2 fresh green chillies, thinly sliced
½ green bell pepper, thinly sliced
2 tomatoes, thinly sliced
½ fresh mango, peeled and thinly sliced
1 tablespoon chopped fresh coriander
1 tablespoon vinegar
1 tablespoon olive or sunflower oil
1 teaspoon fennel seeds
salt to taste

Combine everything in a bowl, adding salt to taste. Cover and chill for up to 24 hours.

Coconut Chutney

Illustrated on pages 150-151

SERVES 4

8 tablespoons desiccated coconut
1 tablespoon mustard blend oil
2 teaspoons black mustard seeds
3-4 dried red chillies, chopped
6-8 curry leaves
milk
salt to taste

1. Have a cold bowl standing ready. Heat up a wok, but keep it dry (i.e. no water, no oil). Add the coconut and briskly dry-fry it, stirring constantly, for the few seconds it takes to start browning. Transfer it at once to the cold bowl. This stops it browning further.
2. Heat the oil in the same wok, and fry the

seeds, chillies and curry leaves for 1 minute. Mix into the coconut in the bowl.

3. Add just enough milk to form a stiff paste. Add salt to taste, and serve cold.

Green Onion Chutney

1 large onion, finely chopped
1 tablespoon finely chopped fresh mint leaves
2 teaspoons finely chopped spring onion leaves
1 teaspoon lemon juice
pinch of green food colouring powder
salt to taste

Combine everything in a bowl, adding salt to taste. Cover and chill for up to 24 hours.

Shredded Carrot with Tamarind

3-4 large carrots
4-6 tablespoons tamarind chutney (*imli*) (see page 45)
juice of 1 lemon
1-2 tablespoons jaggery (palm sugar) or brown sugar
1-2 teaspoons chilli powder
salt to taste

1. Wash and scrape the carrots, then shred them, using a mandolin, grater or a food processor.
2. Mix the remaining ingredients together, adding enough water to make a runny mixture.
3. Combine the tamarind mixture with the carrots, mixing well so that all of the carrot is covered with the liquid. Add salt to taste.
4. Place in a serving bowl, cover and refrigerate for at least 6 hours before serving.

Podina

SERVES 2

2-3 spring onions, leaves and bulbs, very finely chopped
1 teaspoon bottled minced coriander
2 teaspoons bottled mint sauce
4 tablespoons finely chopped fresh mint leaves
juice of 1 lemon
salt to taste

Combine all the ingredients and add enough water to make the chutney mobile. Chill and serve.

Dhania Narial

Fresh coriander and coconut purée

1 large bunch fresh coriander leaves, stalks removed
1 small onion, coarsely chopped
2 tablespoons coconut, fresh or desiccated
1 tablespoon lemon juice
salt to taste

Process all the ingredients together in a blender, using just enough water to make a thick paste. Chill and serve. Use within a few days or freeze.

NOTE: This chutney can be used in cooking in place of fresh coriander.

Fresh Chilli Purée

450 g (1 lb) fresh green or red chillies, stalks removed
1 bunch fresh coriander leaves, stalks removed (optional)
300 ml (½ pint) distilled white vinegar

Combine all the ingredients in a food processor and grind to a purée. You may need a little more vinegar. Stored in a screw-top jar, this chutney will keep indefinitely.

DESSERTS AND SWEETS

A visit to an Asian sweet shop is a must. You'll see a tantalising array of technicoloured treats, such as the sweetmeats at the top of the picture on this page, including Laddu (the ball), Balushahi (the doughnut) and many types of Halva (soft toffee) and Burfi (fudge). In the small tumblers are Supari Mix (left) and Sugar-Coated Aniseed which are enjoyed as part of the Pan experience (see page 14), as digestives after the meal.

In the bowl on the left is Kheer, a sweet milky rice pudding. It is popular all year round, and mandatory every September, when a huge festival is held all over India to give thanks to one of India's most revered gods, the elephant-headed Ganesha, corrector of wrongs and bringer of good luck. Payesh is the Bengali version of this dish.

The Portuguese brought cheese-making to India, and it led to a series of Paneer sweets being invented by a Calcutta *mithai* (sweet) trader in the nineteenth century. In the divided glass dish are four variations. On the left are three Ras Gullas. *Ras* means 'juice' and *Gulla*, 'round'. Also called Ros Golla, they are made by moulding soft paneer into balls, which, after simmering in a translucent syrup, remain firm, white and very juicy. Below are Cham Cham, which are identically made, except they are coloured and a different shape. At the top of the dish are two Gulab Jamun. Meaning 'rosy plums', these are also made exactly as for Ras Gulla, except that they are deep-fried until they become golden. Still hot, the balls are immersed in a hot saffron-enhanced syrup. Usually they are served cold, but try them hot, even flambéed with brandy! On their right are two Kala Jamun. Meaning 'black plums', these oblongs are made identically to Gulabs, except they are made darker by prolonged frying.

The initial cooking of Ras Malai, in the right-hand bowl, is again identical to Ras Gulla. The difference here is that the paneer is moulded into a disc shape, which is immersed in hot cream (*malai*) after being simmered in syrup.

Wild Onion Seed

Kalonji or *Nigella*

NIGELLA SATIVA

Throughout the A to Z of Spices, we see that there is confusion between one spice and another. Wild onion seeds are certainly another of these. Open almost any spice reference book, and you will find this spice mis-named as black cummin (see page 196). It bears absolutely no resemblance to it, nor is it even a member of the same family (Umbelliferae) to which black and white cummin belong. Neither is it a member of the onion (Liliaca) family, wild or cultivated, although the seeds of some Indian onions are somewhat similar, which may have been the cause of the mis-nomer 'wild onion seeds'. An unambiguous name is nigella, the Hindi of which is *kalonji*. It is a member of the Ranunculus family, to which a number of aquatic plants belong, as does the buttercup. Nigella is not aquatic. It is a native of Asia and north India, and grows as a herbaceous annual, up to 60 cm (2 feet) high, also known as love-in-a-mist, with pale blue flowers. Its seed, a matt-coal-black, irregular, pentagonal nugget, is about 1.5–3 mm in size. Nigella has a distinctive, slightly bitter, intensely aromatic, delicious, vaguely peppery taste. It is used whole, in certain curry recipes, especially in the Bengal area. It is one of the five spices in panch phoran, and pressed into naan bread dough, it not only looks good, but it tastes great.

Ras Gulla

Cake-like balls in sugar syrup

MAKES 8 LARGE OR 12 SMALLER
RAS GULLAS

225 g (8 oz) paneer curds (see page 33)
up to 3 tablespoons cornflour
900 g (2 lb) white granulated sugar
2–3 tablespoons rose water

1. Knead the paneer in a bowl with just enough cornflour and water to create a smooth, pliable dough.
2. Divide the dough into 8–12 equal-sized pieces, then roll these into balls.
3. Bring 1.2 litres (2 pints) water to the boil in a large saucepan, and add the sugar. Dissolve it completely (the syrup will be quite thin), then maintain at a simmer.
4. Add the balls, one at a time, and simmer for 20 minutes, ensuring, particularly early on, that they do not stick together. The syrup should not become too thick. If it starts to thicken, add a little more water.
5. By the end of the 20 minutes, the ras gullas should all be enlarged a little, and light enough to float in the slightly thickened syrup.
6. Remove from the heat and transfer to a non-metallic bowl. Cool, then cover and keep overnight in the fridge.
7. Just prior to serving, sprinkle rose water over the ras gullas, and serve cold.

Gulab Jamun

Golden globes in syrup

MAKES 8

225 g (8 oz) paneer curds (see page 33)
up to 3 tablespoons cornflour
900 g (2 lb) white granulated sugar
vegetable oil for deep-frying
20–25 strands saffron
2–3 tablespoons rose water

1. Knead the paneer in a bowl with just enough cornflour and water to create a smooth, pliable dough.
2. Divide the dough into eight equal-sized pieces and mould into balls or plum-shapes.
3. Bring 1.2 litres (2 pints) water to the boil in a large saucepan, and add the sugar. Dissolve it completely (the syrup will be quite thin) and maintain at a simmer.
4. Heat the oil in a deep-fryer to 190°C/375°F. Gradually add the 'balls', one at a time to maintain the oil temperature, and fry for 2–3 minutes until they become quite golden (but not brown).
5. Put the hot fried balls into the hot syrup and simmer 18–20 minutes.
6. Add the saffron, then transfer the balls and syrup to a non-metallic bowl. Cool, then cover and keep overnight in the fridge.
7. Just prior to serving, sprinkle rose water over the gulab jamun, and serve cold.

NOTE: Gulab Jamun can be served warm, immediately after cooking. To achieve a flambé, ensure the warm balls are not swamped in the syrup.

Ras Malai

Sweet balls in cream

MAKES 8

225 g (8 oz) paneer curds (see page 33)
up to 3 tablespoons cornflour
900 g (2 lb) white granulated sugar
200 ml (7 fl oz) single cream
100 ml (3½ fl oz) evaporated milk
2 tablespoons sugar
½ teaspoon ground cardamom
2-3 tablespoons rose water

1.   Knead the paneer in a bowl with just enough cornflour and water to create a smooth, pliable dough.

2.   Divide the dough into eight equal-sized pieces and shape into balls.

3.   Bring 1.2 litres (2 pints) water to the boil in a large saucepan, and add the sugar. Dissolve it completely (the syrup will be quite thin) and maintain at a simmer.

4.   Add the balls to the syrup one at a time, and simmer for 20 minutes, ensuring, particularly early on, that they do not stick together. The syrup should not become too thick. If it starts to thicken, add a little more water.

5.   By the end of the 20 minutes, the balls should all have enlarged a little, and be light enough to float in the slightly thickened syrup. Remove from the heat and leave to cool.

6.   When cold, remove the balls from the syrup. Keep the syrup for another time.

7.   In a non-stick saucepan, bring the cream, evaporated milk, sugar and cardamom to just under a simmer. Try not to boil it.

8.   Take off the heat, then put the balls into the cream and leave to cool.

9.   When cold, transfer to a bowl, cover and keep in the fridge overnight. Serve cold, sprinkled with rose water.

Kheer

Spicy rice pudding

SERVES 4

400 g (14 oz) canned creamed rice
10-12 strands saffron
1 tablespoon sugar
½ teaspoon green cardamoms, ground
¼ nutmeg, freshly grated, to decorate

Simply combine everything in a bowl and allow to stand for at least an hour in the fridge, while the saffron infuses. Sprinkle with nutmeg and serve.

Halva originated as *helve* in the Middle East. India added cardamom, mace and nutmeg, and made it her own. A vegetable or fruit is simmered in ghee and syrup until it thickens considerably, when it can be served, hot and soft. One of the most common ingredients is carrot, shown on the silver tray at the front of the photograph. Other ingredients include mango (yellow), watermelon (red), pistachio (green), fig (brown), date (dark brown) and buff-coloured semolina (*sujee*). When it cools, the halva can be cut into squares, and served as a sweetmeat, as illustrated on page 190. Burfi is made with thickened milk, in an equally varied range of colours and flavours.

Jalebis, pictured on the right, are sweet, golden, squiggly spirals, made by squeezing fermented batter into hot oil, in continuous circles, to produce irregular coils which, after steeping in syrup, become sticky and shiny, but remain very crispy and crunchy, even when cold. Their near relative, the redder Amarti, left, is made in a similar way, with a more regular pattern.

Simple to make, Shrikand is a syllabub, made by beating cream and yoghurt with saffron and ground cardamom. For that bit of elegance, serve it chilled in a stemmed glass.

These days many varieties of mango are available (see page 25). For the hedgehog, you need a sweet mango, the juiciest and lushest of which is the Alphonso, the queen of Indian fruit. Its outer skin should have a predominantly dark pink colour, its flesh should be orangey-gold and firm, and it should be sweet rather than sour.

It may come as a surprise to discover that Kulfi, Indian ice cream, was being made for the Moghul emperors centuries ago, long before refrigerators were invented. The texture is harder than our modern ice cream. Its usual flavours are pistachio (shown in the glass), vanilla, almond, chocolate, and mango. Kulfi is traditionally cone-shaped; sets of moulds like the ones shown here are available, but it is quite acceptable to use small yoghurt pots as your moulds.

Zeera (Black Cummin)

Jeera or *Kala Zeera* or *Shahi Jeera*

CUMINUM NIGRUM

Zeera concludes our A TO Z OF SPICES, and, of course, it is 'cheating' to use its Hindi word, *Zeera*, since everything else is placed alphabetically in English, but as there is no spice starting with 'Z' in English, here it is. Actually, its more widely used name is *kala* (black) *zeera* or *kala jeera* (cummin). On page 192, we see that nigella is incorrectly called *kala jeera*, so too are plantain seeds. And it does not end there. Other spices called *jeera* in Hindi and Urdu, include white cummin, caraway is *shah* (royal) *jeera*, and aniseed is *mitha* (sweet) *jeera*.

Black cummin is a herbaceous plant of the Umbelliferae family, which grows up to 45 cm (18 inches) in height. It yields dark brown seeds with stripy, longitudinal, charcoal-coloured ribs, ending in a short, curved tail. The seeds closely resemble caraway (see page 56), at about the same 3 mm (⅛ inch) length, though they are darker and narrower. White cummin, on the other hand, is much paler, fatter and longer and, in taste, less subtle and more savoury, than *zeera* black cummin, which has an aromatic, astringent flavour, with a hint of liquorice. Its flavour comes from its oils which contain limonenes and cyonene. Its use is limited, but it is worth having in stock, for its great effect in such dishes as pullao rice and certain vegetable dishes.

Jalebi
Crisp spirals in syrup

SERVES 4

225 g (8 oz) plain flour
2 tablespoons natural yoghurt
10 strands saffron
225 g (8 oz) white sugar
½ teaspoon rose water
oil for deep-frying
2 tablespoons chopped pistachio nuts
(optional)

1. Combine the flour, yoghurt and a little warm water to make a thickish batter. Add the saffron and put the batter in a warm place for a maximum of 12-24 hours to allow the yoghurt to ferment.
2. Make the syrup by boiling 300 ml (½ pint) water, then adding the sugar. Simmer until you get a thick syrup, stirring often. Take off the heat, and add the rose water.
3. Stir the batter well. Add a little water if necessary but keep it quite thick. Heat the oil in a deep-fryer to fairly hot.
4. Fill a plastic bag with the batter. Very carefully, cut off one corner of the bag to make a tiny hole. Squirt the batter through this hole into the hot oil in spirals. When the deep-fryer has one complete layer of spirals, stop.
5. The spirals will set firmly. Use tongs to turn them, and don't worry if they break into three or four pieces. When they are golden brown, remove them from the oil and drain on absorbent kitchen paper. Place them in the syrup and serve hot, or leave them for an hour or two, so that they absorb the syrup. Serve decorated with pistachio nuts (optional).

Gajar Halwa
Carrot fudge

SERVES 4

500 g (1¼ lb) carrots, scrubbed and finely grated
1 litre (1¾ pints) milk
150 g (5½ oz) sugar
4 tablespoons ghee
a few drops of rose water essence
1 teaspoon ground cardamom
25 g (1 oz) almonds
25 g (1 oz) pistachio nuts
25 g (1 oz) raisins
4 dried dates, soaked and drained

1. Place the finely grated carrots in a non-stick pan with the milk, and simmer, stirring from time to time, over a medium heat until the mixture turns dry and thick. This will take 1-1½ hours. Towards the end, as it dries out, stir frequently and watch carefully as it burns easily. When you can pull the mixture away from the bottom of the pan easily, with no liquid running out, it is ready.
2. Add the sugar and stir until it is dissolved and absorbed. Adding the sugar will make the mixture runny again, so spend 25 minutes on this, repeating the technique of stage 1.
3. Add the ghee and stir-fry until the mixture turns a pleasant dark orange-brown colour.
4. Mix in the rose water essence and ground cardamom.
5. Serve hot, or leave it to set in a greased shallow baking tin. Mark out the squares with a sharp knife and decorate with nuts, raisins and dates. When set, turn out on to a board and cut into squares.

Kulfi
Indian ice cream

SERVES 4

2.25 litres (4 pints) full cream milk
150 g (5½ oz) sugar
4 drops vanilla essence
a pinch of ground green cardamom
a pinch of salt
50 ml (2 fl oz) single cream

1. Boil the milk over a low heat, stirring consistently, until it has reduced to one-third of its volume.
2. Add the sugar, vanilla essence, ground cardamom and salt, and stir until everything is well combined.
3. Transfer to a bowl and cool for 30 minutes. Stir in the cream and pour into kulfi moulds or yoghurt pots. Put in the freezer until frozen, preferably overnight. To get it out of the mould, run the mould under the hot tap for a few seconds.

VARIATIONS

Any of the flavours listed below can be added at stage 2.

Chocolate

150 g (5½ oz) dark bitter chocolate, broken into pieces

Pistachio

100 g (3½ oz) pistachio nuts, chopped
⅛ teaspoon green food colouring powder (optional)

Mango

100 ml (3½ fl oz) thick mango pulp

Almond

100 g (3½ oz) almonds, toasted and chopped

Kesari Shrikand
Saffron yoghurt syllabub

SERVES 4

550 g (1¼ lb) natural yoghurt
150 ml (5 fl oz) double cream
2 tablespoons ground almonds
3 tablespoons white granulated sugar
1 teaspoon ground green cardamom
6-10 saffron strands

DECORATION

freshly grated nutmeg
1 tablespoon chopped pistachio nuts

1. Combine all the ingredients, except the nutmeg and pistachios, together.
2. Spoon into serving bowls or stemmed glasses, and decorate with nutmeg and pistachio nuts. Chill in the refrigerator before serving.

Fresh Mango Hedgehogs

SERVES 2

1 fresh ripe mango

1. Stand the mango on its base and, using a sharp knife, slice down, running the knife along one side of the stone. Repeat on the other side.
2. Place the mango halves on a plate, flesh-sides up. Score the flesh in straight lines, in a criss-cross pattern, but be careful not to cut through the skin of the fruit.
3. Taking one half of the mango in both hands, gently push the skin inwards and upwards, towards you, almost like turning it inside out. This makes the cubes of sliced flesh separate and stand out, reminiscent of a hedgehog's prickles! Repeat with the second half of the mango.

MENU EXAMPLES

In the lands where curry and spicy food are indigenous, such food is eaten for breakfast, lunch, tea, supper and dinner. Western culture has never favoured spicy breakfasts, but that has not stopped me from giving two breakfast menus, which, believe me, are just wonderful in India, so why not here? There are various other menus for different times of day, and different occasions. Indian food is great for snacks and grazing, and it makes satisfying meals. Curry choice is very flexible, so do not feel obliged to offer elaborate multi-choice meals every time. Sometimes the simplest dishes are the best. Try the rice and *dhal* menu, for example, from the 'Simplest Tastiest Curry'.

When you do want to be more elaborate, as a general rule of thumb, for a lunch or dinner main course, the choice is for a principal curry, on its own, or with one or more accompanying curries, or *dhal*, plus chutneys and pickles, and rice and/or bread to accompany it. The more diners there are, the more choice you can offer. Remember, you can freeze many of the 'overs'.

As the relevant airlines well know, curry, *dhal* and rice can be prepared well in advance, can be chilled or frozen, reheats well, and keeps warm without spoiling. That makes it ideal, and very popular for that party you've been promising to hold! But before that, why not work your way through these menus from breakfast to a midnight binge! That way you'll have tried out most of the recipes in the book, and you'll know which are your favourites. And please do not hesitate to make up your own menu. To locate the relevant recipes quickly, use the index at the back of the book. Have fun!

Light Breakfast

Puri and Mango Chutney
Fresh fruit and coffee or tea

Indian Breakfast

Sambar
Dahi Vada
Aloo Paratha
Mango Hedgehog

Brunch

Mixed Pakoras
Rasam
Mango Pickle

Light Lunch

Chicken Tikka
Tarka Dhal
Yellow Tandoori Raita
Chupatti
Lime Pickle

Afternoon Tea Snack

Pakoras
Samosa
Raita
Mixed Pickle

Snack or Supper

Channa Chaat
Chupatti
Cucumber Raita

The Simplest Tastiest Curry

Tarka Dhal
Plain Rice
Brinjal Pickle
Plain Raita

A TV Dinner

Keema
Lachadar Paratha
Green Onion Salad

Tandoori Mixed Grill

Lamb Chop
Sheek Kebab
Green Chicken Tikka
Red Meat Tikka
Tandoori Fish
Tandoori Naan
Tandoori Yellow Chutney

A Spicy Picnic

Bhel Puri
Cold Tandoori Chicken
Chaamp Lamb Chop
Nargis Kebab
Aloo Tikki
Garam Masala Raita
Sweet and Hot Tomato Chutney

South Indian

Papadoms with Coconut Chutney
Rasam
Masala Dosa
Sajjar Avial
Sambar
Lemon Rice

Vegetarian

Handi Vegetables
Bhindi Bhajee
Mattar Paneer
Vegetable Pullao

Kashmiri

Roghan Josh Gosht
Saffron Rice
Garam Masala Raita

Punjabi

Methi Gosht
Paratha
Plain Rice
Shredded Carrot with Tamarind

Moghul

Korma
Pullao Rice
Puris

Two-Course Dinner

Onion Bhaji with salad

Pasanda
Plain Rice
Maharani Dhal
Cachumber
Red Cabbage Raita

Three-Course Dinner

Prawn Puri

Dhansak
Mattar Valor
Brown Rice
Chilli Jeera Raita

Kheer

Four-Course Dinner

Mixed Papadoms

Hasina Kebab with salad

Chicken Tikka Masala
Brinjal Bhajee
Khoombi Bhoona Bhajee
Green Rice
Podina Chutney

Kulfi

Feast

Mixed Papadoms

Katori Kebab with Salad

Tandoori-Stuffed Quail

Podina Wild Boar
Tarka Dhal
Bombay Potato
Sag Paneer
Keema Biriani
Kulcha Naan

Gulab Jamun

A Party

Mixed Kebabs
Mixed Tandoori
Mint Raita

Chicken Jalfrezi
Punjabi Keema Mattar
Jeera Chicken
Green Thai Pork Curry
Niramish
Kabli Channa
Meat Tikka
Pullao
Peshawari Naan
Dhania Narial
Cachumber
Lemon Pickle

Gajar Halwa

The Fridge Buster
(a midnight feast)

Kebab Pullao with chutneys and pickles

THE CURRY WORLD

Curry eating is not confined to India. Indeed, apart from the new-found aficionados in the West, curry is, and has been for centuries, 'staple' food to over one-third of the world's population. Here are the briefest 'thumbnails' on the main Indian culinary regions, and the other principal curry lands.

Afghanistan

For 7,000 years, invaders have passed through Afghanistan's inhospitable mountain passes, on their way to plunder the treasure pots of India, including the Aryans, Alexander the Great, and Genghis Khan. Marco Polo visited here on his way to China, and the first Moghul emperor, Babur, died in Kabul. In the eighteenth century, Afghanistan became an independent kingdom. Located between Russia, Iran (formerly Persia) and Pakistan (formerly the north-west frontier of India), the cuisine of the Middle East passed through it to India, and vice-versa. To this day, its population is formidably fearsome, tribal, and fundamentally Moslem. Their cuisine is simple, but largely meat-based and dairy orientated. Rice and wheat are available, and fruit and vegetables are plentiful. Cooking is traditionally done over charcoal or wood fires, and in clay ovens. Grills, kebabs, koftas and birianis are popular. The Afghan root vegetable curry on page 124 is lightly spiced with the unique Afghan spice mix, Char Masala.

Balti

In the high mountains of north Pakistan, is the ancient state of Baltistan, sharing its borders with China and India's Kashmir, and once on the spice route to China. These days, with Pakistan and India in a permanent state of war, the few roads connecting the two countries are closed. Little may have been known about Balti food outside its indigenous area, had it not been for a small group of Pakistani Kashmiris, who settled in east Birmingham in the 1960s. There, they opened small cafés in the back streets, serving curries made aromatic with Kashmiri Garam Masala, and herbal with plentiful coriander, in a two-handled pot called the *karahi* in India, but 'balti pan' amongst themselves. Eating with no cutlery, using fingers and bread to scoop up the food, is the norm to the community, but revelatory to Birmingham's white population, who made Balti their own. And it was inexpensive. See pages 58-61 and the index.

Bangladeshi/Bengali

Most of the standard curry houses in the UK are owned by Bangladeshis, and nearly all of those produce standard 'formula' curries, ranging from mild to very hot. Bangladesh, formerly East Pakistan, is located east of the river Ganges. Before partition, the area was known as East Bengal. Today, West Bengal is the mainly Hindu Indian state, containing Calcutta, which shares its border with Bangladesh. The common language is Bengali. In terms of food, Bangladesh is Moslem, so pork is forbidden. Usually in India, beef is eaten, although it is expensive (see page 123) and chicken is popular too (see page 135). The area is prolific in fish, with tasty species such as pomfret, hilsa and ayre and enormous tiger prawns prevailing, and it specialises in vegetable dishes such as Niramish, spiced with *panch phoran* (see page 163). Bengal is most famous for its sweet dishes, and most of those between pages 190 and 197 are from there.

Burma

Burma, now renamed Myanmar, shares its boundaries with Bangladesh, India, China, Laos and Thailand, and all those influences are incorporated into its food. Burma became independent from Britain in 1948, but since then she has been isolated behind a screen of dictatorial communism. The result is the inevitable decline into abject poverty, little tourism, and a virtually non-existent restaurant culture in the West. This is our loss, because Burma is an exquisite country, with a gentle, Buddhist population, whose food combines the spices of India, especially turmeric, tamarind and chilli, with the fragrance of Thailand, in the form of lemon grass, shrimp paste and fish sauce, and the cooking, steaming and stir-fry wok techniques and soy sauce of China. Rice is the staple, and noodles are popular too, although there is no bread-making. Curries are plentiful, and made very spicy and chilli hot. There are no religious objections to eating pork or beef, or other meats, and duck and seafood are commonly used.

Caribbean

When, in 1492, Columbus landed on one of the islands of the archipelago which extends over 1,500 miles from Venezuela to Florida, he presumed he had discovered islands off India, and mis-named them the 'West Indies'. Their primitive Carib people were soon wiped out by the Spanish. And, in turn, the Spanish were ousted by the British, who soon turned these virgin fertile lands into plantations for sugar, cotton, bananas, coffee and cocoa. Lacking a work force, the British imported and utilised black slaves, in shockingly inhumane conditions. Most were simply snatched from West Africa. The indigenous spices, allspice and chilli, were also cultivated, and nutmeg, smuggled in from the, by now, Dutch Indonesian island of Ambon, was found to flourish best on just one Caribbean island, Grenada. The British also brought in an Asian-Indian labour force for the menial, non-slave tasks, and they brought with them their repertoire of curry spices. Today, there are a large number of dishes in the West Indies that are indistinguishable from those elsewhere, from chupattis to chutneys, and birianis to bhajis. There are curries, too, using local produce such as plantain, jackfruit, yams and sweet potato, the most famous of which is Jamaican Goat Curry.

China

There is no curry indigenous to China, but demand compelled the Chinese restaurants in Britain to invent one. It is made by frying a little standard commercial curry powder with Chinese five-spice, then stir-frying in the principal ingredient(s) along with a cornflour sauce, sugar and orange juice. The result is sweet, mild and floury, and bears no resemblance to its Indian counterpart.

India

Post-partition India, even without her previous states, which together made up the subcontinent, is a vast land, nearly as big as Europe, with a population approaching one billion. With our burgeoning curry-house industry, and its 'formula curries', we can be forgiven for believing that there is just one food style in India. In reality, there are many, with changes, no matter how subtle, taking place from north to south, state to state, district to district, even town to town. The following thumbnails briefly outline the better known of these.

BOMBAY The commercial centre of India, Bombay is a most vibrant, buoyant city, with some of the highest property prices in the world, contrasting with some of the most appalling poverty. Bombay has a number of curry houses, some of which sell Punjabi-style curries, but if you visit them, do not expect to find Bombay Mix (see page 36), Bombay Curry (see page 93) or Bombay Potato (see page 157). All are inventions of the British curry house, but, believe it or not, 'coals have been taken to Newcastle'; a few even go as far as selling Britain's Tikka Masala curries. Bombay's indigenous food, Maharashtran, is mild and delicately spiced. Parsee food (see page 203) is also native to Bombay. A further delicious concoction is Bhel Puri, Bombay's favourite delicious kiosk food, served cold, and nowhere better than at Chowpatti Beach. Not seen much at restaurants outside Bombay, it is worth trying yourself (see page 44).

The sweet syllabub Shrikand (page 194) originated here.

GOA Portugal once played a major role in discovering spices. She was the first European colonist to occupy India, and the last to leave. She landed in Goa, on the west coast of India, about 400 miles south of Bombay, in 1498, and left in 1962. (The British did not make their first tentative appearance in India until 1608, and left in 1947.) The Portuguese were as anxious to capture the spice market as they were to instil Christianity into the locals. The result today is a largely Christian Indian population who have no objections to eating pork or beef. The food of Goa is unique, with a fabulous range of chicken and fish dishes, and unusual puddings. From the Portuguese they learned to make chorizo, a spicy bacon sausage, and to marinate pork in vinegar, garlic and wine, to which they add copious quantities of red chilli. One dish made from this base is Piri-piri, another is the better known Vindaloo, derived from the Portuguese *vinha d'alhos* (see page 119). And what better to accompany this than Chilli Rice (see page 173).

GUJARAT Gujarat is a state on India's north-west coastline, some 400 miles north of Bombay.

The first British diplomat docked at the port of Surat in 1608, and the town was used as a British trading post, until Bombay was built in 1674. We saw, on page 12, that the Gujarati soup-like dish, with gram flour dumplings, called Khadi, whose yellow gravy is made with turmeric, spices and yoghurt, may have been the very dish which gave curry its name. Gujarat is home to more vegetarians (about 70 per cent) than anywhere else in India, and their food is also India's least spicy. The Parsees, who lived in Gujarat for 500 years (see page 203), influenced the food, with subtleties of sour and sweet. Khadi is just one dish showing Gujarati adoration of gram flour. The famous bhajia or bhaji (see page 39) also originated here, as did the lesser known Dahi Vada, a gram flour dumpling in a tangy yoghurt sauce (see page 43). The vegetable kebab on page 165 is typically Gujarati.

HYDERABAD Hyderabad was home to the richest royal on earth, the Nizam, until India deposed her royals in the 1960s, and he took umbridge and retirement in Australia. In the south central part of India, Hyderabad is the largest state, with a mainly Moslem population, an enclave hundreds of miles from the main Moslem areas. Consequently, this is a meat-eating cuisine, but it is also one of India's hottest, as indicated by Hare Mirchi Kari, the chilli curry on page 108. Biriani (see page 176) is a favourite in Hyderabad, as are kebabs and koftas (pages 52 and 80).

KASHMIR Kashmir is India's most northern state, being thousands of feet above sea level, in the foothills of the Himalayas. It is snow-bound in the winter, and a beautiful cool retreat in the summer. Indeed, this was so important to the Moghuls that they established their Shangri-La (heaven on earth) there. Kashmiri food is highly aromatic, and, in some cases, coloured with red or yellow spices (see pages 36 and 156). The Kashmiri Moslem wedding feast, the Wazwan, is remarkable. It must contain seven different mutton dishes, including a Kebab (page 52), a Kofta (page 80) and various curries, including Kashmir's most celebrated dishes, Korma (page 84) and Roghan Josh Gosht (page 112), both perfected in Moghul times. Kashmiri red chillies colour and flavour the unique red Mirchwangan Korma (page 109). Being a rice and saffron growing area, a typical staple is Pullao or Saffron Rice (page 171). Note must be made of the restaurant-style Kashmiri Curry (see page 129), which is no relation to the above dishes; it is a standard Medium Curry to which is added fruit, cream and coconut.

LUCKNOW The Nawabs were the rich royals of the Lucknow area in the north of India, who lived over two centuries ago. They were related by blood to the Moghuls, but went their own way in the eighteenth century. Sadly, despite conscientious early rule, the last of the Nawabs' love of the good life led to a reputation for debauchery, and their ultimate demise. One inheritance they left us was their cuisine. Lucknow, being Moslem, enjoys meat, but its cooking is unique. Flavours are spicy and aromatic, but subtle, the food luxurious. One process is called *dum* or *dum puk*. It means slow-cooking by steaming the curry or rice dish, in a *handi* or round pot, whose lid is sealed into place with a ring of chupatti dough. The resulting dish is opened in front of the diners, releasing all those captured fragrances. The Murghi Dum (chicken) dish on page 141 is an example. The Katori, or 'silky textured' kebabs on page 53 are an example of another unique Nawabi technique.

MOGHUL No one on earth was richer than the Moghuls, and it was when their rule was at its peak, in the seventeenth century, that Indian food was taken to its supreme heights. Indeed, they did to Indian food what the contemporary Louis XIV did to French cooking. They perfected creamy sauces with marriages of spices, giving supremely aromatic curries like the classic Korma (page 84), Pasanda (page 100) and Rhogan Josh Gosht (page 112), and the Raan (roast lamb) on page 140. The standard curry house has based some of its formula on mild, rich, creamy dishes such as these, albeit lacking the subtlety of the real thing.

PUNJAB The area called the Punjab was split by the creation of Pakistan in 1947, and it is the Punjabi tastes that formed the basis of the British curry house menu. Glasgow and Southall have sizeable Pakistani populations. The food is very spicy. It is a wheat area, and Parathas and Puris (see page 179) are staples. Robust curries like Punjabi Keema (page 75), Methi Gosht (page 133), Aloo Ghobi Methi (page 156), and Sag Paneer (page 164) are typical.

SOUTH South India is largely vegetarian, with a rice-based cuisine, and no reliance on wheat. Apart from rice itself, of which Lemon Rice (see page 173) is a great example, there are huge thin crisp lentil and rice flour pancakes called Dosas, with a curry filling (*masala*), and Idlis (steamed rice or lentil flour dumplings). Papadoms (see page 37) originate from here. Curries are thinner than those from the north, and are flavoured predominantly with turmeric, pepper, chilli, mustard seed, coconut and curry leaf. Yoghurt and

tamarind provide two quite different sour tastes. Specialities include Avial, with exotic vegetables, Sambar, a lentil-based curry (page 152) and Tarka Dhal (page 169).

Kenyan Asian

Many Indians who had settled in this part of Africa during British colonialisation, had to leave during racial hostilities in the 1970s, to take up residence in the UK. Some opened restaurants, and, though the food is mostly Punjabi, there are some original dishes. Fish curry using the African Talapia, and Jeera Chicken (see page 128) are two examples.

Malaysia/Indonesia

Malaysia's population is composed of Chinese, Indians and Malayans, and this results in a distinctive cuisine also known as Nonya. Satay, meat coated in a lightly spiced peanut sauce, is well known, and a curry version is Inche Kabin, where curry paste is added to a sauce that is used to coat a whole chicken, which is then grilled then grilled. Wet curries are flavoured with lemon grass and shrimp paste, along with the robust spices of India. Soto Ayam and Redang are two of Malaysia's better-known curries. Neighbouring Indonesia also likes its spicy dishes. Ironically, though it contains the celebrated spice islands, the original home of clove, mace and nutmeg, its cuisine never uses these spices. The Malaya curry on page 132 owes its roots to the British curry-house formula, rather than to traditional tastes.

Middle East

Though Middle Eastern cuisine uses certain spices, most of its dishes are quite different from, and more subltly spiced than, their curry counterparts. There are exceptions, the result of many Indian settlements in Arabia, some going back over millenia, to the days when the ancient maritime trade routes linked India to the Gulf. Today you will find spicy dishes in places like the Yemen and Oman. For example, Kiymeh Mashwi, a curried mince dish, is derived from Indian Keema. 'Kaftas' on the other hand, went from Arabia to India to become Koftas.

Nepal

The beautiful mountain kingdom of Nepal, located to the north of India, in the Himalayas, is home to the Gurkas, sherpas, the yeti, and a virgin goddess princess. The Nepalese enjoy curry and rice, and wheat breads, many of which are familiar from the north Indian repertoire. Nepals own specialities are perhaps less well known. Momo, for example, are dumplings with a mince curry filling. Aloo Achar are potatoes in pickle sauce. Achari Murgh (page 124) is chicken in a pickle and curry sauce. Pulses are important, and the superb Rajma Maahn dish (black *urid dhal* and red kidney beans) is typically delicious (see page 136).

Pakistan

Pakistan was created by the partition of 1947, as a Moslem homeland, comprising what had formerly been the northwestern group of Indian states. Located between Afghanistan and India, it contains the famous Khyber Pass. Its people are predominantly meat-eaters, favouring goat and chicken (being Moslems, they avoid pork). Charcoal cooking is the norm, and this area is the original home of tandoori cooking (see page 55). Breads such as Chupatti, Naan and Paratha are the staples. Balti cooking originated in the northernmost part of Pakistan, and found its way to Birmingham centuries later (see page 200). In general, Pakistani food is robustly spiced and savoury, two distinct styles being Sindhi and Punjabi (see page 202). The *chaats* and *chanas* of pages 44, 49 and 168 are typical. The Karachi Karahi Curry on page 129 is an example of original Pakistani cooking.

Parsee and Persia

It is quite common to see 'Persian' dishes listed on the standard curry-house menu. Dishes such as Biriani and Pullao did indeed originate in Persia (now called Iran), but most of these dishes refer to the specialities of Bombay's religious sect, the Parsees, who came from there. They have no religious proscriptions on eating, so in theory they can eat pork and beef as well as lamb and shellfish. They love egg dishes, and the sweet and sour

combinations typified in their Patia (see page 104). The coriander-coated fish dish, Patrani Maachli (page 149) is a Parsee speciality, but their best-knowndish is undoubtedly Dhansak (see page 68), traditionally meat cooked with lentils and vegetables (a Persian concept), accompanied by Brown Rice (page 173).

Sri Lanka

Sri Lanka is the small pearl-shaped island, formerly Ceylon, at the southern tip of India. Its cuisine is distinctive and generally chilli hot. Like south India, it is a rice district, and some of their food is similarly spiced, but their cuisine is less vegetarian orientated, with Sri Lankans also enjoying meat, squid, chicken and duck. Some of their curries are very pungent. Sri Lankan Black Curry is so called because its spices, including black peppercorn and coriander, are roasted until dark in colour. There is nothing like a Sri Lankan Crab and Shellfish Curry (see page 137) served with Tengai Sadam (Coconut Rice, page 173), but the restaurant-style Ceylon Curry (page 125) bears no resemblance to the real Sri-Lankan thing, delicious though it is.

Thailand

Thai curries are nothing like their Indian counterparts. There are six main types of Thai curry. The two from the south of Thailand, Mussaman (Moslem-style) and Panaeng (Malaystyle), being nearest Malaysia, demonstrate the most Indian influences, with their use of turmeric, coconut and other Indian spices that are not used further north. There we find Red, Green, Orange and Yellow Thai Curries, the principal flavourings coming from plentiful tiny chillies of the appropriate colours. Coconut is not used in the curries of the far north, but other ingredients common to all Thai curries are shrimp paste, fish sauce, lemon grass, lime leaf, coriander root and leaf, and the aniseed-tasting holy basil. A representative Thai Green Pork Curry is given on page 137.

THE STORE CUPBOARD

Here is a workable list of items you need to make the recipes in this book, subdivided into essential and non-essential. The essential items appear again and again in the recipes; the non-essential appear only in one or two. This list may look a bit formidable but remember, once you have the items in stock they will last for some time. I have listed the minimum quantities you'll need (as supplied by one or more manufacturers) in metric only, as given on most packaging these days.

Essential Whole Spices

Bay leaf	3 g
Cardamom, black or brown	30 g
Cardamom, green or white	30 g
Cassia bark	30 g
Chilli	11 g
Clove	20 g
Coriander seed	60 g
Cummin seed, white	25 g
Curry leaves, dried	2 g
Fennel seed	27 g
Fenugreek leaf, dried	18 g
Mustard seed	65 g
Peppercorn, black	47 g
Sesame seed, white	57 g
Wild onion seed (nigella)	47 g

Non-Essential Whole Spices

Alkanet root	3 g
Allspice	50 g
Aniseed	25 g
Caraway seed	25 g
Celery seed	25 g
Cinnamon quill	6 pieces
Cummin seed, black (*zeera*)	25 g
Dill seed	25 g
Fenugreek seed	47 g
Ginger, dried	6 pieces
Lovage (*ajwain*) seed	27 g
Mace	8 g

Nutmeg, whole	6 nuts
Panch Phoran	30 g
Pomegranate seed	30 g
Poppy seed	52 g
Saffron stamens	0.5 g
Star anise	30 g

Essential Ground Spices

Black pepper	100 g
Chilli powder	100 g
Coriander	100 g
Cummin	100 g
Garam Masala	50 g
Garlic powder and/or flakes	100 g
Ginger	100 g
Paprika	100 g
Turmeric	100 g

Non-Essential Ground Spices

Asafoetida	50 g
Cardamom, green	25 g
Cinnamon	25 g
Clove	25 g
Galangal	20 g
Lemon grass	20 g
Mango powder	100 g
Salt, black	50 g

Essential Dry Foods

Basmati rice	1 kg
Coconut powder	100 g
Gram flour	500 g
Jaggery	100 g
Massoor (red) lentils	500 g

Non-Essential Dry Foods

Food colouring powder, red E129	25 g
Ditto, natural beetroot powder	25 g

Food colouring powder, yellow E110	25 g
Ditto, natural annatto	25 g

Lentils

Black-eyed beans (*lobhia*)	500 g
Black lentils, split	500 g
Chick peas	500 g
Red kidney beans	500 g
Urid, whole black	500 g

Nuts

Almonds, flaked	100 g
Almonds, ground	100 g
Almonds, whole	50 g
Cashews, raw	100 g
Creamed coconut block	200 g
Peanuts, raw	100 g
Pistachios, green	100 g

Miscellaneous

Papadoms, spiced and plain (pack)	300 g
Puffed rice (*mamra*)	100 g
Rice flour	500 g
Rose water, bottle	7 fl oz
Sev (gram flour snack)	200 g
Silver leaf (*vark* – edible)	6 sheets
Supari mixture	100 g
Tamarind block	300 g

Oils

Mustard blend	250 ml
Sesame	250 ml
Soya	250 ml
Sunflower	250 ml
Vegetable ghee	250 g

Canned Foods

Chick peas	420 g
Coconut milk	400 g
Lobhia beans	420 g
Patra	420 g
Plum tomatoes	420 g
Red kidney beans	420 g

THE CURRY CLUB

quarterly magazine, which has regular features on curry and the curry lands. It includes news items, recipes, reports on restaurants, picture features, and contributions from members and professionals alike. The information is largely concerned with curry, but by popular demand it now includes regular input on other exotic and spicy cuisines such as those of Thailand, the spicy Americas, the Middle East and China. We produce a wide selection of publications, including the books listed at the front of this book.

Curry diners will be familiar with the Curry Club window sticker and restaurant quality certificate, which adorns the windows and walls of the best thousand curry restaurants. Curry Club members form the national network of reporters, which leads to the selection of these restaurants, in the now annual publication, of the highly successful *Good Curry Guide*, with its prestigious awards to the top restaurants.

Obtaining some of the ingredients required for curry cooking can be difficult, but The Curry Club makes it easy, with a comprehensive range of products, including spice mixes, chutneys, pickles, papadoms, sauces and curry pastes. These are available from major food stores and specialist delicatessens up and down the country. If they are not stocked near you, there is the Club's associate, well-established and efficient mail-order service. Hundreds of items are in stock, including spices, pickles, pastes, dried foods, canned foods, gift items, publications and specialist kitchen and tableware.

On the social side, the Club holds residential weekend cookery courses and gourmet nights at selected restaurants. Top of the list is our regular Curry Club gourmet trip to India and other spicy countries. We take a small group of curry enthusiasts to the chosen country and tour the incredible sights, in between sampling the delicious food of each region.

If you would like more information about The Curry Club, write (enclosing a stamped, addressed envelope please) to: The Curry Club, PO Box 7, Haslemere, Surrey GU27 1EP.

Pat Chapman has always had a deep-rooted interest in spicy food, curry in particular, and over the years he has built up a huge pool of information which he felt could be usefully passed on to others. He conceived the idea of forming an organisation for this purpose.

Since it was founded in January 1982, The Curry Club has built up a membership of several thousand. We have a marchioness, some lords and ladies, knights a-plenty, a captain of industry or two, generals, admirals and air marshals (not to mention a sprinkling of ex-colonels), and we have celebrity names – actresses, politicians, rock stars and sportsmen. We have an airline, a former Royal navy warship, and a hotel chain.

We have 15 members whose name is Curry or Curries, 20 called Rice and several with the name Spice or Spicier, Cook, Fry, Frier or Fryer and one Boiling. We have a Puri (a restaurant owner), a Paratha and a Nan, and a good many Mills and Millers, one Dal and a Lentil, an Oiler, a Gee (but no Ghee), a Cummin and a Butter but no Marj (several Marjories though, and a Marjoram and a Minty). We also have several Longs and Shorts, Thins and Broads, one Fatt and one Wide, and a Chilley and a Coole.

We have members on every continent including a good number of Asian members, but by and large the membership is a typical cross-section of the Great British Public, ranging in age from teenage to dotage, and in occupation from refuse collectors to receivers, high street traders to high court judges, tax inspectors to taxi drivers. There are students and pensioners, millionaires and unemployed . . . thousands of people who have just one thing in common – a love of curry and spicy foods.

Members receive a bright and colourful

GLOSSARY

This glossary is very extensive, including some items not specifically mentioned in the recipes. It is intended to be used as a general reference work. If you do not find a particular word here it is worth checking to see whether it is in the index and can be found elsewhere in the book.

The 'Indian' words are mostly Hindi and some Urdu. The English spelling is 'standard' but can vary as words are translated phonetically.

A

Achar – Pickle
Adrak – Ginger
Ajwain or Ajowain – Lovage seeds
Akhni – Spicy consommé-like stock. Also called *yakni*
Alloo – Potato
Am – Mango
Am chur – Mango powder
Anardana – Pomegranate
Aniseed – *Saunf*
Areca – Betel nut
Asafoetida – *Hing*. A smelly spice
Aserio – Small red-brown seeds used medicinally
Ata or Atta – *Chupatti* flour

B

Badain – Star anise
Badam – Almond
Bargar – The process of frying whole spices in hot oil
Basil – Used only in religious applications in Indian cooking, but widely used in Thai cooking
Basmati – The best long-grain rice
Bay leaf – *Tej Pattia*. Aromatic spice
Besan – See *Gram flour*
Bhare – Stuffed
Bhoona or Bhuna – The process of cooking spices in hot oil
Bhunana – Roast
Blachan – see *Shrimp Paste*
Black salt – *Kala namak*. A type of salt

Bombay Duck – A crispy deep fried fish starter or accompaniment
Brinjal – Aubergine
Burfi or Barfi – An Indian fudge-like sweetmeat

C

Cardamom – *Elaichi*
Cashew nuts – *Kaju*
Cassia bark – related to cinnamon
Cayenne pepper – A blend of chilli powder from Latin America
Chana – Type of lentil. See *Dhal*
Charoli – Chirongi. Sweetish pink-coloured, irregularly shaped seeds with no English translation. Ideal in desserts. Sunflower seeds are a good alternative
Chawal – Rice
Chilgoze or Nioze – Pine nuts
Chilli – *Mirch*. The hottest spice
Chor magaz – Melon seeds. Used as a thickener
Chupatti – A dry 15 cm (6 inch) disc of unleavened bread. Normally griddle-cooked, it should be served piping hot. Spelling varies e.g. *Chuppati, Chapati*, etc.
Cinnamon – *Dalchini*
Cloves – *Lavang*
Coriander – *Dhania*
Cummin or Cumin – *Jeera*
Curry – The only word in this glossary to have no direct translation into any of the sub-continent's 15 or so languages. The word was coined by the British in India centuries ago. Possible contenders for the origin of the word are *karahi* or *karai* (Hindi), a wok-like frying pan used all over India to prepare masalas (spice mixtures); *kurhi*, a soup-like dish made with spices, gram flour dumplings and buttermilk; *kari*, a spicy Tamil sauce; *turkuri*, a seasoned sauce or stew; *kari phulia, neem* or curry leaves; *kudhi* or *kadhi*, a yoghurt soup; or *koresh*, an aromatic Iranian stew
Curry leaves – *Neem* leaves or *kari phulia*. Small leaves a bit like bay leaves, used for flavouring
Cus cus – See *Poppy seed*

D

Dahi – Yoghurt
Dalchini or Darchim – Cinnamon
Degchi, Dekhchi or Degh – Brass or metal saucepan without handles also called *pateeli* or *batloi*
Dhal – Lentils. There are over 60 types of lentil in the subcontinent, some of which are very obscure. Like peas, they grow into a hard sphere measuring between 1 cm and 3 mm. They are cooked whole or split with skin, or split with the skin polished off, and are a rich source of protein
Dhania – Coriander
Dill – Heart
Doroo – Celery
Dum – Steam cooking. Long before the West invented the pressure cooker, India had her own method which lasts to this day. A pot with a close-fitting lid is sealed with a ring of dough. The ingredients are then cooked in their own steam under some pressure

E

Ekuri – Spiced scrambled eggs
Elaichi – Cardamom

F

Fennel – *Sunf* or *soonf*
Fenugreek – *Methi*
Fish sauce – *Nam pla* (Thai), *Nga-pya* (Burmese), *Patis* (Philippine). It is the runny liquid strained from fermented anchovies, and is a very important flavouring agent
Five-Spice powder – Combination of five sweet and aromatic spices used in Chinese and Malay cooking. Usually ground. A typical combination would be equal parts of cinnamon, cloves, fennel seeds, star anise and Szechuan pepper
Foogath – Lightly cooked vegetable dish

G

Gajar – Carrot
Galangal or Galingale – A tuber related to ginger, used in Thai cooking where it is called *kha*, and in Indonesian (*laos*) and Malay (*kenkur*)

Garlic – *Lasan*
Ghee – Clarified butter or margarine
Ginger – *Adrak* (fresh), *sont* (dried)
Gobi or Phoolgobi – Cauliflower
Goor or Gur – Jaggery (palm sugar) or molasses
Gosht – Lamb, mutton or goat
Gram flour – *Besan*. Finely ground flour, pale blond in colour, made from *chana* (see *Dhal*)

H

Halva – Sweets made from syrup and vegetables or fruit.
Handi – Earthenware cooking pot
Hing – Asafoetida
Huldi – Turmeric

I

Imli – Tamarind
Isgubul – Vegetable seed

J

Jaifal or Taifal – Nutmeg
Jaggery – See *Goor*
Javatri – Mace
Jeera or Zeera – Cummin
Jinga – Prawns

K

Kabli chana – Chick peas. See *Dhal*
Kadhi – Yoghurt soup
Kaju – Cashew nut
Kala jeera – Black cummin seeds
Kala namak – Black salt
Kaleji – Liver
Kalonji – See *Wild onion seeds*
Karahi – *Karai, korai* etc. The Indian equivalent of the wok. The karahi is a circular two-handled round all-purpose cooking pan used for stir-frying, simmering, frying and deep-frying – in fact it is highly efficient for all types of cooking. Some restaurants cook in small karahis and serve them straight to the table with the food sizzling inside
Karela – Small, dark green, knobbly vegetable of the gourd family
Katori – Small serving bowls which go on a *thali* (tray)
Kecap manis – Indonesian version of soy sauce. It is sweeter and slightly sticky. Soy sauce is a good, though more salty, substitute

Keema – Minced meat curry

Kewra – Screwpine water. An extract of the flower of the tropical screwpine tree. It is a fragrant clear liquid used to flavour sweets. It is a cheap substitute for rose water

Khir – Technique of making a sort of cream. Milk is cooked with cucumber and puréed

Kish mish – Sultanas

Kokum or Cocum – A variety of plum, pitted and dried. Prune-like and very sour. Also known in Malayan as mangosteen

Koya – Reducing milk to a thick sticky solid

Kus Kus – See *Poppy seed*

L

Lasan – Garlic

Lassi or Lhassi – A refreshing drink made from yoghurt and crushed ice. The savoury version is *lhassi namkeen* and the sweet version is *lhassi meethi*

Lavang – Cloves

Lemon grass – *Takrai* (Thai), *serai* (Malay). A fragrant-leafed plant which imparts a subtle lemony flavour to cooking

Lentils – See *Dhal*

Lilva – A small oval-shaped bean which grows in a pod like the European pea

Lime leaves – *Markrut* or citrus leaves. Used in Thai cooking, fresh or dried, to give a distinctive aromatic flavour

Loochees – A type of bread made in Bengal using white flour

Lovage – *Ajwain* or *ajowain*

M

Mace – *Javitri*

Macchi or Macchli – Fish

Makke – Cornflour

Makrut or Markrut – Citrus or lime leaf

Malai – Cream

Mamra – Puffed basmati rice

Mango Powder – *Am chur*

Masala – A mixture of spices which are cooked with a particular dish. Any curry powder is therefore a masala. It can be spelt a remarkable number of ways –

massala, massalla, musala, mosola, massalam, etc.

Massoor – Red lentils. See *Dhal*

Mattar – Green peas

Meethi – Sweet

Melon seeds – Chor magaz

Methi – Fenugreek

Mirch – Pepper or chilli

Mollee – Fish dishes cooked in coconut and chilli

Mooli – Large white radish

Moong – Type of lentil. See *Dhal*

Murgh – Chicken

Mustard seeds – *Rai*

N

Namak – Salt

Nam Pla – Fish sauce

Naryal – Coconut

Neem – Curry leaf

Nga-Pi – Shrimp paste

Nga-Pya – Fish sauce

Nigella – Wild onion seeds

Nimboo – Lime (lemon)

Nutmeg – *Jaifal*

O

Okra – *Bindi*. A pulpy vegetable also known as ladies' fingers

P

Pan or Paan – Betel leaf folded around a stuffing – lime paste or various spices (see *Supari*) and eaten after a meal as a digestive

Palak or Sag – Spinach

Panch Phoran – Five seeds

Papadom – Thin lentil flour wafers. Many spelling variations include popadom, pappadom, etc.

Paprika – Mild red ground pepper made from red bell peppers. Its main use to give red colour to a dish

Pepper – *Mirch*

Piaz, Peeaz or Pyaz – Onion

Pickles – Pungent, hot pickled vegetables or meat essential to an Indian meal. Most common are lime, mango and chilli

Pistachio nut – *Pista magaz*. A fleshy, tasty nut which can be used fresh (the greener the better) or salted

Poppy seed – *Cus cus* or *Kus Kus*. (Not to be confused with the Moroccan national dish cous-cous, made from steamed semolina)

Pulses – Dried peas and beans, including lentils

Q

Quas chawal or Kesar chaval – rice fried in ghee, flavoured and coloured with saffron

R

Rai – Mustard seeds

Rajma – Red kidney beans

Ratin jot – Alkanet root

Rose water – *Ruh gulab*. A clear essence extracted from rose petals to give a frangrance to sweets. See *Kewra*

Roti – Bread

Ruh gulab – Rose water essence

S

Sabzi – A generic term for vegetables

Saffron – *Kesar* or *zafron*. The world's most expensive spice

Sag or Saag – Spinach

Sajjar – Drumstick. A bean-like variety of gourd which looks exactly like a drumstick

Salt – *Namak*

Sambals – A Malayan term describing the side dishes accompanying the meal. Sometimes referred to on the Indian menu

Sarson ka sag – Mustard leaves (spinach-like)

Saunf or Souf – Aniseed

Seenl – Allspice

Sesame seed – *Til*

Shrimp paste – *Blachan* (Malay), *Nga-Pi* (Burmese), *Kapi* (Thai). Very concentrated block of compressed shrimps. A vital flavouring for the cooking of those countries

Sonf – Fennel seed

Sont or Sonth – Dry ginger

Subcontinent – Term to describe India, Pakistan, Bangladesh, Nepal, Burma and Sri Lanka as a group

Supari – Mixture of seeds and sweeteners for chewing after a meal. Usually includes aniseed or fennel, shredded betel nut, sugar balls, marrow seeds, etc.

T

Taipal or Jaiphal – Nutmeg

Tamarind – *Imli*. A date-like fruit used as a chutney, and in cooking asa souring agent

Tava or Tawa – A heavy, almost flat, circular wooden-handled griddle pan used to cook Indian breads and to 'roast' spices. Also ideal for many cooking functions from frying eggs and omelettes to making pancakes, etc.

Tej patia – Cassia bark leaf

Thali sets – To serve your meal in truly authentic Indian fashion use *thali* sets. A great and stylish talking point. Each diner is served a *thali* tray on which is a number of *katori* dishes in which different curry dishes, rice, chutneys, etc., are placed. Breads and papadoms go on the tray itself

Til – Sesame seed

Tindla – A vegetable of the cucumber family

Toor or Toovar – A type of lentil. See *Dhal*

Tukmeria or Tulsi – Black seeds of a basil family plant. Look like poppy seeds. Used in drinks

Turmeric – *Haldi* or *huldi*. Use sparingly or it can cause bitterness

U

Udrak – Ginger

Urid – A type of lentil. See *Dhal*

V

Vark or Varak – Edible silver or gold foil

W

Wild onion seeds – See *Nigella*

Z

Zafron – Saffron

Zeera – Cummin